Redeveloping Communication for Social Change

Critical Media Studies: Institutions, Politics, and Culture

Series Editor:
Andrew Calabrese, University of Colorado at Boulder

This series covers a broad range of critical research and theory about media in the modern world. It includes work about the changing structures of the media, focusing particularly on work about the political and economic forces and social relations which shape and are shaped by media institutions, structural changes in policy formation and enforcement, technological transformations in the means of communication, and the relationships of all of these to public and private cultures worldwide. Historical research about the media and intellectual histories pertaining to media research and theory are particularly welcomed. Emphasizing the role of social and political theory for informing and shaping research about communications media, Critical Media Studies seeks to address the politics of media institutions at national, subnational, and transnational levels. The series will also include short, synthetic texts on "Masters and Concepts" in critical media studies.

Advisory Board

Titles in the Series

Interactions: Critical Studies in Communication, Media, and Journalism, Hanno Hardt

Communication, Citizenship, and Social Policy: Rethinking the Limits of the Welfare State,
edited by Andrew Calabrese and Jean-Claude Burgelman

Public Opinion: Developments and Controversies in the Twentieth Century, Slavko Splichal

Tabloid Tales: Global Debates over Media Standards, edited by Colin Sparks and John Tulloch

Redeveloping Communication for Social Change: Theory, Practice, and Power, edited by Karin Gwinn Wilkins

Forthcoming in the Series

The Information Society in Europe: Work and Life in an Age of Globalization,
edited by Ken Ducatel, Juliet Webster, and Werner Herrmann

Deregulating Telecommunications: A Comparison of American and Canadian Telecommunications, 1844–1997, Kevin G. Wilson

Deliberation, Democracy, and the Media, edited by Simone Chambers and Anne Costain

Redeveloping Communication for Social Change

Theory, Practice, and Power

Karin Gwinn Wilkins

ROWMAN & LITTLEFIELD PUBLISHERS, INC.
Lanham • Boulder • New York • Oxford

ROWMAN & LITTLEFIELD PUBLISHERS, INC.

Published in the United States of America
by Rowman & Littlefield Publishers, Inc.
4720 Boston Way, Lanham, Maryland 20706
http://www.rowmanlittlefield.com

12 Hid's Copse Road
Cumnor Hill, Oxford OX2 9JJ, England

British Library Cataloguing in Publication Information Available

Library of Congress Cataloging-in-Publication Data

Wilkins, Karin Gwinn, 1962–
Redeveloping communication for social change : theory, practice, and power / Karin Gwinn Wilkins.
p. cm. — (Critical media studies)
Includes bibliographical references and index.
ISBN 0-8476-9587-5 (cloth : alk. paper) — ISBN 0-8476-9588-3 (pbk. : alk. paper)
1. Communication in economic development. 2. Social change. I. Title. II. Series.
HD76 .W55 1999
302.2–dc21 99-042086

Printed in the United States of America

∞ ™The paper used in this publication meets the minimum requirements of American National Standard for Information Sciences—Permanence of Paper for Printed Library Materials, ANSI Z39.48–1992.

To Peter and Our Twins

Contents

Acknowledgments

This collection has emerged from a conference on "Redeveloping Communication for Social Change: Issues of Power, Gender and Practice" held in June 1998 at the University of Texas at Austin. For their generous support of this conference, we thank the University of Texas at Austin's College of Communication, Department of Radio–Television–Film, the Institute for Latin American Studies, Center for American History, Center for Women's Studies, Center for Asian Studies, Center for Middle Eastern Studies, and the Population Research Center. For their dedication and diligence in administering the conference, I also thank Elizabeth MacLean and Jody Waters, who also has served as a valuable colleague in this and other projects. In addition, I greatly appreciate the guidance of Brenda Hadenfeldt and the assistance of Jennie Rupertus in helping to prepare this manuscript. The time spent editing this volume would have been much more difficult without the generous provision of a Dean's Fellowship from the Department of Radio–Television–Film. As always, I gratefully acknowledge Peter Siegenthaler for his thoughtful editorial advice and his unfailing support.

1

Introduction

Karin Gwinn Wilkins

In the field of development communication we now face a critical juncture. Through the twentieth century we have witnessed remarkable advances in communication technologies. We are inundated with enthusiastic assessments of our shift from an industrial to an information age, where global knowledge takes precedence over national development. We hear about working with "partners," not "bureaucracies"; to develop "people" in a global village, not "nations"; through "information," not "capital." Yet as this century draws to a close, serious problems, such as poverty, malnutrition, over-population, inequality, and environmental degradation, remain. Despite being designed to resolve these social problems through the strategic application of communication technologies and processes, development communication programs, for the most part, have failed to achieve their objectives. Even though one might believe that development as a discourse has adapted over time to integrate many of these concerns, the burdens of global commercialization and development privatization have weighed heavily on the potential for development communication to foster significant social change.

This anthology begins with the assumption that to reshape the field of development communication we must situate its discourse and practice within contexts of power. Through project intervention, the development industry articulates knowledge about the process of social change facilitated through communication and about the intended beneficiaries of strategic programs. This collection of chapters recognizes the power dynamics manifest in the construction of discourse and the implementation of projects. Many of the authors in this volume urge us to consider the complexity of social change processes, moving away from dichotomous notions of development and power.

The first section of this book addresses different perspectives on reconceptualizing development communication theory, the second considers new ways of approaching development communication practice, and the final section speculates how a framework accounting for power might contribute toward new directions in the field.

Reflecting on the recent history of development discourse, we see that approaches to development have posited different perspectives on power within the process of social change. The early Dominant Paradigm articulated by Lerner, Schramm, and others assumed that media, as a tool to promote national development goals, would have the power to inspire individuals to act and think in modern, Western ways. Dependency scholars reminded us of the global structure within which developing countries work, situating power in the hands of wealthier nations. Participatory approaches to development then drew our attention to the power of local communities to recognize and resolve social concerns. Recent attention to social movements complements participatory approaches by emphasizing the ability of marginal communities to control their own social change.

By situating strategic social change within this context of power, we can recognize both the ability of dominant groups to control hegemonic processes through perpetuating their ideological interests and the potential for marginal communities to resist. We can look for evidence of power dynamics in the political–economic structures that govern the distribution of resources across and within nations in the inequities within regions, nations, and communities that constrain access to services, technologies, and finances, or even in the assertion of particular ideologies that legitimize or resist dominant interests. In development communication, we can explore this context through understanding the global structure within which agencies construct social problems and interventions, the discourse guiding the normative climate for conceiving and implementing projects, the praxis of intervention, and the consequences of these structures, discourses, and interventions.

Contributors in this section work to reconceptualize development communication theory, taking into account power dynamics. In an exploration of the consequences of these power structures, focusing on gender offers an important illustration of a case in which discourse has changed historically to attend to women's issues, but interventions have failed to improve the conditions of women on a global scale. Leslie Steeves explores the critical implications of gender inequities in her discussion of the problems and potentials of "Gendered Agendas." In this informative chapter, she examines gendered power relations and agendas of international development agencies. Like Steeves, Ronald Greene carefully interrogates the role women play in the construction of development policy, specifically focusing on population issues. Greene explores the discursive practices of engaged by agencies as they work to "govern reproduction."

Continuing this focus on power in development communication theory, Srinivas Melkote proposes a new conceptual framework. Elaborating on the notion of empowerment, Melkote respectfully builds from the assumption that promoting social change needs to begin by understanding the differences in power across communities and institutions.

Next, Thomas Jacobson foregrounds cultural hybridization and preservation in his framework for development communication. Basing his work on Habermas's scholarship, Jacobson reminds us of the importance of linking strategies for social change with political processes, such as those directed toward democratization and the promotion of human rights. The chapters in this section contribute to an understanding of power dimensions along ideological, political–economic, and institutional levels.

These theoretical issues need to be explored in relation to development practice engaged in the process of strategic social change. Even though one might believe that development as a discourse has adapted over time to integrate many concerns, we must examine the manifestations and consequences of this rhetoric in project implementation. In the second section, we examine the manifestation of power dynamics in the practice of development communication.

Many of the authors in this section use ethnographic approaches to consider the importance of accounting for power structures and dynamics in development practice. Bridging participatory communication approaches with new social movement frameworks, Robert Huesca provides an innovative assessment of the context in which labor organizing occurs in *maquiladora* assembly plants on the Mexican-U.S. border. Echoing Huesca's emphasis on the process rather than the product of development intervention, Jody Waters suggests thoughtful procedures and considerations for observing power dynamics in conducting research and participating in development communication processes.

As a reflective practitioner himself, Doug Storey then offers a valuable reconceptualization of the role of donor agencies in the practice of development communication through discursive analyses. Applying this framework to several specific USAID projects, Storey suggests that the meanings of interventions are fluid, being negotiated across donors and beneficiaries, particularly in the arena of popular culture.

Using a popular narrative to illustrate his case, Mark Pedelty characterizes the role of popular culture in post-revolutionary Mexico, as a polysemic discourse that both articulates the themes of dominant development concerns as well as the ideas represented in shifting resistance movements.

Continuing this theme on the role of popular culture in strategic social change, Brij Kothari offers a case study of a television project in India, to demonstrate both the importance of literacy in offering access to social power and the constraints involved in implementing interventions. His discussion highlights some of the institutional dynamics encountered in the process of implementation.

As do many of the other contributors in this book, Clemencia Rodríguez provides an important contribution through her bridging of development communication with another field. In her case, linking peace studies with development communication allows her to describe several examples of peace initiatives as tools toward giving voice to those with comparatively less power.

In the final section, we propose new directions for considering social change processes in development communication. Arturo Escobar's work has been inspirational in this regard, articulating development as a discourse that builds knowledge and power through the construction of social problems and institutional interventions. His contribution introduces this section, questioning our assumptions regarding development as an appropriate vehicle for social change. Instead, Escobar articulates the role of place in the process of social change, as local groups act collectively in a global context, given the potential afforded through new communication technologies. Edna Einsiedel continues the attention to this concern with fluidity, proposing that we focus on borders, as permeable and hybrid dimensions, in our conceptualization of social change. In order to establish boundaries as sites for valuable interchange, she advocates we respect differences within social groups and across multiple approaches.

The next two chapters direct our attention to power dynamics in the process of social change. Through her review of the field, Bella Mody demonstrates the contextual nature of introducing particular theoretical positions and of implementing projects. She concludes that future development communication frameworks need to consider both the conditions of media systems and of power structures in order to understand and promote positive social change. In the final chapter, Karin Wilkins summarizes critical debates in the field that move toward reconceptualizing development communication within a context that articulates the role of power in the production of knowledge about people, social problems, and potential solutions.

We can build on these assessments of past experiences with development processes in order to reinvent the field. Instead of mourning the demise of development communication, this volume is intended to provoke critical debate that will help us change our approaches to meet new challenges.

Part I

Reconceptualizing Development Communication Theory

2

Gendered Agendas

Dialogue and Impasse in Creating Social Change

H. Leslie Steeves

This chapter centralizes concerns of women in development (WID), while discussing communication and dialogue as crucial to achieving WID goals, and some of the obstacles that must be confronted. Success depends on dialogue, which suggests key roles for feminist communication scholars and activists. The effectiveness of our contributions, however, depends on our understandings of communication. Processes of communication and development are inseparable from the cultural contexts in which they occur. Therefore, an analysis of communication in development must consider the cultural values of the groups involved. Culturally grounded communication barriers are many and complex. Here they are divided simply as "material" and "nonmaterial," e.g., economic class and religion/spirituality.

DEVELOPMENT

There are many ways of conceptualizing development, ways that foreground economics, politics, culture, or a combination, and within each of those realms, ways that emphasize processes or structures or both and their relationships. Further, in some perspectives development is geographically inclusive, whereas in others the focus is the so-called Third World or developing countries and their aid needs.[1]

Certainly one's perspective on development may be different working in the field than reading development texts in academia. A former Peace Corps volunteer in Nepal writes:

> What does development mean in this village? Villagers do not debate the fine points of development definitions or models. Theirs is a world of few options and little choice. They cannot affect long-term outcomes of their own lives. They do not ask "What is development?" or "Why should a country develop?" People want to grow more food and have more clothes. They want to fulfill their family and social obligations [. . . and properly perform] the religious ceremonies that define the daily dimensions of life and death. (Tisch & Wallace, 1994, p. 3)

Robert Agunga, who comes from a small village in the Northern Region of Ghana, writes similarly:

> Growing up on a subsistence farm unquestionably led me to my choice of a professional career. I wanted to be an agriculturist to help subsistence farmers increase their productivity, which would lead to increased incomes and better standards of living. Having lived amid underdevelopment for much of my life, I have never had a problem deciding what development is. It is getting rid of hunger, illiteracy and ill-health, having better roads, protecting the environment and similar improvements. (1997, p. 217)

All conceptual writings on development contribute to our understandings of development, including the values and structures that determine why and how this process occurs and its consequences. However, I am most persuaded by theories that begin by recognizing real human experiences of deprivation—for instance, by delineating what it means fundamentally to be a human being or what sorts of human functional capabilities are required for a good life. That is one reason Paulo Freire's works are so compelling (e.g., 1970). There are others who ground their work in philosophical conceptions of what it means to be human. The feminist philosopher, Martha Nussbaum, for instance, has been building this type of argument (e.g., 1995).[2]

Most people around the world experience severe conditions of poverty, unemployment, hunger, illiteracy, sanitation, and health and have few options to improve their lives. Refugee conditions are among the worst. The numbers of refugees globally have increased dramatically in the past two decades. The United Nations High Commissioner for Refugees estimates that there are fifty million people displaced either within or from their countries. The majority of them are female (1997, pp. 2, 58–63).

A key observation of Women in Development (WID) scholars beginning in the 1970s, which still has not made its way into many international and development communication texts,[3] is that conditions of deprivation are unequal. Women's and girls' circumstances are substantially *worse* than those of men and boys in nearly every area of human need, and human right. Although progress has been made in some places, and on some issues, great inequities do remain in most areas of basic need, however defined, as well as in political and organizational access. This is evident by scanning recent statistics, for instance, in United Nations publications (e.g., UN Development Programme, 1997, 1998; United Nations, 1995; World Bank, 1999), and in *The State of the Women in the World Atlas* (Seager, 1997).

Statistics show that no society treats its women and girls as well as its men and boys. In developing countries there are still nearly two-thirds more women than men among illiterate adults. Even at the primary school level, where progress has been made, female enrollment averages 13 percent lower than male enrollment (Seager, 1997, pp. 74–75; UNDP, 1997, p. 39). In both developing and industrialized countries female wages are lower than male wages, and unemployment is higher among women than men. At the same time, women constitute the vast majority of the unpaid family workers (Seager, 1997, pp. 66–71; UNDP, 1997, p. 39).[4] Statistics are plentiful showing these and other disparities. Further, in each context, breakdowns by age, ethnicity, and by other social divisions usually show much more desperate conditions for women and girls. In sub-Saharan Africa the conditions of deprivation are the most extreme, as are the gender disparities (Seager, 1997; United Nations, 1995, p. xviii).

Gathering and exposing these comparative statistics has been part of the work of WID scholars and activists. But statistics tell only part of the story, as statistical gender inequalities certainly predated colonial and postcolonial development. A major contribution of WID scholars is their critique of economic development assistance for ignoring gender roles and worsening existing gender inequalities, sometimes creating new inequalities. The credit for first making this argument, as well as for helping inspire the movement that led to the 1975–1985 Decade for Women, often goes to the Danish economist Ester Boserup (1970). Boserup showed how colonial and postcolonial assumptions about public and private distinctions undermined women's traditional areas of power and responsibility. For instance, in East Africa men were encouraged to leave the home and work on cash crops or in cities. Women, who traditionally farmed, were left at home to do everything, such as grow family food, gather fuelwood, care for children, and earn needed cash by working on plantations or in the informal market. At the same time, development projects failed to consider the gendered context of the situation and focused on men.

The WID scholarship and activism that followed Boserup's observations sought to challenge and transform development studies and practice. The pattern of feminist challenge has been similar to that in many fields of study, including feminist communication studies. In the 1970s the emphasis was on integrating women in development, that is, deliberately including women as participants and recipients. Many studies in the 1980s, some focusing on communication issues, documented women's continued marginalization and worsened situation as a result of development. For instance, despite the fact that female subsistence farmers produce 80 percent of the family food in much of sub-Saharan Africa, extension communication workers bypassed these women, seeking out male farmers or wealthier women (e.g., Staudt, 1985). Sophisticated persuasive communication projects to promote contraceptive technologies have also been insensitive and harmful to women (e.g., Luthra, 1988, 1991).

Anecdotes abound of projects whose planners failed to consult with women initially and failed, usually worsening women's situation in the process. For instance, a colleague describes a U.S. Agency for International Development (USAID) project in

Pakistan to build a mine. The project's social impact study surveyed men in the nearby village. This study showed that the men were enthusiastic, but that there were not enough local men to staff the mine. Therefore, migrant workers would be needed as well. A shelter for migrant workers was built on a direct path between the village and the well, where women went daily to get water. Women then had to walk around the shelter to get to the well. The result was much suspicion of infidelity and enormous social turmoil between the village men and the migrant mine workers as well as between the village men and women. Eventually the whole project collapsed. Yet the project probably would have succeeded and the community spared this trauma if the shelter had been put in a different place. This was not done because women were not consulted (Weiss, personal communication, 1998).[5]

By the 1980s, as women continued to be neglected and many development projects continued to fail as well, it became obvious that the discourse of inclusion was not the most productive direction, that inclusion alone—to the extent it occurred at all—would not solve the problems. Women already are central to the most fundamental concerns of development, such as meeting basic needs, sustaining the environment, and contributing economically. Therefore, women's needs and societal improvement are closely entwined. Scholars and activists making this argument often cite statistics showing that gender inequality is strongly associated with human poverty, or the reverse, that societal progress is correlated with improvements in women's lives.[6]

The argument also can be made merely by reading each country's annual National Development Report. Areas prioritized are always ones where women have central roles, including agriculture, labor productivity, environment and sanitation, population, nutrition, health, and human rights. Women's key contributions in many of these areas have been highlighted in major global conferences this decade: the 1992 Environment and Development Conference in Rio; the 1993 Human Rights conference in Vienna; the 1994 Population and Development Conference in Cairo; the 1995 World Summit on Social Development in Copenhagen; and of course, the 1995 Beijing conference. Therefore, as WID scholars suggest, women must be central to all development planning.

Parallel to the women-are-central theme has been the more nuanced gender and development theme (GAD), which rightly argues that the central consideration in development is not necessarily women, but *gender,* that is, a socially constructed division that needs to be understood in each context. For a combination of conceptual and political reasons, I have favored a position that argues for the centrality of *women* while recognizing the complexity of gender roles. According to the authors of a collection written in preparation for the pre-Beijing conference of the Association for Women in Development (AWID),

> The problem for today is not to include women in a gendered development process carried out mostly by men but to enlist the cooperation of men (and the resources they control) in the gendered development process that is [already] under way and carried out mostly by women. (Kusterer, Samarasinghe, & Young, 1993, p. 2)

Women *are* in fact central to development, yet women have little voice in development. The gendered nature of women's centrality varies by context and by level of consideration, as does women's empowerment. Women often wield power at the grassroots, but lose power at higher levels of resource allocation.

Purportedly reflecting a new gender focus, in March, 1996, USAID instituted an agency-wide "Gender Plan of Action," to "ensure the integration of gender considerations into its programs and to continue to foster the institutional changes needed to support women in development" (*Gender Action,* 1997, p. 4). In the past, where feminist arguments have reached the level of policy, there has been little real impact. This was the case, for instance, with the 1973 Percy Amendment to the U.S. Foreign Assistance Act, which mandated that all USAID projects consider impacts on women. As hegemony theory predicts, U.S. bilateral aid policy (like much multilateral aid policy) has readily incorporated small amounts of activism, but without becoming truly progressive. Studies have documented that WID initiatives have been underfunded and that USAID has not routinely monitored the impacts of projects on women.[7]

Also, it is important to note that neither the Percy Amendment nor the new Gender Plan even apply to the majority of the projects funded by USAID. Most USAID money is classified as either Development Assistance (DA) or Economic Support Funds (ESF). The Economic Support Funds, the greater amount, go to countries that are important to the United States for political or strategic reasons (Hoy, 1998, pp. 18–19). Pakistan was an ESF country when the mine project described above took place. So technically, while a social impact study was required, a women impact study was optional (Williams & Rudel, 1988, p. 121). Obviously one was not done in that case. Clearly, USAID's new Gender Plan will have little or no effect on ESF projects. It's unclear to what extent this plan may allow openings for improvements in DA projects.

COMMUNICATION AND CULTURE

There are many ways to challenge gendered power relations and agendas—that is, gendered agendas of power—at all levels of society. These challenges or resistances originate from within as well as outside of the mainstream. Feminist communication scholars are ideally situated to contribute—for instance, by critically examining project communications, by examining the structures and discourses of aid organizations, by documenting the roles played by formal and informal women's groups, including women's media groups, and by studying media representations of development and of women in developing countries. All of these areas of resistance and challenge are worthwhile. They may eventually accumulate and create new openings for change.[8] But we can resist more effectively when we recognize shared goals within and between sites of resistance and when we can talk in ways that empower instead of alienating and disparaging each other. My optimism increases to the extent that feminists globally are able to continue to talk, listen, share information, and negotiate goals and strategies.

There are many encouraging examples of dialogue and coalition-building. Probably most significant, because they resulted in hundreds of feminist initiatives, including communication projects,[9] and inspired so much global discussion, were the three Decade for Women Conferences, as well as the 1995 Fourth World Conference on Women in Beijing. Planning for the Beijing conference emphasized a *trialogue* from the grassroots up among scholars, activists, and policy makers. The draft document for the Beijing Platform for Action, with its twelve critical areas of concern, was the result of several years of grassroots discussions globally. Local community meetings were followed by regional meetings on every continent in 1993 and 1994,[10] leading to meetings in New York in March, 1995, where the UN Commission on the Status of Women prepared the final draft document for presentation in Beijing.

This trialogue was good and encouraging, but it takes a long time to effect change, and it is important to find ways to sustain the post-Beijing momentum. How can we encourage the continuation of the trialogue? Work to monitor and participate in post-Beijing discussions is a potential area of contribution for communication scholarship. Aside from process, as "women and the media" is one of the twelve critical areas of concern, we can also focus specifically on what is happening in this particular area. It is disheartening to look at post-Beijing reports from our government and find that "women and the media" represents the smallest section. In fact, the 1998 and 1999 reports include just one four-line item each: a Peace Corps project in Lesotho that published a women's role model calendar for classrooms (Update to America's Commitment, 1998); and a Peace Corps project in Guinea that launched a girls' health magazine (President's Interagency Council on Women, 1999b).

In all areas of dialogic initiative between and among women globally, there remain many obstacles and corresponding opportunities that we need to consider. In my view, the most fundamental reality that links issues of gender, development, and communication is culture. Culture is crucial to dialogue, yet exceedingly complex. Raymond Williams calls it "one of the two or three most complicated words in the English language" (1976, p. 76).[11] The anthropologist Edward Hall notes broad agreement on three characteristics of culture: that culture is shared by members of groups, and helps define them; that culture is learned, not innate; and that this learning is interrelated: "you touch a culture in one place and everything else is affected" (1976, p. 16).[12]

Also, culture is inseparable from communication. James Carey, among others, began linking the concepts in the idea of communication as shared meaning, versus information transmission or persuasion (e.g., 1989). Communication is the maintenance, modification and creation of culture. In this sense, the processes and institutions of communication, of culture and of development (or social change) are all woven together. Development communication scholars and practitioners still tend to be split between those who view communication as an organizational delivery system versus those who view communication more broadly, as inseparable from culture and social change.

Two dimensions of culture constitute on-going challenges in global dialogue among women and in development communication. These two dimensions may be described as extremes of material and nonmaterial culture: economic class and religion.

Material Culture

Economic class, which relates to education, remains a huge barrier to dialogue and is certainly inseparable from culture, development, and communication. In developing countries class is created by development and communication. The notion of cultural hybridity sometimes refers to the educated elite in developing countries; those who have economic privilege and have adopted consumer values because of a Western education and resulting opportunities, yet still identify with their traditional culture. This educated elite is very small and contrasts sharply with the large poor majority, which is disproportionately female and helps account for the unequal global gender statistics discussed previously.

Class and culture in this sense are created not only by Western educational experience and influence, but by other development priorities as well, for instance, of infrastructural development, of privatization, and of increased Gross National Product (GNP), calculated to exclude women's unpaid work. These priorities and measures are supported by development communication, which often is marketing communication, and may be culturally insensitive.

In USAID development projects, communication increasingly equates with social marketing, which means using principles of commercial marketing to promote ideas or products that are believed to be in the public interest (e.g., Kotler, 1984). This commercial marketing orientation often privileges mass communication and therefore neglects informal communication channels that may be most salient to the majority of women. A marketing approach is rapidly spreading to nongovernmental organizations (NGOs), which increasingly are the implementers of bilateral and multilateral aid. Some NGOs are actually created with bilateral grants to perform consistent functions. The Ghana Social Marketing Foundation is an example, as an NGO in Accra that was started by USAID. It seeks funds from aid organizations, including USAID, which allow it to hire consultants who do research and create materials for social marketing campaigns. All of this perpetuates and spreads a commercial orientation that is often class, gender, and urban-biased, and also neglects traditional forms of communication in the process.

In global dialogue, economic class is most evident in simple *access,* in that even grassroots discussions about social change exclude most of the people who supposedly are recipients of change. The Beijing trialogue of scholars, activists, and policy makers has comprised mostly more privileged women. If we look globally at who took part in pre-Beijing conversations, it had to be people *who found out about them,* which suggests class indicators of access to communications, discretionary time, and education. On a related note, class is a key theme in discussions about the democratic potential of the internet in linking women.

Beyond simple access to dialogue, unequal class status makes a huge difference in finding common ground in dialogue, a problem that has been discussed extensively by scholars writing about participatory action research and about feminist method. In multiethnic, multilingual societies, as in Africa, I find that it is relatively easy to communicate with my academic colleagues, who tend to come from privileged backgrounds, speak English, have studied overseas, and usually are interested in collaboration. Significant differences remain, although class and education do provide much common ground in these relationships. They also may create much distance between academics (regardless of nationality) and village women. Of course, ethnicity and language are factors here too. But economic class status and the things that go along with it—knowing a European language, education, professional employment, travel opportunities—together constitute a huge obstacle to real dialogue.

When attempts are made to implement Freirean dialogic pedagogies or consistent research methodologies such as Participatory Action Research (PAR), economic privilege remains a threat to the process. These difficulties may create opportunities as well, but we seldom have enough time to build the relationships necessary to realize the opportunities, nor is it always humanly possible to follow up in all the ways promised once the research is over.

This is not to say that our class and privilege make it impossible to relate. Rather, a commitment to dialogue is easier announced than accomplished, and each of us needs to sort out our own threshold for conflict and difference, our feminist values, our personal and political motives, and what is realistic in the time available. Some argue that individual personality is the key to success in dialogue, that only certain people are capable of engaging in true participation, those who have an unusual level of energy, intelligence, sensitivity, and inner freedom, and who are capable of a high degree of self-reflexivity. These arguments appear to describe Mother Theresa. Few of us are saints, willing or able to give up material possessions for dialogic communion. I do not think we have to be saints to do ethical work across class lines, yet individual personality is an undeniable factor. Our degree of attachment to material reality, to the rewards of class status, and our sensitivity and self-awareness of these limitations do play a role in dialogic capacity.[13]

Nonmaterial Culture

This leads to religion and spirituality, the second aspect of culture discussed here, as these realms are especially problematic for Westerners, including Western feminists. There seem to be a couple of extremes. At one extreme is a New Age tendency to elevate or romanticize indigenous traditions, including indigenous spirituality, as key to peace, environmental protection, and human understanding. Aside from issues of appropriation and colonization, while this direction may reveal important insights in going against materialism (and of course we have much to learn from non-Western beliefs), some go too far down this path to the neglect of other issues. Difference cannot be erased in shared spiritual experience. We cannot solve profound problems of material need and inequity via any one path or set of assumptions, including spirituality. Global patriarchy and capitalism are much more complex than that, as are women's experiences, and the processes and organizations of feminist resistance.

The *much* bigger problem with religious difference in development is the other extreme, that is, our widespread secular orientation and consequent discomfort with religion and spirituality. Most Westerners, including feminists, are products of Enlightenment philosophy, which views the world dualistically and assumes a separation between material and spiritual concerns. Our consideration of religion in global dialogue and development is usually absent or negative. If we think about religion at all, we usually see the many ways in which religious values and organizations devalue and oppress women. We see that women are denied access to certain roles and positions of power. Therefore, we view religion as an obstacle or barrier to development, to development communication and to finding common ground in dialogue.

Yet religion, culture, and dialogue are inseparable in most of the world. Unlike what most of us experience, religious rituals and values are a part of everyday life in many other societies. Often, religion provides the foundational framework for behavior in just about every area of life—food traditions, styles of dress, friendship networks, work and study priorities, and certainly values and behaviors related to family.

Also, and again because of our secular orientation, we in communication studies seldom consider that the most profound forms of religious practice, including meditation and prayer, are in fact forms of communication. While these forms of communication are seldom examined in our research or considered when planning development strategy or coalition building, many people around the world do consider spiritual practice perhaps the most significant and empowering form of communication. Further, religious organizations make use of many other forms of communication besides prayer and meditation, including storytelling, song, drama, and controlled media and mass media. Storytelling, especially, is a powerful part of religion and culture in general, as well as of education, and development communication (and there are scholarly literatures on the role of storytelling or narrative in all of these areas). Our shared stories constitute important cultural and dialogic bonds.

Women have traditional roles in many cultures as story tellers and keepers of oral tradition. Also, smaller informal groups within religious communities often are gender- and age-divided and may be significant in development. Many have argued the importance of coordinating projects with indigenous women's groups that often exist for political, economic, or religious purposes. Women's religious groups are different from other types in that they exist not only for tangible purposes but also provide a culturally meaningful and divinely sanctioned frame for women's actions (March & Taqqu, 1986, p. 67).

Given the centrality of many forms of religious communication globally, why not consider all this in the context of development communication? Some do, especially those influenced by forms of liberation theology;[14] but, for the most part, religious practice tends to be overlooked and rarely considered under the communication umbrella, except in a negative sense—as a resistance point to be overcome, or sometimes as a cultural tool in persuasive campaigns. This gap in our consciousness is a problem in development communication, as well as in our efforts to collaborate.

Because religious stories and sacred texts often have not been interpreted by organizational leaders in ways that favor women's empowerment, feminists and others globally are critically examining sacred texts and traditions and finding new interpretations or contradictions that suggest new ways of thinking. I have become acquainted with the Muslim component of a UN Population Fund (UNFPA) Family Life Education project involving nine religious organizations in Ghana.[15] The project began in 1990, based on the recognition that traditional (including gendered) distributions of power within families often are grounded in religious beliefs, which are supported by religious organizations. Therefore, improvements in family welfare cannot succeed without involving these organizations. Each of the religious groups began the project with its own specific concerns as well. Muslim leaders were concerned about the marginalized status of Muslims in Ghana and the deprived and depressed conditions in their communities, where family sizes were large and there were high rates of teen pregnancy, child delinquency, HIV infection, overcrowding, malnutrition, and dropping out of school, especially among girls.

The Muslim component of the project began by gathering Islamic scholars and teachers to discuss what the Qur'an says about family responsibilities, family size, gender roles, and family health. While most of these scholars and teachers were men, leaders of Muslim and national women's groups were invited to present their views. In the end this analysis argued strongly against all forms of gender discrimination in the family context, including an educational preference for boys, and all practices threatening the health of women and girls. With regard to family size, the consensus was that Muslims in the past have focused disproportionate attention on the Prophet's command to multiply so he would have many followers on the day of judgment. Other Qur'anic passages suggest that what the Prophet wants is quality followers who are well-educated and healthy. This suggests healthy parents and a manageable family size, compatible with family resources. As these new interpretations have been agreed upon, women's group leaders have served as natural facilitators in subsequent dialogue and discussion among women and girls.

Martha Nussbaum argues that all major religions share a certain common moral core, which has grounded, for instance, Ghandi's attack on the caste system in India and Lincoln's attack on slavery (1998). Yes, religious organizations are patriarchal and oppress women. Yet there are conservative and liberal wings and feminist and liberation theologies and activists in every religion. The nature of the feminist positions may be complex and not easily understood by Westerners. For instance, often there are differences in the nature of religious practice by gender, and these differences do not necessarily indicate patriarchal oppression. Within all religious frameworks, women do usually lead quite creative lives with more possibilities for leadership and power than may be initially assumed.

Class privilege and religious difference constitute two major and complex challenges to global dialogue among women, as well as to development communication. But cultural barriers to dialogue and development communication are numerous, and all of them are gendered, including one's native language and the modes of thought and expression that go along with language. Where a colonial language like English or French is shared, the meanings may not be. Our words are always encoded to carry an agenda of priorities, an agenda that may or may not be consistent with what is decoded. A word like feminist is risky in many contexts, as are all words and labels of difference, of privilege, of disadvantage, and of social change. A Ghanaian educator makes this point in her description of the deadlock between Western and African women at the 1980 mid-Decade conference in Copenhagen. Communication broke down around issues of female genital mutilation, polygamy, bridewealth, and women's proper roles in political conflicts. Clearly the words and labels used by participants alongside considerable cultural insensitivity played a role in impeding dialogue in this instance (Dolphyne, 1991, pp. x–xiii).

Of course, cultural mistakes are inevitable. But to succumb to paralysis and stop talking is the worst impediment to dialogue. There are other cultural issues, and the essays in this volume explore many of them in specific contexts. All of these areas of difference create problems, but they also may suggest opportunities for mutual understanding, personal growth, and new and creative forms of communication.

Two Examples

One problem where all the issues raised so far intersect—issues of gender inequity, development, communication, culture, class, religion, human rights—is violence against women and girls in its many forms, including battering, rape, child abuse, incest, child prostitution and slavery. Gender violence also has been a major focus of dialogue among women globally in recent years. There have been at least two overlapping arguments.

First, women have argued that gender violence is a major obstacle to development. This argument builds on considerable evidence that sustainable development is impossible unless women participate. But how can women participate while oppressed by and fearing violence? The United Nations Development Fund for Women (UNIFEM) has led the way in making these arguments (Carillo, 1992; Heise, 1992). Increasingly other multilateral agencies and religious groups are arguing similarly, as in the Muslim family life project in Ghana described previously.

The salience of gender violence for me personally rose dramatically in 1991 when I was in Kenya, conducting research on women's participation in development communication projects. My plans changed in mid-July when 306 boys attacked 271 girls at St. Kizito Mixed Secondary School in Meru, Kenya. Nineteen schoolgirls died and more than 70 survivors were raped or gang–raped. In the subsequent months, as I studied Kenyan media reports of the crime and listened to public discussions, I observed a blatant absence of concern for the victims and little attention to the larger context of gender violence and oppression in Kenyan society (Steeves, 1997). The overwhelming question that struck me was this: How can we promote equal participation in development projects until girls are safe in school, in their homes and on the streets, until societies reject gender violence?

Second, women have argued that freedom from gender violence is an international human right, one that must be addressed at human rights conferences and in resulting actions (Schuler, 1993, p. 4). In 1979 the UN General Assembly adopted the Convention on the Elimination of All forms of Discrimination Against Women (CEDAW), which remains the most comprehensive international treaty addressing the human rights of women, including the right to freedom from gender violence. Further, the 1993 UN Human Rights conference recognized gender abuse and violence as human rights violations and said the UN should encourage the universal ratification of CEDAW by the year 2000. The 1995 Beijing Declaration and Program for Action reiterated these statements. So far 161 nations have ratified CEDAW. The United States is not yet among them. However, in honor of International Women's Day in March, 1998, President Clinton asked the Senate to prioritize the issue. The President's Interagency Council on Women, which is implementing the Beijing Platform, is also urging ratification (President Clinton, 1998; President's Interagency Council on Women, 1999a).

While the widespread ratification of CEDAW seems encouraging, the treaty can only be as effective as the national and local mechanisms in place to interpret and enforce it. Also, new questions of cultural influence and intervention may be raised. Madeleine Albright, who chairs the President's Interagency Council on Women, has suggested making state initiatives to curb gender violence a criterion for foreign aid. In other words, just as our foreign aid decisions involve criteria of democratization as we understand it, USAID may additionally seek and promote evidence of state action on violence against women.[16] This is happening in the extreme case of Afghanistan, where the Taliban militia are breaking every human rights treaty that exists by imprisoning females in their homes. Women who leave the home without following strict rules of attire and male accompaniment are being beaten and killed. The United States says that while we are neutral regarding the factional fighting, our neutrality does not extend to the Taliban's human rights violations against women. Therefore the United States has not extended diplomatic recognition to the Taliban Government. Further, our aid decisions in 1997 prioritized programs benefiting Afghan women and girls.[17] President Clinton also has committed an extra $10 million in 1998 and 1999 for projects globally combating violence against women (President Clinton, 1998).

What about this new direction? First, like other policy rhetoric such as the Percy Amendment mentioned earlier, it's hard to predict what implementation measures actually will be taken. But to the extent that they are, questions of where, what, and how must be raised. The Afghanistan situation is extreme and has united feminist and human rights activists. But just as critics have asked whether our ideas about democracy are appropriate everywhere, will they not also ask whether our understandings of gender violence apply everywhere? To what extent do our policies at times reflect what Chandra Mohanty calls "discursive colonization" (1991)?

The discourses that help shape national policies and their modes of implementation come from at least two places: global conferences and mass media. Certainly considerable misunderstanding and conflict around gender violence characterized the Copenhagen Conference. Yet the cultural misunderstandings or "acts of colonization" that take place in meetings among people with common interests, no matter how severe, pale compared to how these events get represented in the media. When global women or women's activism are covered, the stereotyping is blatant and context provided is abysmal. The *New York Times* and *Washington Post* coverage of the Beijing Conference is summarized in the title of a recent article in *Critical Studies in Mass Communication:* "'Radical' Feminists and 'Bickering' Women: Backlash in U.S. Media Coverage of the United Nations Fourth World Conference on Women" (Danner and Walsh, 1999).

When Third World women are covered by mainstream media, the topic is typically sensational and emotional, reinforcing stereotypes about class, race, nation, and religion. The press coverage of gender violence that may influence and be influenced by aid policy on gender violence fits with this observation. Other widespread problems usually are neglected, like illiteracy, child pregnancy, and systemic economic disadvantage. News reports almost never include Third World women's own analyses and activism. In my study of the international coverage of the St. Kizito murders and rapes, I found editorials by American feminists that rejected the violence but also revealed blatant class, ethnic, and racial ignorance and prejudice as well. I do not know of a study as yet of the coverage of the Taliban situation, but it is likely the coverage reveals Western prejudices and misconceptions about Islam and Islam's oppression of women, as well as about Third World women as passive victims. Global media coverage certainly influences and reinforces policy decisions, as well as modes of implementation. We lobby for gender-sensitive policy and projects, but new questions and conundrums surface.

Another aid issue that raises potentially troubling questions is in the area of microcredit and microenterprise for women. This idea has been embraced with enthusiasm by donor agencies, who are giving large sums of money for this purpose. USAID launched a "Microenterprise Initiative" in 1994, allocating $120 million per year for microenterprise projects in 1996 and 1997. Many of the projects focus specifically on women (Hoy, 1998, p. 36). Clearly aid agencies are assuming that credit for income generation projects will help transform women's lives by making them economically independent. Yet the idea of microenterprise, like other development directions, may suggest an imposition of foreign values—for instance, of economic individualism in societies that value collective enterprise (e.g., Rapley, 1996, pp. 170–172). Some microcredit projects at least appear to have a collective orientation, like the Grameen Bank in Bangladesh, but many do not.[18]

Further, it appears that at least some microenterprise schemes have not made the conceptual leap from the old WID framework to a more flexible and realistic GAD way of thinking. For instance, Christine Kellow gathered data for her master's thesis while doing an internship at a UN High Commission on Refugees camp in Uganda. Her job was to develop a credit scheme with money specifically earmarked for "Special Services for Women." Therefore loans would be limited to females. She quickly found that the women in the camp already were overworked doing subsistence gardening, fuelwood gathering, cooking, and child care. It was the men who had the time and motivation for income generation, but the funding was not for men (Kellow, 1998, p. 74).

CONCLUSION

The research questions and political projects that need to be addressed encompass all levels and areas of development, including development organizations and discourses. Ideally feminist research and practice are mutually reinforcing, collaborative, involve dialogue between people from different backgrounds and with different strengths, and include everyone involved in a project. This ideal is rarely achieved because of some of the differences and constraints reviewed here, and much more. Although this ideal seems remote, there are many lessons in the struggle, and we have to keep trying and recording our insights.

There is plenty of work to do at home without big travel grants. Questions and problems of gender, power, development, and discourse are everywhere. There is a need for the close study of aid organizations and how they function, work with other organizations and respond to organizational challenges. We also need to keep exposing hegemonic processes by decoding discourses of development. This includes policy and project documents and academic texts. It also includes news reports and other media representations of the Third World, which are mostly absent, but when present do affect our policies and views of other cultures and groups.

Finally, in struggling with these intersecting themes, of gender, development, power, communication, and dialogue, I often am overwhelmed by the complexity of the questions. Our interdisciplinary work crosses many fields of study, including women's studies, ethnic studies, development studies, communication studies, education and pedagogy, religious studies, critical studies, cultural studies, and every geographic area of study. No one can master the relevant literatures in all of these areas. We may work uneasily at the intersection of these many areas of literature, but should find strength in this interdisciplinary approach.

Therefore, this chapter and the others in this volume should at best be considered starting points for our collective conversations. The idea of privileged speech contradicts feminist and Freirian assumptions that we should be equal partners in dialogue and discovery. Yet processes of dialogue, coalition building, and hegemonic challenge continue, and many modes of communication may be useful. The essays published here began as talks and were challenged by the discussion that immediately followed. Hopefully the publication of this book will extend that conversation, leading to further dialogue, research, and publication, as well as to global feminist communication projects.

NOTES

The author acknowledges Anita Weiss for many helpful suggestions in the preparation of this manuscript and thanks Karin Wilkins for her vision and work in planning the conference and this volume.

1. In describing development, Robert Agunga uses the metaphor of the blind feeling an elephant—it appears completely different depending on your perspective (1997, p. 137). I use the term "Third World" in a political sense, implying poverty, opposition, and struggle. See Isbister (1991, pp. 15–16) and Mohanty (1991, p. 7).

2. See especially pages 82–85. Nussbaum argues that *capability,* not actual functioning, should be the goal of public policy. She also argues that if people are granted the functional capabilities she outlines, they are also capable, with effort, of *good* functioning.

3. I do not know of any general texts on international or development communication that devote more than a paragraph or a passing mention to gender inequality. Edited collections that focus primarily on gender are Gallagher and Lilia Quindoza-Santiago (1994), Riaño, (1994), and Allen, Rush, and Kaufman (1996).

4. At the 1995 Fourth World Conference on Women in Beijing, delegates pushed to have women's unpaid labor factored into national accounts. This alone would greatly alter understandings of development, as most Third World countries would rise rapidly in the ranks on measures of GDP. For an extended analysis of this issue, see Waring (1988).

5. This project took place in the Sind region of Pakistan in the mid-1980s. Anita Weiss found out about it while assisting with a report reviewing U.S. Economic Assistance to Pakistan, 1982–1987 (Williams and Rudel, 1988). For many other examples, see Rogers (1980).

6. See especially UNDP (1997, 1998) for extensive analyses comparing and correlating national indices of human development and gender-related development. UNDP's human development index (HDI) combines measures of average life expectancy, educational achievement (literacy plus education), and GDP per capita. The gender-related development index (GDI) is the same as the HDI, considering inequalities in achievement between women and men (e.g., 1998, pp. 14–15).

7. For an evaluation of the effectiveness of Percy Amendment actions, see Staudt (1985b). Additionally, Hoy (1998, p. 24) reports that in December, 1993, the General Accounting Office was requested to evaluate the outcome of the Percy Amendment mandates. The conclusion was that progress in implementing the mandates had been slow with much evidence of noncompliance. For an excellent analysis, though dated, of the ineffectiveness of WID policy for both multilateral and bilateral aid, see Rogers (1980).

8. This can be argued conceptually via Gramsci and Habermas. See Seidman (1989) and Mouffe (1979).

9. For examples, see Sreberny-Mohammadi (1996).

10. For instance, 1993–1994 regional meetings with hundreds in attendance were held in Manila, Philippines; New York (several meetings); Jakarta, Indonesia; Turku, Finland; Mara del Plata, Argentina; Buenos Aires, Argentina; Vienna, Austria; Amman, Jordan; and Dakar, Senegal.

11. Williams assumes a web of significance among many facets of nonmaterial and material culture, including lifestyles, modes and processes of intellectual, spiritual and artistic work, and the concrete products of all this work (pp. 80–81).

12. I thank Christine Kellow (1998, p. 26) for suggesting this synopsis in Hall.

13. For a discussion of PAR as a tool of resistance, see Escobar (1984). For a critical examination of the concept, see Rahnema (1990). For an excellent discussion of the economic privilege as an obstacle to PAR, see Patai (1991).

14. Ariyaratne (1987) describes group meditation as one of several strategies within the Sarvodaya movement in Sri Lanka, which is rooted in Buddhism and aims simultaneously to develop individual spiritual consciousness and change societal conditions characterized by large economic gaps between the haves and have-nots. See also Dissanayake (1991) for a discussion of the movement. Taylor (1994) describes the value of group meditation and other spiritual rituals for problem solving and enhancing group process for women's groups in Thailand and Newfoundland.

15. The three religious groups that participated at the start of the project were Muslim Family Counseling Services, the Christian Council of Ghana, and the National Catholic Secretariat. By 1993, seven others were involved: Adventist Development and Relief Agency; Ahmadiyya Movement in Islam; Church of Pentecost; Ghana Pentecostal Council; Islamic Research and Reformation Centre; Salvation Army; Seventh–Day Adventists. The lead funding organization is the UNFPA. The Planned Parenthood Association of Ghana is the primary implementing partner, reviewing budgets and carrying out evaluations under UNFPA. Other organizations involved include the Inter-Africa Committee for the Eradication of Traditional Practices Affecting the Health of Women, the National Council for Women in Development, the Ghanaian Association for Women's Welfare, the Ghana Ministry of Health, the National AIDS Control Programme, and the Ghana Social Marketing Foundation.

16. USAID administrator Brian Atwood led the post-Cold War streamlining of USAID's goals from thirty-three to the following five, set forth in 1994: provision of humanitarian relief, stabilization of population growth, promotion of democracy, environmental protection, and broad-based economic growth (Hoy, 1998, p. 35).

17. In 1997 the U.S. government contributed $26.4 million to three organizations that run programs benefiting Afghan women and girls: UNHCR, the International Red Cross, and the World Food Program (President's Interagency Council on Women, 1997).

18. The bank loans are provided to self-formed groups. Each group is given a capital sum, and designates two members to receive the loan. No other members of the group may receive loans until the first two have begun their weekly repayments (Hoy, 1998, p. 122).

REFERENCES

Agunga, R. A. (1997). *Developing the Third World: A communication approach.* Commack, NY: Nova Science Publishers.

Allen, D., Rush, R. R., & Kaufman, S. J. (Eds.) (1996). *Women transforming communications: Global intersections.* Thousand Oaks, CA: Sage.

Ariyaratne, A. T. (1987). Beyond development communication: Case study on Sarvodaya, Sri Lanka. In N. Jayaweera & S. Amunugama (Eds.), *Rethinking development communication* (pp. 239–251). Singapore: Asian Mass Communication Research Centre.

Boserup, E. (1970). *Women's role in economic development.* New York, NY: St. Martin's Press.
Carey, J. (1989). *Communication as culture: Essays on media and society.* Boston, MA: Unwin Hyman.
Carillo, R. (1992). *Battered dreams: Violence against women as an obstacle to development.* New York, NY: UNIFEM.
Danner, L., & Walsh, S. (1999) 'Radical' feminists and 'bickering' women: Backlash in U.S. media coverage of the United Nations Fourth World Conference on Women, *Critical Studies in Mass Communication,* 16(1), 63–84.
Dissanayake, W. (1991). Ethics, development, and communication: A Buddhist approach. In F. L. Casmir (Ed.), *Communication in development* (pp. 319–327). Norwood, NJ: Ablex.
Dolphyne, F. A. (1991). *The emancipation of women: An African perspective.* Accra, Ghana: Ghana University Press.
Escobar, A. (1984). Discourse and power in development: Michel Foucault and the relevance of his work to the Third World. *Alternatives,* 10(3), 377–400.
Freire, P. (1970). *Pedagogy of the oppressed* (M. B. Ramos, Trans.). New York, NY: Continuum.
Gallagher, M., & Quindoza-Santiago, L. (Eds.) (1994). *Women empowering communication: A resource book on the globalization of media.* New York, NY: International Women's Tribune Centre.
Gender action, A newsletter of the USAID Office of Women in Development (1997), 1(3).
Hall, E. T. (1976). *Beyond culture.* Garden City, NY: Anchor Press.
Heise, L. (1992). *Fact sheet on gender violence: A statistics for action facts sheet.* New York, NY: IWTC/UNIFEM Resource Centre.
Hoy, P. (1998). *Players and issues in international aid.* West Hartford, CT: Kumarian Press.
Isbister, J. (1991). *Promises not kept: The betrayal of social change in the Third World.* West Hartford, CT: Kumarian Press.
Kellow, C. L. (1998). Refugee needs and donor agendas: Communication and coordination of services in refugee aid programs. Unpublished master's thesis, University of Oregon, Eugene, Oregon.
Kotler, P. (1984). Social marketing of health behavior. In. L. W. Frederiksen, L. J. Solomon, & K. A. Brehony (Eds.), *Marketing health behavior: Principles, techniques and applications* (pp. 23–39). New York, NY: Plenum Press.
Kusterer, K., Samarasinghe, V., & Young, G. (1993). Introduction. In G. Young, V. Samarasinghe & K. Kusterer (Eds.), *Women at the center: Development issues and practices for the 1990s* (pp. 1–7). West Hartford, CT: Kumarian Press.
Luthra, R. (1988). *Communication in the social marketing of contraceptives: A case study of the Bangladesh project.* Unpublished Ph.D. dissertation, University of Wisconsin-Madison.
Luthra, R. (1991). Contraceptive social marketing in the Third World: A case of multiple transfer. *Gazette,* 47(3), 159–176.
March, K. S., & Taqqu, R. L. (1986). *Women's informal associations in developing countries: Catalysts for change?* Boulder, CO: Westview Press.
Mohanty, C. (1991). Under western eyes: Feminist scholarship and colonial discourse. In C. T. Mohanty, A. Russo, & L. Torres (Eds.), *Third World women and the politics of feminism* (pp. 51–80). Bloomington, IN: Indiana University Press.
Mouffe, C. (1979). Hegemony and ideology in Gramsci. In C. Mouffe (Ed.), *Gramsci and Marxist theory* (pp. 168–204). London, UK: Routledge & Kegan Paul.

Nussbaum, M. (1995). Human capabilities, female human beings. In M. Nussbaum & J. Glover (Eds.), *Women, culture and development: A study of human capabilities* (pp. 61–104). Oxford, UK: Oxford University Press.

Nussbaum, M. (1998). International feminism: The role of religion, Colin Raugh Thomas O'Fallon Memorial Lecture in Law and American Culture, Eugene, University of Oregon, Feb. 20.

Patai, D. (1991). U.S. academics and Third World women: Is ethical research possible? In S. B. Gluck, & D. Patai (Eds.), *Women's words: The feminist practice of oral history* (pp. 137–153). New York, NY: Routledge.

President Clinton: An Historic Commitment to International Human Rights, Wednesday, March 11, 1998. Available: http://secretary.state.gov/www/picw/archives/980311_clintons_women.html.

President's Interagency Council on Women (1997). Unpublished document.

President's Interagency Council on Women (1999a). Highlights from NGO Briefing Meeting, Department of State, June 3, 1999. Available: http://secretary.state.gov/www/picw/990603_ngo_pb.html.

President's Interagency Council on Women (1999b). Update: America's Commitment, Department of State, June 3, 1999. Available: http://secretary.state.gov/www/picw/media.html.

Rahnema, M. (1990). Participatory action research: The 'last temptation of saint' development. *Alternatives,* XV, 199–226.

Rapley, J. (1996). *Understanding development: Theory and practice in the Third World.* Boulder, CO: Lynne Reinner.

Riaño, P. (Ed.) (1994). *Women in grassroots communication: Furthering social change.* Thousand Oaks, CA: Sage.

Rogers, B. (1980). *The domestication of women: Discrimination in developing societies.* New York, NY: St. Martin's Press.

Schuler, M. (Ed.) (1993). *Claiming our place: Working the human rights system to women's advantage.* Washington, DC: Institute for Women, Law, and Development.

Seager, J. (1997). *The state of women in the world atlas,* New Edition. London, UK: Penguin.

Seidman, S. (Ed.) (1989). *Jurgen Habermas on society and politics.* Boston, MA: Beacon Press.

Sreberny-Mohammadi, A. (1996). Women communicating globally: Mediating international feminism. In D. Allen, R. R. Rush, & S. J. Kaufman (Eds.), *Women transforming communications: Global intersections* (pp. 233–242). Thousand Oaks, CA: Sage.

Staudt, K. (1985a). *Agricultural policy implementation: A case study from Western Kenya.* West Hartford, CT: Kumarian Press.

Staudt, K. (1985b). *Women, foreign assistance and advocacy administration.* New York, NY: Praeger.

Steeves, H. L. (1997). *Gender violence and the press: The St. Kizito story.* Athens, OH: Ohio University Press, Monographs in International Studies.

Taylor, S. (1994). Communicating for empowerment: Women's initiatives to overcome poverty in rural Thailand and Newfoundland. In P. Riaño (Ed.), *Women in grassroots communication: Furthering social change* (pp. 235–250). Thousand Oaks, CA: Sage.

Tisch, S. J. & Wallace, M. B. (1994). *Dilemmas of development assistance: The what, why, and who of foreign aid.* Boulder, CO: Westview.

United Nations (1995). *The world's women 1995: Trends and statistics.* New York, NY: United Nations.United Nations Development Programme (UNDP) (1997). *Human development report, 1997.* New York, NY: Oxford University Press.

United Nations Development Programme (UNDP) (1998). *Human development report, 1998.* New York, NY: Oxford University Press.

United Nations High Commissioner for Refugees (UNHCR) (1997). *The state of the world's refugees 1997–1998: A humanitarian agenda.* Oxford, UK: Oxford University Press.

Update to America's commitment: Federal programs benefiting women and new initiatives as follow-up to the UN Fourth World Conference on Women. April 1998 supplement. Available: http://secretary.state.gov/www/picw/archives/May1997_report/1998_april_supplement.html.

Waring, M. (1988). *If women counted: A new feminist economics.* New York: Harper Collins.

Weiss, A. (1998). Personal communication, June 5.

Williams, M. & Rudel, L. (1988). *U.S. economic assistance to Pakistan: Review of the period 1982–1987, Final report.* Bethesda, MD: Devres, Inc., April 28.

Williams, R. (1976). *Keywords: A vocabulary of culture and society.* New York, NY: Oxford University Press.

World Bank. (1999). *World development report: Knowledge for Development.* New York, NY: Oxford University Press.

3

Governing Reproduction

Women's Empowerment and Population Policy

Ronald Walter Greene

Girl Power has attached itself to the goals of the United Nation's Fund for Population Activities (UNFPA). In November of 1998, Geri Halliwell, the former Ginger Spice, declared to the world that she would use her fame to promote family planning in the "developing world" (*Time,* 1998). The use of celebrity spokespersons is nothing new, but here we have a blend of popular culture and population policy made possible by the empowerment rhetoric of girl power. Halliwell's association with the rhetoric of empowerment might suggest the need for a more careful investigation into how population policy is being put together for the twenty-first century.

During the last fifteen years, women's empowerment has emerged as a way to transform women into active subjects, as opposed to passive objects targeted by international development plans (Sen & Grown, 1987; Townsend, 1993; UNFPA, 1989). While Geri Halliwell's use value as a celebrity spokesperson might be getting smaller by the day, her appearance on the terrain of international population policy might not be as absurd as one might first imagine. Geri Halliwell's use value is her association with the rhetoric of empowerment (girl power), a rhetoric increasingly deployed to support the incorporation of Southern women into the programs associated with international population policy. The popularity of the Spice Girls is, no doubt, limited by the forces of uneven development that characterize capital flows between the Northern and Southern Hemispheres. Yet, the complex path linking the youth cultures of London and Calcutta does point to at least one place where the UNFPA might be hoping to cash in on Geri Halliwell's ability to communicate the link between women's empowerment and family planning.

I would like to take this opportunity to problematize how we think of power in population policy. More specifically, I want to focus on how "women's empowerment" functions as a "technology of the self" (Foucault, 1988) to invent "modern" women through the regulation of their reproductive lives. This chapter supports a more general tendency to perform a critical interrogation of development communication. At the center of this critical turn is a problematization of development and the ways in which a host of discursive practices contribute to the taken for granted idea that the "Third World" needs development (Escobar, 1995).

To contribute to the critical interrogation of development, I analyze how women's empowerment is being linked to two different governing rationalities of reproduction: the Malthusian modern and the feminist modern. The Malthusian modern promises health, happiness, and economic mobility in and through the regulation of reproduction (Greene, 1999). In opposition to the Malthusian modern, the feminist modern supports the economic, political and cultural rights of women as the foundation for improving the welfare of particular populations (Greene, 1999). The Malthusian modern and the feminist modern battle over women's empowerment in population policy, and the feminist modern is displacing the Malthusian modern on the plane of population policy. However, to appreciate fully the problems and possibilities associated with the feminist modern requires that we abandon a bipolar model of power for a more productive sense of power that focuses on how subjects are brought into being, not merely as objects manipulated by an external force.

ON THE ROAD TO CAIRO

Since World War II, a global network of institutional actors has emerged in an effort to invent, circulate, and regulate a demographic panic (Greene, 1999) associated with population growth. This demographic panic, most famously described as "the population bomb" (Ehrlich, 1968), circulates an anxiety about how the growth and compositional dynamics of world population threaten the economic and environmental security of individual subjects, nations, and the planet. The promotion of this Malthusian panic is one of the primary ways the population apparatus—a complex assemblage of discourses, institutions, technologies, and populations—generates a "will to govern" population growth (Greene, 1999). Of course, this fear about population growth is, more often than not, specifically located in Latin America, Africa, and Asia. In order to govern population growth, the population apparatus increasingly makes visible the reproductive lives of Southern women as a threat to individual, national, and global welfare. The effect of this regime of visibility is, according to Maria Mies and Vandana Shiva, to "see women only as aggregated uteruses and prospective perpetrators of overpopulation. Women of the South are increasingly reduced to numbers, targets, wombs, tubes, and other reproductive parts" (1993, pp. 282–283).

Feminists in the United States and elsewhere challenged the population apparatus for its authoritarian tendencies and its ability to co-opt the feminist struggles for reproductive rights (Balasubrahmanyan, 1989; Beal, 1970; Bradotti et al., 1994; Gordon, 1976; Petchesky, 1990). However, the most serious challenge to the population apparatus was waged in the 1980s by conservatives, led by the Reagan administration at the United Nations (UN), for its role as a provider of abortion services. The Reagan administration set out its challenge to the population apparatus at the United Nations Population Conference held in Mexico City in 1984. The Reagan administration advanced the argument that population growth was not inherently harmful, but neutral in regard to its effect on economic development. It also attempted to intensify the restrictions on the use of U.S. funds by making it more difficult for nongovernmental organizations (NGOs) and the U.S. Agency for International Development (USAID) to "indirectly" deploy those funds to provide abortion services. The effect of Reagan's Mexico City policy was to attenuate the U.S. leadership role severely in promoting the goals of the population apparatus (Finkle & Crane, 1985). For advocates of the population apparatus, the Mexico City policy set in motion a "lost decade," intensifying the harms of population growth and making it more expensive to solve those problems (Camp, 1993).

At the same time, U.S. feminists began to interrogate the effect of the Mexico City policy on women's reproductive rights and reproductive health. Sylvia Law and Lisa Rackner evaluated the consequences of the Mexico City policy this way:

> The Mexico City policy drastically impairs women's control of their reproductive biology. First, the policy effectively restricts the actual availability of abortion services. Second, [it] virtually insures that the counseling women receive in a USAID funded clinic will be biased, incomplete, and simply inadequate. . . . Finally, [it] grossly and blatantly discriminates against women by preventing women and health care workers who serve them from obtaining unbiased written information on abortion. The Mexico City policy plainly oppresses and degrades women. (1987, pp. 222–224)

The support that the population apparatus received, intentionally or not, from U.S. feminists challenging the Reagan policy helped to recode the population apparatus as an advocate of reproductive rights eliding the many "reproductive wrongs" (Hartmann, 1995) done in the name of population stabilization. Due to the conservative challenge, the population apparatus was once again able to position itself as a defender of reproductive rights. As Betsy Hartmann writes: "Ironically, the policy statement [produced by the Conference] served to legitimize the position of the population establishment by casting it in the role of the defender of reproductive rights" (1995, p. 130).

As the Clinton administration prepared for the International Conference on Population and Development held in Cairo, Egypt in October of 1994, it signaled to the world that the United States would abandon the Mexico City policy. Timothy Wirth, the Clinton administration's representative during the preliminary meetings leading to Cairo, declared the reversal of policy:

> President [Clinton] has reversed the so-called Mexico City policy, lifting restrictions that prohibited some family planning organizations from receiving U.S. funding because of related abortion services. . . . The world and U.S. policy has moved past the misconception that population growth is a neutral phenomenon. (1993, p. 397)

The Clinton administration built its case for reversing the Mexico City policy out of three interlocking arguments. First, a commitment to reducing population growth was consistent with the international goals of sustainable development. Second, reducing population growth was part of the solution to control the migration of people, particular from the Southern to the Northern hemisphere. Finally, support for population policy was an important site for the promotion of women's reproductive rights and maternal health as part of an empowerment strategy to offer alternatives to the cultural pressures for children (Wirth, 1993). I want to focus on the how the link between population control and women's reproductive rights/health was assembled and challenged at the Cairo Conference.

The Clinton administration used the Cairo Conference to support a reorganization of the population apparatus to support the goal of women's sexual and reproductive health. The Clinton administration advanced its support for the population apparatus to support an emphasis on "sexual and reproductive health" in four steps. First, it identified the health risks of pregnancy due to inadequate access to maternal health care, contraception, and safe abortion. Second, it linked the goals of women's empowerment to reproductive health and reproductive rights. Third, it supported the claim that a large unmet demand for safe and effective methods of fertility control existed throughout the world. Finally, the Clinton administration supported the view that family planning and reproductive rights and health care were mutually re-enforcing objectives of population policy (Wirth, 1993).

Perhaps the most important document attempting to transform population policy in the direction of sexual and reproductive health was prepared by the International Women's Health Coalition in cooperation with the Harvard Center for Population and Development Studies and the Swedish International Development Authority. *Population Policies Reconsidered: Health, Empowerment, and Rights,* edited by Gita Sen, Adrienne Germain, and Lincoln C. Chen, is a complex and internally contested document that nonetheless sets out to challenge population policy by placing "central importance on overcoming poor health, lack of reproductive choice, poverty, and oppression" (1994, p. xiii). The overall development strategy supported by *Population Policies Reconsidered* is "human development." Human development advocates that the areas of health, education, water, sanitation, housing, and social services take priority in development assistance. This document values the economic, political, and cultural needs of Southern women as a higher priority than the population apparatus's need to reach particular demographic targets.

To support the goals of women's health the document reports that the

> basic message of the women's health agenda is clear: access to quality health services—particularly reproductive health services that include safe and effective contraception and abortion—and respect for reproductive rights are fundamental demands from women worldwide. (Garcia-Moreno and Claro, 1994, p. 53)

The emphasis on empowerment argues for treating women as subjects, that is, active and equal agents in the decision-making process of both development and population policy and not simply as means to reduce fertility. The desire to transform women into subjects is an effort to correct the tendency to treat women merely as objects targeted for change by development and population agencies. The defense of reproductive rights takes on a strong autonomy demand that a woman should "decide for herself matters of sexuality and childbearing with no interference from her partner, family, health care professionals, religious groups, the state or any other actor" (Boland et al., 1994, p. 100). At the same time, the documents support an emphasis on a broad interpretation of reproductive rights that places them within a larger system of "social welfare, personal security and political freedom" (Correa & Petchesky, 1994, p. 107).

The interaction between the Clinton administration and the feminist challenges to the population apparatus, represented by *Population Policies Reconsidered,* proved a powerful combination at the Cairo Conference. While the Vatican attempted to build an alliance with more conservative elements associated with Islam to resist an emphasis on sexual and reproductive health, the plan of action adopted at the Cairo Conference represented an important change in direction for the population apparatus. McIntosh and Finkle claim that "a new definition of population policy was advanced, giving prominence to reproductive health and the empowerment of women while downplaying the demographic rational for population policy" (1995, p. 223). Charles Westoff, a former director of the Office of Population Research at Princeton, expressed the unease felt by many long-term advocates of the population apparatus: "The Cairo Conference was a resounding success for the advocates of women's reproductive health but a disappointment of many concerned about population growth. . . . The two are not synonymous" (1995, p. 16).

The primary challenge represented in the mainstream press to the population apparatus was the conservative opposition launched by the Holy See. However, the Cairo Conference's emphasis on sexual and reproductive rights and the programs associated with women's empowerment did not go unchallenged from the perspective of feminists with a more radical political agenda of destabilizing the articulations between capitalism, racism, and sexism. Betsy Hartmann (1995) suggests that the hard-fought victories at the Cairo Conference may be too easily co-opted to pursue the same old development and population plans. She worries that a narrow interpretation of women's empowerment, a lack of investment in public health (caused by International Monetary Fund and World Back restructuring programs), and skewed funding priorities that earmark family planning as the number one beneficiary of health investments will contain the more radical potentials hoped for in the construction of women's empowerment as a mechanism to fight forms of oppression.

THE FEMINIST MODERN AND THE POPULATION APPARATUS

Women's empowerment, reproductive rights, and maternal health make up a governing rationality that I call the feminist modern. To understand the relationship between the feminist modern and the population apparatus, however, will require a respecification of how to think about power. To be more specific, the on-going debate over women's empowerment is too often hampered by a bipolar model of power that conceptualizes the population apparatus as an external top-down threat to the interests of Third World women. I think this conceptualization of the population apparatus, while often correct, might fail to recognize the problems and possibilities associated with the feminist desire to improve the economic, political, and cultural power of women. All too often an overemphasis on the powerlessness of Third World women fails to recognize how this portrait serves to authorize First World intellectuals to speak for the political, economic and cultural interests of Third World women (Mohanty, 1991; Parpart, 1995; Spivak, 1988).

As a possible escape route from the problems associated with a bipolar model of power, an alternative approach might be offered by thinking of women's empowerment as a "technology of the self." Michel Foucault describes a technology of the self as a practical logic that

> permit(s) individuals to effect by their own means, or with the help of others, a certain number of operations on their own bodies and souls, thought, conducts, and way of being, so as to transform themselves in order to attain a certain state of happiness, purity, wisdom, perfection, or immortality. (1988, p. 18)

A technology of the self helps us to understand how subjects are transformed into subjects, a process Foucault describes as subjectification. For Foucault (1983), the process of subjectification is not limited to the constitutive force of language use, that is, how language use creates an image of a person. Instead the process of subjectification focuses on how a norm is folded onto the body of a subject through a series of practices that help to define the subject as an individual. In other words, the process of subjectification approaches power from the direction of how it produces a person or individual as an active agent in their own self formation.

The bipolar model of power pushes critics to track down how individuals are targeted as objects in order to promote the interests of some external force. To be sure, the population apparatus has been complicit in forms of domination and exploitation that include forced sterilizations, lack of informed consent, the testing of contraceptive devices on Third World women, and the infanticide of girl children. My argument is not that these things do not happen, but to suggest that power works in other ways and that it is important for those of us committed to the creation of a different future, a future free from the Malthusian imagination of development planners and the population apparatus, to begin to approach these other forms of power.

A form of power based on the insights of subjectification requires that we think about how power works to produce individuals or subjects who pursue and promote, often with the help of others, their own normative conception of the good life. Foucault describes the process of subjectification as a form of power that

> applies itself to immediate everyday life which categorizes the individual, marks him [or her] by his [or her] individuality, attaches to him [or her] his [or her] own identity, imposes a law of truth on him [or her] which he [or she] must recognize and which others have to recognize in him. It is a form of power which makes individuals subjects. (1983, p. 210)

I suggest that the investment in women's empowerment as a technology of the self points to the emergence of a particular process of individualization that I have called the feminist modern (Greene, 1999). The feminist modern is committed to the production of women as autonomous subjects who make decisions for themselves and about themselves free from the constraining pressures of kinship and social network. In order to promote the creation of autonomous subjects who speak and reason, the feminist modern supports the expansion of economic, cultural, and political power for women. At this point I want to unravel the relationship between modernity, reproduction, and feminism.

Foucault suggests that modern forms of government ground their legitimacy in the desire to take responsibility for the administration of life. In order to do so, the art of government takes on an investment into the life processes of individuals and populations. Thus, a whole ensemble of knowledges and practices are invented and deployed to inquire into and keep track of such things as birth rates, death rates, fertility rates, the distribution of populations, and the like (Foucault, 1991). This investment in the welfare of a population circulates for Foucault as a form of biopower and generates what he calls biopolitics. Biopower offers itself as a productive form of power that inaugurates the creation of individual subjects through the invention of truths formed by the desire to promote the well-being of a population.

It is important to think of government in a broader sense than the power invested in the state. Government is, for Foucault, a more abstract form of power that focuses on conduct and how certain manners, morals, and behaviors can be harnessed in order to promote the administration of life. In this sense, government is much broader than simply state power, or what Foucault calls juridical power, instead working at the intersection of the technologies of power and technologies of the self, generating a site of contestation and a struggle over how to best govern the self and others. In this way the state is enlisted as an active agent in the promotion of a particular governing rationality as opposed to occupying a central location as a point of origin for the dispersion of forms of government. For Foucault, one cannot escape government, but one can always demand to be governed in other ways. It is in the struggle over forms of government directed at the administration of life that a biopolitics takes place.

If we keep in mind that modern forms of government work through biopower, the body itself often becomes the ground of resistance and transformation. In this way we can understand the struggle over reproductive rights as a contest that takes place on the ground of biopolitics as subjects and populations battle over forms of government. As Jana Sawicki writes: "The history of modern feminist struggles for reproductive freedom is a key dimension of the history of biopower" (1991, p. 68). This relationship between reproduction and government points to what I am trying to characterize as the feminist modern. The feminist modern is a form of reproductive government that attempts to invest in women the final authority to make judgments about having children. In so doing, it offers itself as mode of reproductive government that is different from those forms of government that attempt to use the family, the state, or men as the primary agents in regulating reproduction. However, along with Michel Foucault (1980) and Rosiland Petchesky (1990), I suggest that this authority to make judgments about having children functions as a sign of cultural distinction. Thus the feminist modern offers a governing model that takes women's control over reproduction as a primary technology of the self making possible the invention of modern women. To put this differently, a modern woman is a subject whose truth status as modern resides in her ability to govern herself through the regulation of her reproduction.

It is from this perspective that the uptake of women's empowerment within the administrative logics of the population apparatus becomes particularly acute. The feminist modern's form of reproductive government runs headlong into the Malthusian modern often associated with the population apparatus. The Malthusian modern replicates a demographic panic as part of its ability to promise an improvement in the status of the subject in and through the regulation of reproduction. As Claudia Garcia-Moreno and Amparo Claro write, "a fundamental dilemma for feminists continues to be how to campaign for access to birth control and reproductive health services without being seen as colluding with proponents of population control" (1994, p. 53). Yet, the collusion is perhaps unavoidable in a historical moment when birth control and reproductive health services are often not available without the help of the family planning services provided by the population apparatus. The population apparatus's complicity in women's subordination is often expressed as being a "top-down" approach more concerned with demographic targets than the empowerment of women (Hartmann, 1995). What is usually meant by this description is that the population apparatus enlists institutional agents to support the goals of population reduction in coercive ways. Even in the absence of coercion, the top-down critique also challenges the role of the population apparatus as being complicit in forms of discrimination against women. Yet, the Programme of Action put together by Cairo calls for "Countries to act to empower women . . . eliminating all practices that discriminate against women; assisting women to establish and realize their rights, including those that relate to reproductive and sexual health" (United Nations Programme of

Action, Sec. 4.4–4.4C). As McIntosh and Finkle (1995) point out, the Cairo Conference looks to be the beginning of a new paradigm for the population apparatus.

It may be time to abandon the top-down/bottom-up rhetoric associated with the critique of the population apparatus. This rhetoric would seem to be implicated in a bipolar model of power that may be too quick to assume that the rhetoric in support of women's rights emerging from the population apparatus is a co-optation of feminist struggles. If we are to take seriously the Cairo Conference, we might be justified in arguing that the population apparatus has not so much co-opted women's empowerment as the feminist modern has captured the population apparatus. In other words, the population apparatus is being aligned with other global agencies to support the development, education, and reproductive rights of women as part of an empowerment strategy to "modernize" women.

Once we can begin to conceptualize the feminist modern as a governing rationality in competition with the Malthusian modern, then the population apparatus can be refigured as a site of contestation and debate, open to capture by different governing rationalities. In this way, the population apparatus is less implicated in a form of bipolar power that already subjugates women, but instead can be given a history and a new direction, its resources used for other means than a top-down approach to population control. Yet, to refigure the population apparatus is to think of women's empowerment less as a rhetoric capable of co-optation then as a particular technology of the self that helps to generate a particular type of individual. To appreciate women's empowerment as a technology of the self suggests that we see it as part of the governing rationality of the feminist modern, a global force that engages with other global, national, and local forces in order to promote the decision-making power of women. In the area of biological reproduction, the feminist modern supports the judgment of women as the primary governing agent. In this way, women's empowerment makes possible the creation of a modern woman in and through her status as an active participant in her own cultural, political, and economic life.

CONCLUSION

The promise of the Malthusian modern is one of economic mobility in and through the regulation of reproduction. In the European context, the Malthusian modern also allowed for the self-government of reproduction to serve as a sign of cultural distinction. The key move in this process was the recoding of biological reproduction as governable, something that couples could take responsibility for by making a decision to have or not to have a child. In other words, having children was no longer simply assigned to the realm of the natural, but was taken up as a practice amenable to regulation, planning, timing, and spacing. The feminist modern, while committed to a far more radical restructuring of the relationship between men and women, nonetheless supports the governing of reproduction. The difference is that the Malthusian modern is open to forms of direct coercion in the name of demographic targets. In opposition to this authoritarian tendency of the Malthusian modern, the feminist modern offers a women-centered approach to the governing of reproduction. The feminist modern makes its intervention as a form of biopolitics at the level of the decision-making process. This emphasis on decision making points to the creation of modern subjects whose truth resides in their ability to make judgments as free from external control as possible. In order to promote this participation, the feminist modern supports a broad range of programs to promote the empowerment of women to make decisions in line with their desires and interests.

Yet the feminist modern's use of women's empowerment as part of a technology of the self generates the desire for the population apparatus. The cultural distinction associated with governing reproduction still remains. The feminist modern helps women to signal their status as modern through their ability to regulate their reproduction. This sense of regulation does not require the absence of children. However, as Mielle Chandler (1998) suggests, a feminist politics committed to the creation of autonomous subjects does threaten to code motherhood itself as a threat to women's emancipation. It is for this reason that it becomes important to pull back from a strictly bipolar model of power. The bipolar model of power views women as objects without resources being manipulated to serve the interests of some external force. A different approach is to focus on the process of subjectification as a form of power that creates individuals through a set of truths about their status as individuals with their own voices, interests, and desires. Yet, motherhood can be just such a form of subjectification, defining the truth of women in and through their status as mothers. The feminist modern is an alternative process of subjectification and as such it works to challenge other forms of subjectification that might be too easily articulated to forms of domination, but it is nonetheless a form of power that circulates to create particular types of individuals. In the area of population policy, the feminist modern is committed to producing modern women by helping women to govern their reproduction.

If we abandon the top-down/bottom-up rhetoric associated with a bipolar model of power, it becomes possible to see how the feminist modern might be capable of capturing the population apparatus for its own purposes. The population apparatus's support for population control based on a Malthusian model of reproductive government should not be taken for granted. In the aftermath of the Cairo Conference, the population apparatus might be in the process of being turned in the direction of a feminist model of reproductive government. This capturing of the population apparatus blocks a coercive Malthusianism by supporting women's empowerment, reproductive rights, and maternal health. It may be important to rethink how the population apparatus remains a force without resorting to the argument that it co-opts the rhetoric of feminism. Instead, it might be possible to think about how the feminist modern captures the population apparatus so as to empower women by making its expertise and resources for governing reproduction more available and more democratic. To be sure, the feminist modern wants to reorganize how expertise functions particularly in the way in which it tends to disenfranchise women in the decision-making process. But it is this very call to activate women as experts, as equal participants, that, perhaps ironically, brings women into a more active relationship with the population apparatus. In other words, women are no longer the mere objects of population control, but empowered subjects directing the resources of the population apparatus to support their reproductive rights and maternal health.

REFERENCES

Balasubrahmanyan, V. (1989). Women as targets in India's family planning policy. In R. Arditti, R. Klein & S. Mindin (Eds.), *Test-Tube women: What future for motherhood* (13th Chapter). London, UK: Pandora.

Beal, F. (1970). Double jeopardy: To be black and female. In R. Morgan (Ed.), *Sisterhood is powerful: An anthology of the writings from the women's liberation movement* (pp. 382–396). New York, NY: Vintage.

Boland, R., Rao, S. & Ziedstein, G. (1994). Honoring human rights in population policies: From declaration to action. In G. Sen, A. Germain, & L. Chen (Eds.), *Population policies reconsidered: Health, empowerment, and rights* (pp. 89–106). Cambridge, MA: Harvard University Press.

Bradotti, R., Charkiewicz, E., Hausler, S., & Wieringa, S. (1994). *Women, the environment and sustainable development.* London, UK: Zed.

Camp, S. (1993). Population: The critical decade. *Foreign Policy* (April), 132–147.

Chandler, M. (1998). Emancipated subjectivities and the subjugation of mothering practices. In S. Abbey & A. O'Reilly (Eds.), *Redefining motherhood: Changing identities and patterns* (16th Chapter). Toronto, CAN: Second Story Press.

Correa, S. & Petchesky, R. (1994). Reproductive and sexual rights: A feminist perspective. In G. Sen, A. Germain, & L. Chen (Eds.), *Population policies reconsidered: health, empowerment, and rights* (pp. 107–126). Cambridge, MA: Harvard University Press.

Ehrlich, P. (1968). *The population bomb.* New York, NY: Ballentine.

Escobar, A. (1995). *Encountering development: The making and unmaking of the Third World.* Princeton, NJ: Princeton University Press.

Finkle J. & Crane, B. (1985). Ideology and politics at Mexico City: The United States at the 1984 conference on population. *Population and Development Review,* 11(2), 1–24.

Foucault, M. (1980). *History of sexuality,* vol. 1. Trans., Alan Sheridan. New York, NY: Vintage.

Foucault, M. (1983). Afterword: The subject and power. In H. Dreyfus & P. Rabinow (Eds.), *Michel Foucault: Beyond structuralism and hermeneutics* (pp. 208–226). Chicago, IL: University of Chicago Press.

Foucault, M. (1988). Technologies of the self. In L. Martin, H. Gutman, & P. Hutton (Eds.), *Technologies of the self: A seminar with Michel Foucault* (pp. 16–49). Amherst, MA: University of Massachusetts Press.

Foucault, M. (1991). Governmentality. In G. Burchell, C. Gordon, & P. Miller (Eds.), *The Foucault effect: Studies in governmentality* (pp. 87–104). Chicago, IL: University of Chicago Press.

Garica-Moreno, C. & Claro, A. (1994). Challenges from the women's health movement: Women's rights versus population control. In G. Sen, A. Germain, & L. Chen (Eds.), *Population policies reconsidered: Health, empowerment, and rights* (pp. 47–63). Cambridge, MA: Harvard University Press.

Gordon, L. (1976). *Women's body, women's right: A social history of birth control in America.* New York, NY: Grossman Publishers.

Greene, R. (1999). *Malthusian worlds: U.S. leadership and the governing of the population crisis.* Boulder, CO: Westview.

Hartmann, B. (1995). *Reproductive rights and wrongs. The global reproductive politics of population control.* Boston, MA: South End Press.

Law, S. & Rackner, L. (1987). Gender equity and the Mexico City policy. *New York University Journal of International Law and Politics,* 20(1), 193–228.

Mies, M. & Shiva, V. (1993). *Ecofeminism.* London, UK: Zed.

McIntosh, A. & Finkle, J. (1995). The Cairo conference on population and development: A new paradigm? *Population and Development Review,* 21(3), 222–245.

Mohanty, C. (1991). Under western eyes: Feminist scholarship and colonial discourses. In C. Mohanty, A. Russo, & L. Torres (Eds.), *Third world women and the politics of feminism* (pp. 1–31). Bloomington, IN: Indiana University Press.

Parpart, L. (1995). Deconstructing the development "expert": Gender, development and "vulnerable groups." In M. Marchand & J. Parpart (Eds.), *Feminism postmodernism development* (pp. 221–243). London, UK: Routledge.

Petchesky, R. (1990). *Abortion and women's choice: The state, sexuality, & reproductive freedom.* Boston, MA: Northeastern University Press.

Sawicki, J. (1991). *Disciplining Foucault: Feminism, power and the body.* New York, NY: Routledge.

Sen, G., Germain, A., & Chen, L. (Eds.). (1994). *Population policies reconsidered: Health, empowerment, and rights.* Cambridge, MA: Harvard University Press.

Sen, G. & Grown, C. (1987). *Development, crisis and alternative visions: Third world women's perspectives.* New York, NY: Monthly Review Press.

Spivak, G. (1988). Can the subaltern speak? In C. Nelson & L. Grossberg (Eds.), *Marxism and the interpretation of culture* (pp. 272–285). Urbana, IL: University of Illinois Press.

Time (1998). Next: Menudo to Join Security Council (November 4), 36.

Townsend, J. (1993). Gender studies: Whose agenda? In F. Schurman (Ed.), *Beyond the impasse: New directions in development theory* (pp. 169–186). London, UK: Zed.

United Nations (UN) (1994). *Programme of Action United Nations International Conference on Population and Development* (1994). New York, NY: United Nations.

United Nations Fund for Population Activities (UNFPA) (1989). *Investing in women: The focus of the nineties.* New York, NY: United Nations.

Westoff, C. (1995). International population policy. *Society* (Winter), 11–16.

Wirth, T. (1993). U.S. statement on population and development. *U.S. Department of State Dispatch,* May 31, 1–5.

4

Reinventing Development Support Communication to Account for Power and Control in Development

Srinivas R. Melkote

> There are neither inadequate persons nor inadequate environments but rather that the fit between persons and environment may be in relative accord or discord.
>
> (Rappaport, 1977, p. 2)

The field of development support communication is presently undergoing a "middle-age crisis." Indeed, the growth was robust during its heyday. Until the 1970s, scholars, policy makers, and administrators saw great potential for the role of communication in Third World development. However, after nearly fifty years of research, some scholars have already written an obituary for development support communication (Hornik, 1988). Is there no useful role for communication in development? Or are we declaring the wrong patient dead? It is premature to declare development support communication as dead. What really needs an overhaul is the conception of the omnibus term "development."

Empirical evaluations of the role of communication in development projects showed unimpressive results (Hornik, 1988), mainly because the goal of "Third World Development" was too broad, inadequately operationalized, and riddled with cultural and historical biases. In this scenario, communication media became the vehicles for top-down transmission of prepackaged development messages of governments or other authorities using the much-maligned Dominant Paradigm (Rogers, 1976) of modernization and development. In this paradigm, the information and transmission values of the communication media were massaged to the hilt, but the rich potential of the organizational value of communication media was virtually untouched. Today, as we approach a new millennium, much of the current work in development support communication is premised and maintained in pluralistic and participatory approaches, as opposed to the top-down prescriptive transmission models of the past. However, even today, the frameworks offered for understanding social change in the newer participatory approaches do not differ significantly from the earlier models in the Dominant Paradigm, insofar as the discursive practices do not attempt to dismantle the structures and practices that maintain power inequities in societies.

It is important that we account for power in development theory and practice. Real change is not possible unless we deal squarely with the lack of power among individuals and groups especially at the grassroots. The construct of empowerment identifies the "real" constraints in Third World development and helps to articulate a more appropriate and useful role for development support communication (DSC) and DSC personnel.

EXPLICATION OF CONSTRUCTS, PROCESSES AND OUTCOMES

From Development Communication to Development Support Communication

A major reconceptualization in academic literature and professional praxis was the transition from development communication to development support communication. Development communication was guided by the organizing principles of the Dominant Paradigm. Initially, the emphasis in this approach was on economic growth as the main route to development. Later, as disenchantment grew with the notion of just economic growth, people-oriented development variables were included under the umbrella of the paradigm. Development Support Communication (DSC), a term coined and popularized by practitioners (Childers, 1976), was the response of field workers to the ground realities in developing countries. With this term the emphasis changed from looking at communication as an input toward greater economic growth to visualizing communication as a support for self-determination of people, especially those at the grassroots (Ascroft & Masilela, 1994; Jayaweera, 1987). The development communication model and the development support communication model are compared in table 4.1.

Participatory Decision Making

The idea of development support communication, after some initial resistance, gained acceptance among several multilateral development agencies such as the United Nations Development Program (UNDP), United Nations International Children's Emergency Fund (UNICEF), and Food and Agriculture Organization (FAO). An FAO (1987) report urged the integration of multimedia with interpersonal commu-

Table 4.1 Differences Between the Development Communication and Development Support Communication Constructs

Development Communication	*Development Support Communication*
Source:	
University based Structure:	Development agency based
Top-down, Authoritarian	Horizontal knowledge sharing between benefactors and beneficiaries
Paradigm:	
Dominant paradigm of an externally directed social change	Participatory paradigm of endogenously directed quest to maintain control over basic needs
Level:	
International, National Media:	Grassroots, Local
Big media; TV, Radio, Newspapers	Small media, Video, Film strips, Traditional media, Group and interpersonal communication
Effects:	
To create a climate of acceptance by beneficiaries for exogenous ideas and innovations	Create a climate of mutual understanding between benefactors and beneficiaries

Source: Ascroft and Masilela, 1989, pp. 16–17.

nication approaches and strongly recommended participatory communication that involved the people who would be the targets of development projects. It was also understood that participatory decision making required knowledge sharing between the "experts" and the "beneficiaries" of development projects (Chambers, 1983, 1997). However, this strategy has never really taken root among development agencies, partly due to the unwillingness of the experts to give up control over the process and partly due to the inability of development support workers to appreciate and operationalize true participatory communication approaches at the grassroots. "Few understand its implications because few, very few, have ever been directly involved in projects in which theirs was the task of operationalizing the concept and implementing it in real life situations" (Ascroft & Masilela, 1994, p. 281).

Meanwhile, the term "participatory communication" itself has been misunderstood and misused. Participation has been defined and operationalized in many ways: from pseudoparticipation to genuine efforts at generating participatory decision making (Alamgir, 1988; Ascroft & Masilela, 1989; Bamberger, 1988; Díaz Bordenave, 1989; Freire, 1973; White, 1994). There is a great deal of confusion about the outcomes desired and the contradictions between exemplars and phenomena of interest. While the practice of participatory communication has stressed collaboration between the people and the experts, knowledge sharing between the people and experts on a coequal basis, a local context, and cultural proximity (all of which fall under the empowerment model), the phenomenon of interest, in most cases, has not been true empowerment of the people, but the attainment of some indicator of development as articulated in the modernization paradigm (see table 4.2 under the modernization paradigm). Thus, participatory approaches have been encouraged, though the design and control of messages and the development agenda have remained with the experts. Also, issues of power and control by the authorities, structures of dependency, and power inequities have not been addressed at all within Third World settings. Thus, most of the participatory approaches are essentially old wine in new bottles.

The reality of the social and political situation in most developing countries is such that the urban and rural poor, women, and other people at the grassroots are entrapped in a dependency situation in highly stratified and unequal social and economic structures. The low status accorded to these groups prevents the realization of the newer approaches, such as the participatory strategies or the knowledge-sharing model described above. In the absence of tangible efforts to empower these "unequal" partners, the terms "participatory" or "coequal knowledge sharing" will remain as mere clichés.

Paradigm of Empowerment

Much work has been done on empowerment in the fields of community organization, education, and community psychology, and we may do well by borrowing and adapting this useful concept to development support communication. The construct of empowerment has been mentioned quite often in the communication and development literature, but the terms, exemplars, levels of analysis, outcomes, and so on have not been thoroughly explicated. Thus, the material in table 4.2 offers an attempt to provide a conceptual framework; it compares and contrasts the development communication model that was informed by the Dominant Paradigm with development support communication as influenced by the Empowerment Paradigm (Melkote & Steeves, forthcoming).

The basic premise guiding theory and practice in development communication (as articulated in the Modernization Paradigm) has been the notion that human societies are just and fair in their distribution of resources to individuals and groups within them and that all people, with a little bit of effort and help, can achieve the benefits that societies have to offer. Thus, according to the Dominant Paradigm of development, if an individual or group does not possess "desirable" attitudes, opinions, behaviors, or other attributes, or does not participate effectively in a society's affairs, it is the individual who is deficient and thus needs to be taught skills and provided help. The earlier development communication models have subscribed to such a victim–blame hypothesis. However, large sections of the population in the Third World continue to be impoverished and lack access to necessities that would make a qualitative improvement in their lives.

The concept of empowerment is heuristic in understanding the "real" constraints in Third World development. It clarifies the real outcomes we should work for in our development-related work and provides a useful niche for development support communication (DSC).[1] Further, what sets empowerment apart from the models informed by the Modernization Paradigm is that the locus of control in this process

Table 4.2 Comparison of Development Communication in the Modernization Paradigm with Development Support Communication in the Empowerment Paradigm

Development Communication in the Modernization Paradigm

Phenomenon of Interest/Goal: National and regional development, People development, Community improvement

Belief: Underdevelopment due to economic, political, cultural, geographic, and individual inadequacies; Existence of a single standard (as articulated by experts)

Bias: Cultural insensitivity, Nonecological, Standardization

Context: Macro and micro settings

Level of Analysis: National, Regional, Individual

Role of Change Agent: Expert, Benefactor, Nonparticipant

Communication Model: Linear, Top-down, Transmission of information

Type of Research: Quantitative, One-shot surveys, Post hoc analysis

Exemplars: Prevention of underdevelopment; Remedy through/by experts; Blame the victim; Individual adjustment to a dominant norm; Use of the mass media to spread standardized messages and entertainment; Messages that are preachy, prescriptive, and/or persuasive

Outcomes Desired: Economic Growth, Infrastructural Development

Development Support Communication in the Empowerment Paradigm

Phenomenon of Interest/Goal: Empowerment of people, Social Justice, Building capacity and equity

Belief: Underdevelopment due to lack of access to economic, political, and cultural resources; Underdevelopment due to lack of power and control on the part of the people; Diversity of standards

Bias: Cultural proximity, Ecological, Diversity

Context: Local and community settings

Level of Analysis: Individual, Group or organization, Community

Role of Change Agent: Collaborator, Facilitator, Participant, Advocate for individuals and communities, Risk-taker

Communication Model: Nonlinear, Participatory, Used to convey information as well as build organizations

Type of Research: Quantitative and qualitative, Longitudinal studies, Labor intensive

Exemplars: Activate social support systems, social networks, mutual help, and self-help activities; Encourage participation of all actors; Empower community narratives; Facilitate critical awareness; Facilitate community and organizational power; Use communication to strengthen interpersonal relationships

Outcomes Desired: Increased access of all citizens to material, psychological, cultural and informational resources; Honing of individual and group competence, leadership skills, useful life and communication skills at the local level; Honing of critical awareness skills; Empowerment of local organizations and communities rests on the individuals or groups involved and not with the experts, the DSC persons, or the sponsoring organizations. Although professionals may have a part to play in terms of designing intervention strategies, they are not the key actors. The key players are the people handling their problems in local settings and learning and honing their competencies in the concrete experiences of their existential realities.

Power and Control in Development

It is important to provide a context for the discussion on empowerment by explicating carefully the concept and practice of power and control in Third World social settings. A review of literature from both theory and practice in community organization and Third World development indicates the following:

1. Power is exemplified through organized money or organized people (Alinsky, 1971) or through connections with such entities.
2. Power is exercised through control of important economic, political, cultural, and informational resources. These resources are necessary in some measure for individuals, organizations, and communities to make qualitative improvements in their lives, and in developing countries this could also imply the fulfillment of basic needs.
3. Entities that wield power can also reward or punish targets by withholding or decreasing access to important resources (Gaventa, 1980; Polsby, 1959; Speer & Hughey, 1995).
4. Power is exercised through control of the development agenda; i.e., what gets included or excluded in policy statements, development plans, or public debate is carefully controlled. Entities with power can stymie participation or slant perspectives by erecting many barriers: control of the topics and timing of discussions and the range of issues discussed (Speer & Hughey, 1995).
5. Power is also exercised by influencing or shaping the shared consciousness of a people, community, or nation. This may be operationalized through the propagation of myths, stories, ideology, or outright control over sources of public information (Lukes, 1974; Speer & Hughey, 1995). Thus, power is the ability to create, interpret, or tell stories about an individual, a group, community or nation (Rappaport, 1995). For example, marginalized groups, such as the peasants in the Third World or "welfare mothers" in the United States, have had their stories expropriated and interpreted by outside entities.

Definitions of Empowerment

Before describing the process of community empowerment that can act as a countervailing power to forces of domination and control in Third World societies, and the specific roles that development support communication can play in the process, it is necessary to articulate clearly what is meant by the term *empowerment.* While empowerment as a construct has a set of core ideas, it may be defined at different levels: individual, organization, and community; and operationalized in different contexts.

Several working definitions of empowerment are available. However, given the nature of our work, which can be described as directed social change, and given the power inequities in societies that I posit as the major impediments to achieving meaningful development, it is important that the working definitions be linked directly to the building and exercise of social power (Speer & Hughey, 1995).

The following definitions and descriptions of the empowerment term are useful. According to Fawcett and colleagues, "community empowerment is the process of increasing control by groups over consequences that are important to their members and to others in the broader community" (1984, p. 146). Rappaport describes empowerment as

> a psychological sense of personal control or influence and a concern with actual social influence, political power, and legal rights. It is a multilevel construct applicable to individual citizens as well as to organizations and neighborhoods; it suggests the study of people in context. (1987, p. 121)

Another definition describes empowerment as

> an intentional, ongoing process centered in the local community, involving mutual respect, critical reflection, caring and group participation, through which people lacking an equal share of valued resources gain greater access to and control over those resources. (Cornell Empowerment Group, 1989, p. 2)

In summary, empowerment is the "manifestation of social power at individual, organizational, and community levels of analysis" (Speer & Hughey, 1995, p. 730).

Empowerment is the mechanism by which individuals, organizations, and communities gain control and mastery over social and economic conditions (Rappaport, 1981; Rappaport, Swift, & Hess, 1984); over democratic participation in their community (Rappaport, 1987; Zimmerman & Rappaport, 1988); and over their stories. While we read scholarly papers or theses about local peoples' stories, we seldom get to listen to their actual voices (Rappaport, 1995). Local stories document individual or community narratives about their or others' lives, histories, experiences, values, and so on. Like all other resources, the power to create, select, and tell stories about one's self, one's group, or other people is controlled by the elites through their organizations, agents, or genres that usually control the mass media channels that bombard communities with selective stories, messages, or mainstream populist entertainment fare. Thus, minorities, the poor people, and local communities lose control of an important cultural resource: the right to tell their own stories to their children and to significant others. Community empowerment attempts to give people control over this resource. Peoples' right to communicate their stories should be at the heart of the participatory strategies leading to empowerment.

As a process, empowerment may have different outcomes. For some it could lead to a perception of control over their lives while for others it may mean actual control (Rappaport, 1987; Young, 1994); it could be an internalized attitude or an externally observable behavior; it could be an individual achievement (Zimmerman, 1990; Zimmerman & Rappaport, 1988), a community experience (Chavis & Wandersman, 1990), or a professional intervention using strategies that are informed by the local realities. The process itself defies easy definition and may be recognized more easily by its absence: "powerlessness, real or imagined; learned helplessness; . . . (and) alienation" (Rappaport, 1984, p. 3).

Perspectives on Interventions

Premise

As long as societies distribute needs and power unequally within their populations, it is unethical for communications and human service professionals to help solve minor and/or immediate problems while ignoring the systemic barriers erected by societies that permit or perpetuate inequalities among citizens. Real change is not possible unless we deal with the crucial problem in human societies: lack of economic and social power among individuals at the grassroots. Latin American communication scholars such as Beltrán (1976) and Díaz Bordenave (1976), among others, reminded us almost twenty-five years ago about the oppressive social, political, and economic structures that exist in many developing countries. Yet the models and strategies that were developed have failed to address directly these constraints. Individuals are impoverished or sick or do not consume a balanced diet or are slow in adopting useful practices, not because they lack knowledge or rationality but because, more often than not, they do not have access to opportunities for enhancing the quality of their lives. This is largely due to their lack of social, political, and economic power. Unless we are willing to recognize this and act on it, our work will either be ineffective or function as mere bandages, temporary palliatives to a larger and long-standing problem. If DSC is to continue to play an effective role in social change processes, researchers have to deal squarely with the problem of unequal power of people at the grassroots.

Focusing on unequal power dynamics has a direct consequence on the traditional objective of development support communication, i.e., the delivery of new information and technological innovations. In the future, mere transmission of information and diffusion of innovations will be inadequate. Empowerment requires more than just information delivery and diffusion of technical innovations. It calls for grassroots organizing (Kaye, 1990) and communicative social action on the part of the poor, women, minorities, and others who have been consistently and increasingly marginalized in the process of social change. The implication for DSC, then, is a reconceptualization of its role. A greater importance should be placed on the organizational value of communication and the role of communicative efforts in empowering citizens. In essence, what this author is advocating for DSC is a move away from effecting "development" (as articulated by the Dominant Paradigm and the helping professions) to assisting in the process of "empowerment."

What I am advocating is a social system change model. This is not an easy task. It not only requires dealing with enclaves of power and influence that are usually deeply anchored in the structures of a society/nation, but the process also requires the active participation of individuals and communities in the intervention efforts affecting their welfare (Swift, 1984). However, it is the right thing to do if we are truly interested in the empowerment of people in the rural areas or the urban slums. This role is in consonance with the role of the DSC practitioner (see table 4.2) as an advocate of the people and as a risk-taker (Wolff, 1987).

Guiding Tenets for Practice

Speer and Hughey (1995) prescribe three tenets in their analysis of community organization. First, empowerment is achieved through effective organizations. Many external forces such as the government, development organizations, and other outsiders (both individuals and groups) act upon local communities and individuals. Some of these interactions are positive and beneficial and the interventions may require the consensus of the community. However, many of the interventions may be coercive and not require the consensus of the community. External (or internal) organizations are most often operating in their own self-interest. There are several competing self-interests and usually the most powerful groups prevail. Thus, the marginalized groups need effective organizations of their own that work for their self-interest, network with similar organizations, and compete with other forces. Saul Alinsky (1971) made the point long ago that social power comes either through organized money or organized people. All of this has many implications for development support communication (DSC) practice. The organizational value of communication is clearly indicated here. Individuals will need help in forming effective organizations, developing leadership skills, communication skills such as negotiation, and critical skills such as problem solving.

The second tenet specifies that effective organizations are sustained by strong interpersonal relationships (Speer & Hughey, 1995). Viable and self-sustaining organizations are built from the ground up through interactions with people who share values. These are superior to ad hoc organizations built on temporal issues, however important they may be. Relation-focused organizations do not atrophy when the issue goes away and a few individuals who could dominate in issue-charged organizations cannot hijack them. This fact again has useful implications for DSC personnel. They can facilitate strong interpersonal links through one-on-one communication, as well as shared values through the use of the indigenous communication media and technological media, such as the videotape cameras as used in Nepal or the Fogo community in Canada (Belbase, 1994; Williamson, 1991).

The third tenet deals with individual empowerment and involves the concept of action–reflection. Individuals need to activate their critical consciousness (Freire 1970, 1973); however, they need to go beyond reflection to social action as part of an organization. Organizations act as vehicles for cognitive insights and emotional factors to be challenged and tested behaviorally; they also act as laboratories wherein behavioral actions may be reflected upon (Kieffer, 1984; Speer & Hughey, 1995; White, 1994; Zimmerman, 1995). Over time, increased participation and reflection on the part of individuals are associated with individual empowerment (Zimmerman & Rappaport, 1988). The communication and organizational implications of this tenet are immense for DSC practitioners. Grassroots groups in India and the Philippines have used drama and other traditional theater to facilitate critical awareness, identify real constraints, and plan collectively to overcome problems (Kidd, 1984; Van Hoosen, 1984).

Role for the DSC Professionals

Who is a DSC professional? Ascroft and Agunga state that:

> it is a role which in the ultimate analysis, must be able to create the situational and psychological conditions in which development benefactors and their intended beneficiaries can participate together in mutual co-equality in making development decisions. (1994, p. 310)

The role is yet to be systematically codified. However, attempts have been made to describe the qualities and functions of this person (Ascroft & Agunga, 1994; Ascroft & Brody, 1982; Melkote, 1991). The DSC professional is not a development specialist like the agriculture extension or health extension workers. Extension workers are primarily subject-matter specialists in agriculture, health, or nutrition, with only a smattering of training in social-scientific communication techniques. They also lack the broad education in the social sciences and humanities to observe and appreciate the socioeconomic and cultural barriers to empowerment of the people at the grassroots. This makes the extension personnel unequipped to act as advocates for the people. In many development projects, the DSC person is seen as a development functionary of the project, the development agency, or the government. Ascroft and Brody (1982) caution that this role reduces DSC personnel to mere mouthpieces of development, doing the bidding of the development planners. In this mode, the DSC practitioners, while attempting to improve the efficiency and effectiveness of development agencies, may not necessarily be promoting the interests of the people (Melkote, 1991).

The Westley-MacLean (1957) model may be used to anchor the role of the DSC professional (Ascroft & Agunga, 1994; Melkote, 1991). In this model, designed originally to explain the role and impact of mass media in society, there are three principal actors: the receivers who need information to help satisfy needs; the advocates or authorities who can supply the information and help satisfy needs of the receivers but are usually purposive or self-serving; and the mass media channel. This model may be adapted to describe the role and functions of the DSC professional. The DSC person acts as the communication channel and as an advocate for the receivers, i.e., the marginalized individuals and groups who need to access resources and solve security problems. The DSC professional can assist the receivers in identifying and articulating possible solution alternatives, can help identify resources that may solve their security problems, and can identify and gain access to the relevant authorities crucial to meeting the receivers' needs or solving their problems. Thus, the DSC professional can extend the receivers' environment by acting as a collaborator, facilitator, and, importantly, as an advocate. As a development support communicator, he/she is uniquely qualified to organize and lead groups and has the communication skills to train people to present issues cogently, to negotiate, to arbitrate, to resolve conflicts, and so on. The DSC professional is more than just a communication specialist. He/she is also a social worker trained in community organization skills, a social scientist trained in research methods and problem-solving strategies, and a management person trained in organizational development and strategic planning methods.

The previous discussion of power and control in development laid out the different ways in which powerful groups or individuals could dominate. In order to effectively counter this, marginalized individuals/groups should have the capacities:

1. to perceive and articulate their social, cultural, historical, economic, and political realities;
2. to operationalize their needs;
3. to identify resources they need;
4. to identify, articulate, and operationalize possible solution alternatives;
5. to identify and gain access to individuals, agencies, or organizations crucial to meeting their needs or solving their problems;
6. to build communication skills to present issues cogently, conflict resolution skills, negotiation skills, and arbitration skills; and
7. to organize and lead.

When individuals, groups, or communities lack some or all of these capacities, DSC professionals have a niche in which to act as facilitators or enablers.

Fawcett and her colleagues (1995, pp. 686–687) provide a list of activities for facilitating the process of community empowerment. The abbreviated version of this list reproduced below provides an excellent inventory of activities for DSC personnel in the Third World development context:

1. Enhancing experience and competence: encourage listening sessions to identify local issues, resources, barriers, and alternatives; conduct surveys to identify community issues, concerns, and needs; create an inventory of community assets and resources; determine the incidence and prevalence of identified prob-

lems; provide training in leadership skills; provide technical assistance in creating action plans; provide consultation in selection, design, and implementation of early projects.
2. Enhancing group structure and capacity: provide technical assistance in strategic planning; help develop an organizational structure; provide technical assistance in recruiting, developing, and supporting members and volunteers; provide technical assistance in securing financial resources.
3. Removing social and environmental barriers: conduct focus groups to assess interests of community members; use social marketing techniques to promote useful programs, policies, and practices; provide training in conflict resolution; develop media campaigns to counter arguments of opponents.
4. Enhancing environmental support and resources: provide ongoing information and feedback about community change, behavior change, community satisfaction, and community-level outcomes; help locate and develop ties to existing community sectors, organizations, and groups; reinvent innovations to fit local needs, resources, and cultural traditions; arrange opportunities for networking among those with relevant experiential knowledge; provide access to outside experts in matters of local concern.

Thus, while the locus of control in empowerment activities rests with the community members, the DSC professional has important roles to play in the intervention process. The roles include that of a facilitator and consultant throughout the process and that of an initiator and a leader in the initial stages.

CONCLUSION

Development may be described more appropriately as "community betterment" (Fawcett et al., 1995). While the objective is to bring about a positive change, the locus of control rests with people and organizations outside the community. "Community empowerment," on the other hand, signifies positive change where members of the community control the agenda, design, and processes.

There are some important caveats, though. First, empowerment is a long-term process. The structures of domination and their cumulative effects on societies cannot be removed in a short-term frame. Second, empowerment is not something that can be acquired in a quick seminar or workshop setting. It evolves through practice in real-life situations. It is constructed "primarily through actions in, and on, the environment" (Kieffer, 1984, pp. 27–28). Third, it is a labor-intensive process. Last, the DSC professional is important but is not the central figure in the empowerment activities. The role of the DSC professional is that of a facilitator, collaborator, advocate, and risk taker.

Social change is a complex, disordered, unstructured, and quite often uncontrollable process. Empowerment is a process that is well suited to deal with social change in general and with inequitable structures in particular. It provides individuals and communities with the necessary skills, confidence, and countervailing power to deal effectively with social change in a world that distributes needs, resources, and power unequally. Empowerment privileges multiple voices and perspectives and truly facilitates equal sharing of knowledge and solution alternatives among the "beneficiaries" and "benefactors."

NOTES

1. I am tempted to replace "development support communication" with "empowerment support communication," but there is no need to throw the baby out with the bathwater! The term "development" carries negative baggage, but it has provided our field with an identity and a great degree of visibility. Therefore, I am comfortable incorporating empowerment as an important objective within the development framework.

REFERENCES

Alamgir, M. (1988). Poverty alleviation through participatory development. *Development, 2/3*, 97–102.

Alinsky, S. D. (1971). *Rules for radicals.* New York, NY: Random House.

Ascroft, J. & Agunga, R. (1994). Diffusion theory and participatory decision making. In S. A. White, K. S. Nair, & J. Ascroft (Eds.), *Participatory communication: Working for change and development* (pp. 295–313). New Delhi, India: Sage.

Ascroft, J. & Brody, A. (1982). The role of support communication in knowledge utilization: Theory and practice. Paper presented at the seminar on Communication and Change, the University of Hawaii and East–West Center, Honolulu, Hawaii.

Ascroft, J. & Masilela, S. (1989). From top–down to co–equal communication: Popular participation in development decision–making. Paper presented at the seminar on Participation: A key concept in communication for change and development. University of Poona, Pune, India.

Ascroft, J. & Masilela, S. (1994). Participatory decision–making in Third World development. In S. A. White, K. S. Nair, & J. Ascroft (Eds.), *Participatory communication: Working for change and development* (pp. 259–294). New Delhi, India: Sage.

Bamberger, M. (1988). The role of community participation in development planning and project management. EDI Policy Seminar Report, No. 13. Washington, DC: The World Bank.

Belbase, S. (1994). Participatory communication for development: How can we achieve it? In S. A. White, K. S. Nair, & J. Ascroft (Eds.), *Participatory communication: Working for change and development* (pp. 446–461). New Delhi, India: Sage.

Beltrán, L. R. (1976). Alien premises, objects, and methods in Latin American communication research. In E. M. Rogers (Ed.). *Communication and development: Critical perspectives* (pp. 15–42). Beverly Hills, CA: Sage.

Chambers, R. (1983). *Rural development: Putting the last first.* New York, NY: Longman.

Chambers, R. (1997). *Whose reality counts? Putting the first last.* London, UK: Intermediate Technology Publications.

Chavis, D. M. & Wandersman, A. W. (1990). Sense of community in the urban environment: A catalyst for participation and community development. *American Journal of Community Psychology,* 18, 55–82.
Childers, E. (1976). Taking humans into account. *Media Asia,* 3(2), 87–90.
Cornell Empowerment Group (1989). Empowerment and family support. *Networking Bulletin,* 1(2), 1–23.
Díaz Bordenave, J. (1976). Communication of agricultural innovations in Latin America. In E. M. Rogers (Ed.), *Communication and development: Critical perspectives* (pp. 43–62). Beverly Hills, CA: Sage.
Díaz Bordenave, J. (1989). Participative communication as a part of the building of a participative society. Paper presented for the seminar on Participation: A key concept in communication for change and development. University of Poona, Pune, India.
Food and Agriculture Organization (FAO) (1987). *Report of FAO expert consultation on development support communication.* (8–12 June). Rome, Italy: FAO.
Fawcett, S. B., Paine–Andrews, A., Francisco, V. T., Schultz, J. A., Richter, K. P., Lewis, R. K., Williams, E. L., Harris, K. J., Berkley, J. Y., Fisher, J. L., & Lopez, C. M. (1995). Using empowerment theory in collaborative partnerships for community health and development. *American Journal of Community Psychology,* 23(5), 677–697.
Fawcett, S. B., Seekins, T., Whang, P. L., Muiu, C., & Suarez de Balcazar, Y. (1984). Creating and using social technologies for community empowerment. In J. Rappaport, C. Swift, & R. Hess (Eds.), *Studies in Empowerment: Steps Toward Understanding and Action* (pp. 145–172). New York, NY: The Haworth Press.
Freire, P. (1970). *Pedagogy of the oppressed.* New York, NY: The Seabury Press.
Freire, P. (1973). *Education for critical consciousness.* New York, NY: The Seabury Press.
Gaventa, J. (1980). *Power and powerlessness: Quiescence and rebellion in an Appalachian Valley.* Urbana, IL: University of Illinois Press.
Hornik, R. C. (1988). *Development communication: Information, agriculture and nutrition in the Third World.* New York, NY: Longman.
Jayaweera, N. (1987). Rethinking development communication: A holistic view. In N. Jayaweera & S. Amunugama (Eds.), *Rethinking development communication* (pp. 76–94). Singapore: Asian Mass Communication Research and Information Center.
Kaye, G. (1990). A community organizer's perspective on citizen participation research and the researcher–practitioner partnership. *American Journal of Community Psychology,* 18(1), 151–157.
Kidd, R. (1984). The performing arts and development in India: Three case studies and a comparative analysis. In G. Wang & W. Dissanayake (Eds.), *Continuity and Change in Communication Systems* (pp. 95–125). Norwood, NJ: Ablex.
Kieffer, C. (1984). Citizen empowerment: A developmental perspective. In J. Rappaport, C. Swift, & R. Hess (Eds.), *Studies in Empowerment: Steps Toward Understanding and Action* (pp. 9–36). New York, NY: The Haworth Press.
Lukes, S. (1974). *Power: A radical view.* London, UK: Macmillan.
Melkote, S. (1991). *Communication for development in the Third World: Theory and Practice.* New Delhi, India: Sage.
Melkote, S. & Steeves, L. (Forthcoming). *Communication for development and empowerment in the Third World: Theory and Practice.* New Delhi, India: Sage.
Polsby, N. W. (1959). The sociology of community power: A reassessment. *Social Forces,* 37, 232–236.

Rappaport, J. (1977). *Community psychology: Values, research, and action.* New York, NY: Holt, Rinehart and Winston.

Rappaport, J. (1981). In praise of paradox: A social policy of empowerment over prevention. *American Journal of Community Psychology,* 9(1), 1–25.

Rappaport, J. (1984). Studies in empowerment: Introduction to the issue. In J. Rappaport, C. Swift, & R. Hess (Eds.), *Studies in empowerment: Steps toward understanding and action* (pp. 1–7). New York, NY: The Haworth Press.

Rappaport, J. (1987). Terms of empowerment/exemplars of prevention: Toward a theory for community psychology. *American Journal of Community Psychology,* 15(2), 121–144.

Rappaport, J. (1995). Empowerment meets narrative: Listening to stories and creative settings. *American Journal of Community Psychology,* 23(5), 795–807.

Rappaport, J., Swift, C., & Hess, R. (Eds.). (1984). *Studies in empowerment: Steps toward understanding and action.* New York, NY: Haworth.

Rogers, E. M. (1976). Communication and development: The passing of the dominant paradigm. *Communication Research,* 3, 121–133.

Speer, P. W. & Hughey, J. (1995). Community organizing: An ecological route to empowerment and power. *American Journal of Community Psychology,* 23(5), 729–748.

Swift, C. (1984). Empowerment: An antidote to folly. In J. Rappaport, C. Swift, & R. Hess (Eds.), *Studies in Empowerment: Steps Toward Understanding and Action* (pp. xi–xv). New York, NY: The Haworth Press.

Van Hoosen, D. (1984). The barefoot actors: Folk drama and development communication in Asia. In G. Wang & W. Dissanayake (Eds.), *Continuity and Change in Communication Systems* (pp. 127–137). Norwood, NJ: Ablex.

Westley, B. H. & MacLean, M. (1957). A conceptual model for communication research. *Journalism Quarterly,* 34, 31–38.

White, S. A. (1994). Introduction: The concept of participation. In S. A. White, K. S. Nair, & J. Ascroft (Eds.), *Participatory communication: Working for change and development* (pp. 15–32). New Delhi, India: Sage.

Williamson, A. H. (1991). The Fogo process: Development support communication in Canada and the developing world. In F. L. Casmir (Ed.), *Communication in Development* (pp. 270–288). Norwood, NJ: Ablex.

Wolff, T. (1987). Community psychology and empowerment: An activist's insights. *American Journal of Community Psychology,* 15(2), 151–167.

Young, I. M. (1994). Punishment, treatment, and empowerment: Three approaches to policy for pregnant addicts. *Feminist studies,* 20(1), 33–57.

Zimmerman, M. A. (1990). Taking aim on empowerment research: On the distinction between individual and psychological conceptions. *American Journal of Community Psychology,* 18(1), 169–177.

Zimmerman, M. A. (1995). Psychological empowerment: Issues and illustrations. *American Journal of Community Psychology,* 23(5), 581–599.

Zimmerman, M. A. & Rappaport, J. A. (1988). Citizen participation, perceived control, and psychological empowerment. *American Journal of Community Psychology,* 16(5), 725–750.

5

Cultural Hybridity and the Public Sphere

Thomas L. Jacobson

This chapter addresses two aims that are sometimes treated as being contradictory. One concerns analysis of cultural influences from the West as has been undertaken previously in studies of cultural imperialism and more recently in hybridity and postcolonial studies. The other aim concerns conceptualization of democratic prospects. These are contradictory insofar as democracy and human rights represent values often treated as "Western," and whose diffusion can therefore be seen as culturally imperialistic.

The preservation of tradition is of fundamental importance but cannot be meaningfully discussed in isolation, separated from political analysis. It must be discussed in connection with a theory of democracy that explains how cultural differences can be protected. The argument is drawn from Habermas's theory of communicative action, particularly its treatment of the reflective appropriation of tradition and the role played by the public sphere in reflective appropriation.

The warrant for this kind of analysis can be drawn in part by comparing it to the recent work of Arturo Escobar. Escobar's 1995 book, *Encountering Development,* argues persuasively within the framework of development anthropology that the failures of development programs in the Third World were not accidents. Instead, the entire development effort should be conceived in a Foucaultian manner as disciplinary discourse whose every element has been articulated within the expansion of Western hegemony. With this, Escobar advances insights that postmodernist thought has contributed to studies of social change in the Third World over the past decade or two, in addition to those from the postcolonial school of thought, from individual works such as Edward Said's (1978) and other sources.

My own concern parallels this theoretical argument, and assumes that power must be construed not only in terms of armies and money but also in terms of discourses. But I am specifically interested in a complementary problem. Rather than analyze the subversion of general will by illegitimate power, I would like to focus on discourses employed for the purposes of empowerment. To borrow once again from Foucault, scholars can identify insurrectionary discourses and can conduct genealogical studies. But if empowerment stops here, then the halls of parliaments will forever be safe from the people. Discursive theory must engage the theory of politics, including theories of democracy in the contemporary setting. Pursuing this argument means treating the subject of global cultural influences.

The global diffusion of Western cultural products portrays a picture of cultural influence that is often disturbing. However, theoretical analyses of what is disturbing about this picture, and why, have not produced any widely held formulation (Featherstone, 1990). Early analyses of such cultural influences were largely conducted under the assumptions of a neo-Marxist framework (Mattelart, 1979; Schiller, 1976). Apologetic responses, such as Read's (1976), replied that America's "mass media merchants" were not part of a domineering ideological apparatus, but merely a by-product of an honest attempt to make a profit. Other contributions sought a middle ground by narrowing the focus of attention from broadly conceived cultural effects to the analysis of "media" imperialism, as in Boyd-Barrett's study (1977). The phrase "cultural imperialism" has had quite a staying power, testimony to the durability of the impression that cultural influences from North to South have been domineering (Golding & Harris, 1997; Tomlinson, 1991).

While cultural critique may previously have been modeled on the economic-styled hegemony associated with neocolonial economic relations, cultures are now seen as more resilient than suggested by theories of cultural imperialism. Research into cultural "hybridity" shows that local cultural forms survive by incorporating elements of imported cultural forms (Pierterse, 1995). Studies of globalization (Albrow, 1997; Waters, 1995), and local/global intermixing (Wilson & Dissanayake, 1996) have explored spaces created when aesthetics from the Center are intermixed with those of the Periphery. Postcolonial studies have combined these concerns with a focus on power's implication in the creation of difference (Ascroft, Griffiths & Tiffin, 1995; Chambers & Curti, 1996).

These more recent approaches, which I refer to simply as "hybridity" studies, were greatly enabled by postmodernism. If cultural influences are to be approached satisfactorily, then a nonprivileging discourse is required, one that is sensitive to differences overlooked by standard Western analytical categories. Said (1978), for one, has shown how complicit the academy has been in colonialist ideological constructions. In addition, a debate over "African philosophy" addresses the problem of developing reflective thought on the basis of indigenous intellectual resources (Appiah, 1992; Masolo, 1994; Mudimbe, 1992). In this context, Marxism is as much an expression of the West as is behaviorism, and the categorical assumptions of the cultural imperialism hypothesis are also merely Western. From a postmodernist perspective the cultural imperialism hypothesis falls victim to charges it sought itself to make; i.e., it is itself Western, insensitive to "difference," and hence culturally imperialistic.

Thus the study of cultural influences has advanced considerably beyond the cultural imperialism approach through the analysis of hybridity. However, the hybridity approach has its Achilles' heel, too. Even on its own terms postmodernism's usefulness for political analysis is questionable (Haber, 1994). Following Derrida, any attempt to resist a dominant discourse also necessarily serves to inscribe that discourse even more deeply. What is needed in the Third World cannot be "spoken" (Spivak, 1995, p. 26). Insofar as studies of cultural influence rely on deconstruction, it becomes difficult to analyze possibilities for rectifying unjust economic institutions or building political institutions (Dirlik, 1994; Hall, 1996; Shohat, 1992).

From this perspective the study of hybridity requires addressing two analytical aims that may seem contradictory. One aim concerns the analysis of cultural influences from the West, i.e., the problem of cultural preservation in the face of Western influences and a conceptualization of democratic prospects. These are contradictory insofar as democracy and human rights represent values that were widely institutionalized first in the West and then forcefully diffused through modernization programs. Advocating democratic institutions and the rights regimes associated with them would seem to betray intended loyalties to local traditions elsewhere.

Jurgen Habermas's theory of communicative action contains an analysis of cultural change processes in relation to a theory of democracy. Parts of his theory are sometimes cited in connection with development issues (Gonzalez, 1989; Servaes, 1989), but it has not been systematically explored. Perhaps this is due to the fact that in the theoretical environment briefly reviewed above on hybridity studies, informed by postmodern thought, Habermas has often been perceived as part of the problem. His defense of modernity is sometimes taken as a defense of modernization theory and most of its biases. In addition, his theory has often been rather badly misunderstood, including poor treatment even by prominent critics, including Lyotard (Holub, 1991, pp. 133–161).

The universalistic claims of the theory of communicative action have been treated in a number of critiques and related debates (see Benhabib & Dallmayr, 1990; Passerin d'Entréves & Benhabib, 1997; Rasmussen, 1982). Many of these critiques and claims are philosophical. Others are empirical in connection with theories of language and cognitive development upon which Habermas in part relies. He has a number of major statements on the subject (Habermas, 1990, 1993).

But there are good reasons to reconsider his approach. The first and most obvious reason is perhaps that it remains a critical theory. Even if modernist, it nevertheless, at a minimum, provides a powerful indictment of the influences of large-scaled power. This is embodied primarily in his thesis on lifeworld colonization. More importantly, his analysis of colonization relies on a logically prior analysis of the cultural repository that is the lifeworld. Analysis of the lifeworld provides concepts that lend the theory resources for analyzing culture. Particularly useful are those related to the theory of social evolution. When these are tied together with analysis of the public sphere, it is possible to consider cultural hybridization not only from the viewpoint of the victim of cultural imperialism who is attempting to fashion a form of cultural compromise, but also from the perspective of a social agent, whose hybridized culture includes modern institutions such as those of formal law and self-governance. While the law is often turned against the general interest, legal institutions must eventually be harnessed to the general interest if there is to be any hope of improvement in life opportunities. Any theory of hybridity that can address this must include some form of a theory of politics, roughly including theories of the public and of the state.

Habermas by no means provides the only current theory of the state that might be of use. Claus Offe's (1996) recent work is excellent. But it is also an example that does not include a theory of social evolution. In any case, my argument is not advanced so much on behalf of Habermas's theory as it is on behalf of research that combines the basic elements of a theory of social evolution, political institutions, cultural hybridization, and discourse. I intend to explore some of the complexities that must be faced in any approach to hybridity studies that claims to have political relevance under contemporary conditions.

PART I: REASON AND SOCIAL EVOLUTION

Reason and Social Rationalization

The original and enduring intent of Habermas's work has been to construct a critical theory of society, but at its heart lies a communicative theory of reason. Similarly, Habermas's theory contains an elaborate account of cultural change, but here again his approach begins with communicative reason. Perhaps we can most easily observe the connection between cultural change, critical theory, and communicative reason with reference to his critique of Max Weber's theory of social rationalization. Weber's is the theory of rationalization upon which rested much of the modernization theory that was applied in development research and whose treatment of culture was so impoverished.

Weber equated reason with scientific and technical thought and saw modernity as the progressive application of scientific and bureaucratic thought throughout society. It was means–ends reasoning oriented toward causal analysis, prediction, and control. He modeled this philosophical conception on the autonomous ego whose internal subjectivity is separated from the external, physical world and whose reason represents the effort to grasp the world objectively, or "instrumentally," in thought. In this model, values, including cultural values, can only cloud reason.

The edifice of communicative action has been constructed as an alternative to this account of reason. This alternative explains the operations of reason instrumentally with regard to so-called objective and technical matters. But it also explains the operation of reason noninstrumentally with regard to normative matters, that is, matters concerning value-oriented issues. Furthermore, it explains the operation of reason with regard to internal subjectivity. The idea of the "ideal speech situation" is designed to support the argument that reason is broader than technical instrumental thought. Specifically, reason is treated as being tripartite, and culture is treated as part of reason rather than as reason's antithesis.

Communication, as speech, plays a central role in this multidimensional account of reason. This role can be seen in speech's use for debate over three different kinds of matters, i.e. those pertaining to (1) truth, (2) normative appropriateness, and (3) truthfulness (sincerity). These represent three different "validity spheres" in which reason operates. The nature of these spheres, the claims that are made within them, the kinds of discourse appropriate to each, the nature of argument, and more comprise the basic elements of the theory of communicative action.

In brief, communicative action refers to "action oriented towards understanding," which can take place with regard to any of the three validity spheres. The theory recognizes the deceptions of power, of lying, and so on, which it treats as allies of "strategic" communication (Habermas, 1984, pp. 285–6). But it focuses on the reciprocal expectation of an orientation toward understanding without which communication of any kind would be impossible. Therefore, communicative reason is treated as universal. In this way, Habermas shifts his account of reason from an epistemological orientation toward a pragmatistic one (see figure 5.1). Understanding serves the coordination of action among individuals.

One of the most common criticisms of the theory of communicative action is that it is idealistic, i.e., that it suggests people are always trying to understand one another and that it ignores the ways that communication enacts power relations. Both Foucault's analysis of power/knowledge and Lyotard's treatment of "agonistics" argue that power is inextricably bound up with interaction, and that understanding is seldom at the heart of intentions (Foucault, 1980; Lyotard, 1984). In this context, the notion that an "orientation to reach understanding" underlies all communication is naive.

Figure 5.1 Formal Pragmatic Features and Cultural Value Spheres

	Formal Pragmatic Features			
Validity Claims	*World Relations*	*Functions Sphere*	*Cultural Value Component*	*Lifeworld*
Truth	Objective World	Represent States of Affairs	Science & Technology	Culture
Rightness	Social World	Establish Interpersonal Relations	Law & Morality	Society
Truthfulness (Sincerity)	Subjective World	Self-Representation	Art & Literature	Person

Source: Modified from Habermas, 1984, p. 329

From Habermas's perspective this is over-reading the theory, because the theory does not deny agonistics. It does argue that without the presumption of an orientation to reach understanding, even agonistics is unthinkable. And as noted, the theory specifically recognizes power-laden forms of interaction, labeling them as "strategic" action.

Habermas's program has in the past been vulnerable to the charge that it underanalyses the power dynamics attending communication, but it does recognize power and difference. As Bernstein explains, the theory of communicative action is intended not to dispute the prevalence of power or difference, but rather to outline a program of research into difference, "without ignoring or repressing the otherness of the Other" (Bernstein, 1992, p. 313). More recent studies have elaborated Habermas's analysis of power, making the implications of his theory much clearer in this regard. In *Between Facts and Norms* (1996), he examines the relation between law and political theory and includes an updated treatment of civil society and the public sphere given contemporary conditions. In a number of other recent studies Habermas explores rights claims in the context of "struggles for recognition" by minority or otherwise excluded groups (Habermas, 1998).

This account of communicative action as reason provides the foundation for Habermas's theory of social evolution (Habermas, 1979). Just as Weber saw modernization as the progressive application of reason throughout society, so does Habermas. The difference between their theories results from the different conceptions of reason. For Weber, one kind of reason, i.e., instrumental reason, pervades all spheres of society. For Habermas, three different aspects of reason pervade three different spheres of society. Technical reasoning is employed in social subsystems related to science and technology. Reasoning over normative appropriateness is employed in social subsystems related to "law and morality." Reasoning over matters of sincerity is employed in social subsystems related to "art and literature."

Each aspect of reason is enacted through institutionalized forms of speech, or discourse. Each kind of discourse is uniquely suited to its sphere. For example, scientific and technical discourse is not suitable for adjudicating normative issues of value-oriented preferences. Conversely, normative discourse cannot solve technical problems. It follows that aesthetic canons employed in art and literature are suitable for solving neither technical nor normative problems. Each kind of discursive reason can be used somehow in conjunction with the other, but the freedom to use the appropriate kind of discourse for its natural task is seen as an achievement of modernity.

In any case, within such a macrosociological framework the nature of reason is treated not as a philosophical question but rather as an historical project. "The release of a potential for reason embedded in communicative action is a world-historical process" (Habermas, 1992, p. 180). The release of this potential refers to the progressive institutionalization of the three kinds of discourse in what by now are widespread institutions embodying science, law, and modern art. This is what Habermas sees as social rationalization.

The Structural Differentiation of the Lifeworld

The process of social rationalization provides a dimension along which Habermas categorizes stages of social evolution. In this system of stages, a framework emerges for the analysis of reason's relationship to cultural change. At the stage of modernity, the three spheres operate, ideally, with relative autonomy from one another, but with some input from the others.

> With science and technology, with autonomous art and the values of expressive self-presentation, with universal legal and moral representations, there emerges a differentiation of three value spheres. (Habermas, 1984, pp. 163–164)

More systematically, Habermas refers to these three value spheres as "cultural value spheres." Each cultural value sphere performs characteristic functions and accumulates knowledge and tradition. This process of rationalization begins early in what is sometimes called the rise of civilization, proceeds through three stages, including stages of preconventional, conventional, and postconventional social formations, and represents what he calls a "directional variation of lifeworld structures" (Habermas, 1987, p. 145). This variation represents an increasing social capacity for collective participation in justification and legitimation of the social order generally, and for the effective pursuit of differentiated social practices.

In preconventional societies the organization principle is reflected in kinship systems. Natural, social, religious, and artistic norms are interwoven within mythic systems. Conventional societies have class stratification as their organizing principle, where the production and distribution of wealth shifts away from regulation by family lineage and into the hands of a state. The justification of this situation takes place through "dogmatized knowledge," in which the authority of king, pharaoh, or Caesar is proclaimed. Postconventional society begins to emerge with what we know as the rise of modernity. The forces of tradition and dogma wane. The basis of legitimation for social practices is raised for examination and becomes for the first time arguable.

One problem with Habermas's theory, seldom discussed but of pressing importance for the study of globalization, resides in his claim that structural differentiation is universal. The theory allows that the cultural value spheres interact. For example, an economy's allocations are determined, even if insufficiently, in part by welfare policies regarding poverty. However, the theory asserts that there is a point beyond which the involvement of one sphere in another becomes an imposition. This is the basis upon which Habermas's theory endorses what is treated in the West as a necessary separation between economy, church, and state.

Habermas maintains that structural requirements do not determine cultural content; i.e., traditions that a society may wish to retain within such differentiated structures can be freely chosen. Any religion can find expression in a society's normative value sphere, and the content of aesthetic trends is free to vary in the sphere of art and literature. However, it is clear that differentiation is not entirely independent of content. Tradition must be abandoned wherever it would block differentiation and would justify transgressions across cultural value spheres, for example when a religiously legitimated state curbs artistic freedom. The charge against the theory holds that all social structures are equally deserving of respect, differentiated or otherwise.

Habermas's defense against this claim is based on the position that in order to resolve the issue an historical perspective must be taken. In the nineteenth and twentieth centuries, cultures have been forced into close proximity with one another. This has taken place not only through colonization but also through dramatic increases in trade and immigration. The issue, therefore, is not one of preserving cultures in their pristine condition but rather of preserving cultures in relation to one another, by protecting each against all. This requires the universalizing perspective provided only by reason and justice.

This represents Habermas's approach to cultural relativism. He does not argue that his reconstruction of reason is harmless, not being a threat to cultural variety and to difference, but that reason and its social institutionalization through structural differentiation of the lifeworld are necessary in order to protect the freedoms required for the exercise of otherness and difference.

> The universalist position does not have to deny the pluralism and the incompatibility of historical versions of "civilized humanity"; but it regards this multiplicity of forms of life as limited to cultural contents, and it asserts that every culture must share certain formal properties of the modern understanding of the world, if it is at all to attain a certain degree of "conscious awareness. (Habermas, 1984, p. 180)

The phrase "conscious awareness" is intended to suggest that difference can be tolerated only within the framework of a system of law that protects it and that such systems of law presuppose the exercise of reason.

Yet another place where lifeworld differentiation may be found objectionable, on related grounds, is in Habermas's thesis of a directional variation in lifeworld structures, which proceeds through a series of stages. Due to the superiority associated in modernization theory with countries at higher stages, this element of the theory of communicative action theory is suspect (Giddens, 1985; Rasmussen, 1982).

Habermas formalizes his conceptualization by drawing from the developmental psychology of Jean Piaget (1970). He does not intend to suggest that individual psychological processes can be used to explain social processes, but to borrow, at an abstract level, Piaget's model of developmental stages. In Piaget's model each cognitive stage is able to process more complexity than its previous stage, and thus some stages presuppose others (Habermas, 1984, pp. 66–74). Similarly, Habermas argues that history follows a developmental logic, with social stages presupposing certain other stages.

This logic does not require that development be inevitable, as generally was held in modernization theory. Progress gained can be lost. It might be "eroded—even finally crushed" (Habermas, 1992, p. 196). Progress itself is not treated very hopefully. Habermas sees modernity simply as the enhanced capacity for responding to survival challenges. Quality of life, as inferior or superior, is not at issue (Habermas, 1992, pp. 204–205; 1994, p. 107). So, the theory of communicative action is directional, but neither teleological nor middle-class utopian in the fashion of modernization theory.

Debates surrounding the universalism claim and the charge of idealism are complex and too involved to explore further here. But the difference between Habermas's approach to modernity and that embodied in earlier theories of modernization is considerable. His triadic approach to social rationalization differentiates the theory of communicative action from Max Weber's and others' work. It provides a framework that makes possible a more adequate grasp of the historical evolution of the legal, moral, and aesthetic characteristics of modern society, in addition to those associated with science and technology. It also provides a framework within which the role of cultural traditions in social change can be analyzed, against the background of the cultural "lifeworld."

PART II: LIFEWORLD AND THE PUBLIC SPHERE

Even in its differentiated form, the lifeworld comprises a storehouse of tradition and cultural background knowledge. This background knowledge is fundamental to the transmission of norms, to the integration of social institutions, and to the formation of individual identity.

Habermas's treatment of the lifeworld is best known in connection with the thesis of "lifeworld colonization." Colonization is said to occur when instrumental reason is inappropriately used in place of more appropriate discourse in an attempt to fulfill lifeworld functions. It occurs, for example, when science and/or bureaucracy are used in place of normatively oriented family interaction to make determinations on matters of child rearing; when market values come to determine the direction of aesthetic and artistic trends, or when bottom-line reasoning moves from the business to the editorial side of newspapers.

Readers of earlier Frankfurt School theorists (Horkheimer & Adorno, 1972; Jay, 1973) tend to read colonization simply as the advance of instrumental reason. Against the background of the theory of structural differentiation, the picture is different and more complex. Colonization represents an unbalanced form of development, as a "selective pattern of rationalization."

This same Frankfurt reading tends to see the public sphere as a place where public discourse is a force leveled solely against the forces of instrumental reason, particularly those embodied in capitalist institutions and aims (Habermas, 1989). However, again, the public sphere is more than this, for it operates not only to negate instrumental reason and inappropriate effects of capital. The public sphere is more accurately construed in a broader manner, as the necessary forum in which interactions among all cultural value spheres may take place.

Whenever the resources of one sphere are not sufficient to handle a contingency, then this matter must be thrown open to public consideration of the most general sort. Such contingencies may be related, therefore, to matters that are aesthetic, normative, technical, traditional, political, gender based, and so on. The public sphere is the place where all issues that cannot be handled in a specialized fashion come to roost, where society can raise for consideration any and all traditions that it may want to retain, abandon, protect, or condemn. Another way of putting it is to ask: Where do the resources come from to resist instrumental reason if not from normative and aesthetic reason?

Communicative Action and the Reflective Appropriation of Tradition

A considerable literature has developed analyzing and applying Habermas's approach to the public sphere (Benhabib, 1996; Chambers, 1996; Dahlgren, 1995). Almost without exception, these analyses take as their context of application problems facing fully industrialized countries. Here, the hypercommercialization of mass media is decried and distortions in news coverage and aesthetic standards are delineated. Most if not all of these studies assume the form of a defense of constitutional values against the interests of capital, and so they should. In the United States, for example, "progressive" political forces struggle to defend traditional constitutional freedoms of free speech against commercialization of the press. Thus, the discourse envisioned as fully democratic is largely oriented toward critical political economy.

Both reason and the public sphere should be more broadly conceived, however. This should be no more clear than in the South. Compared to the North, public sphere debates within the South must have the broadest of concerns. For one thing, the struggle for free and unfettered speech against the impositions of capital is less a matter of maintaining constitutional provisions than it is of establishing such provisions. This involves importing, or deciding whether to import, for example, the idea of constitutionally protected free speech from outside the lifeworld of traditional culture. In many cases, of course, traditional cultures have cultural equivalents of free speech. But even here, if the people living within such a culture do wish to pursue modernity, then community debate must reconcile the more traditional expressions of free speech with institutionalized forms of free speech. Critical political economy is important, but deeper normative matters have a prior importance.

In any given Third World culture, the choices must be fashioned from options including mixtures of local cultural traditions and cultural values from outside, including from the West. As differences among Western democracies illustrate, in the United States and Sweden for example, a variety of trade-offs between solidarity and individualism can abide within modern society. A particular African culture might reflect on the nature and desirability of retaining collective solidarity as a core element of individual identity. But when the specific form of solidarity originates in a nonindustrial society, fashioning a fit must be a complex endeavor.

In any case, public reflection in the South must be preoccupied with fashioning a fit between traditional cultural values and newer social structures. This emphasizes the role that the public sphere plays in a process Habermas refers to as the reflective appropriation of tradition. In Habermas's stage theory, the idea of treating modern societies as being "postconventional" highlights a "relative" freedom from convention as opposed to traditional (either preconventional or conventional) societies. In this stage, tradition is not observed simply due to the fact that "it has always been done that way." Rather, practices can be evaluated and determined as preferable, i.e., appropriated or not in a reflective manner. Tradition can be seen *as* tradition. This reflective appropriation is, of course, selective. By definition, the adoption of new practices involves abandoning or modifying at least some traditions.

> Under modern conditions of life none of the various rival traditions can claim prima facie general validity any longer. Even in answering questions of direct practical relevance, convincing reasons can no longer appeal to the authority of unquestioned traditions. (Habermas, 1993, p. 151)

Habermas does not treat tradition as bad, saying only that it is no longer relied upon for authority unquestioningly. On the other hand, it should be clear that it is not possible to abandon tradition entirely. The concept of the lifeworld is a reminder that a cultural background of preunderstandings is necessary for the very existence of language and of individual identity. Any abandonment of tradition therefore must be a matter of particulars and not totalities. The hybridity debates illustrate just this tenacity of culture. Western culture might be a global juggernaut, but colonized lifeworlds survive just as do colonial subjects.

Therefore, the important question is not whether to retain or abandon tradition and replace it with modernity. There must be a mix. The question is this: How are decisions about tradition to be made? Are they to be made by subjects or visited upon objects, made in freedom or in dependency, made democratically or as a part of hegemonic practice, communicatively or strategically? Here, the idea of reflective appropriation against a lifeworld background links up with analysis of the structural differentiation of cultural value spheres and with the need for a public sphere as a site for "interpretive accomplishments" mediating among more specialized discourses in novel circumstances.

CONCLUSION

This analysis was introduced with reference to two conflicting aims. One aim is to develop an analysis of cultural preservation, a topic at one time treated as cultural imperialism. The other is to develop the analysis in such a manner that it can be linked with a theory of democracy and rights.

Previous research based on the cultural imperialism thesis has served to highlight the problem, but that research generally suffered from an underestimation of culture's complexity and resilience. Hybridity studies subsequently rectified this weakness, making clear the persistence of cultural difference even in the face of persistent influence from the West. However, the limitations of the hybridity formulation are significant. Although hybridity studies are generally "critical" in intent, little basis is provided for enacting progressive change. Even democracy is eschewed as a proving ground for desirable hybrids, because democracy is associated with Western-styled technical and scientific reason that justifies current global processes of hypermarketization.

By way of conclusion we can ask whether the theory of communicative action achieves both. Does the model offer a productive approach to studying the preservation of culture? And is this approach compatible with a promising theory of democracy?

Certainly, the theory intends to do both. The analysis of cultural influence is treated within the framework of the reflective appropriation of tradition against the background of the lifeworld. The analysis of democratic prospects is treated in terms of the full realization of communicative action within the context of a public sphere. The two analyses are not merely compatible, for they in fact depend one upon the other. The preservation of culture requires democratic processes, because the selective appropriation of tradition requires communicative action within a public sphere. Conversely, the public sphere requires preservation of at least a broad portion of traditional culture, because discourse of any kind takes place against the essential background of a lifeworld.

Conditions in the North and South differ in a great many respects. For this reason, it is necessary to consider possible ways in which the general ideas of lifeworld colonization and the public sphere may not be applicable.

First, system rationality did not arise within indigenous Southern social systems, as it did in the North, but rather was introduced from outside. In the North even as lifeworld colonization began, autonomous spheres of law and morality, art, and literature had already evolved. Because system rationality was introduced to the South from outside, a well-balanced evolution in all three cultural value spheres has been even more absent than in the North. Can the resulting damage be meaningfully diagnosed as lifeworld colonization?

The second and related difference concerns the pace and mechanisms of change. Even where governments of new nations have had some influence on the process and direction of change, pressures from the outside encourage change at a breakneck pace. What cultural resources can be brought to bear in this process? The specific mechanisms for public reflection must vary given the specific conditions of each nation and each cultural environment. Is the public sphere too sluggish and slow-moving to facilitate a coherent process of change in many of the South's settings?

The intrusion of system rationality from outside the South and the pace with which it has been introduced represent two marked differences between the North and the South. But the significance of these differences is an open question. The violence done to traditional cultures is undeniable. However, as hybridity studies show, these cultures have not disappeared. The cultural resources remaining are considerable and have every chance of forming the fabric of modern, multiplicity cultures if allowed to develop with public input.

In any case, the theoretical point to be made here is that the kind of theory embodied in Habermas's work provides a framework within which such meaningful questions can be asked. Far from being aloof from studies of culture and cultural change, it contains an ambitious account of cultural change. Far from being insensitive to difference, it provides a theory of social evolution that intends to be culturally relativistic. The theory of communicative action represents an account of modernity, but it goes to great lengths in its attempt to avoid the ethnocentrism of previous universalistic theories of modernity.

In closing, I shall return to the question of trends. Some theory must be employed that simultaneously addresses cultural and political change. The reason is simple: Studies of cultural change divorced from political theory provide little guidance for political action. The challenges facing emancipatory social change efforts are daunting, of course. This chapter has barely even alluded to them, being limited to a schematic outline of the issue in general. The prospects for progressive change in a practical sense will in any case vary in every given situation. Nevertheless, a praxiological theory is necessary for action. Postcolonialism and other schools influenced by postmodernism provide insight into the lineaments of power, but only with regard to disciplinarity and difference, with regard to illegitimate power. Questions of preferred orders for society, for legitimate power, are vastly underanalyzed. Making, or remaking, this connection is a step the field needs to take.

REFERENCES

Albrow, M. (1997). *The global age.* Stanford, CA: Stanford University Press.

Appiah, A. (1992). *In my father's house: Africa in the philosophy of culture.* Oxford, UK: Oxford University.

Ascroft, B., Griffiths, G., & Tiffin, H. (Eds.) (1995). *The post-colonial studies reader.* London, UK: Routledge.

Benhabib, S. (Ed.) (1996). *Democracy and difference: Contesting the boundaries of the political.* Princeton, NJ: Princeton University Press.

Benhabib, S. & Dallmayr, F. (1990). *The communicative ethics controversy.* Cambridge, MA: The MIT Press.

Bernstein, R. J. (1992). *The new constellation: The ethical-political horizons of modernity/postmodernity.* Cambridge, MA: The MIT Press.

Boyd-Barrett, O. (1977). Media imperialism: Towards an international framework for the analysis of media systems. In J. Curran, M. Gurevitch, & J. Woolacott (Eds.), *Mass communication and society* (pp. 87–103). London, UK: Arnold.

Chambers, I. & Curti, L. (1996). *The post-colonial question: Common skies, divided horizons.* London, UK: Routledge.

Chambers, S. (1996). *Reasonable democracy: Jurgen Habermas and the politics of discourse.* Ithaca, NY: Cornell University Press.

Dahlgren, P. (1995). *Television and the public sphere: Citizenship, democracy and the media.* London, UK: Sage.
Dirlik, A. (1994). The postcolonial aura: Third World criticism in the age of global capitalism. *Critical Inquiry,* 10, 328–56.
Escobar, A. (1995). *Encountering development: The making and unmaking of the Third World.* Princeton, NJ: Princeton University Press.
Featherstone, M. (1990). *Global culture: Nationalism, globalization and modernity.* London, UK: Sage.
Foucault, M. (1980). *Power/Knowledge: Selected interviews and other writings 1972–1977.* Edited by C. Gordon. New York, NY: Pantheon.
Giddens, A. (1985). Reason without revolution? Habermas' Theorie des kommunikativen Handelns. In R. J. Bernstein, (Ed.), *Habermas and modernity* (pp. 95–124), Cambridge, MA: The MIT Press.
Golding, P. & Harris, P. (1997). *Beyond cultural imperialism: Globalization, communication & the new international order.* London, UK: Sage Publications.
Gonzalez, H. (1989). Interactivity and feedback in Third World development campaigns. *Critical Studies in Mass Communication,* 6, 295–314.
Haber, H. F. (1994). *Beyond postmodern politics: Lyotard, Rorty and Foucault.* London, UK: Routledge.
Habermas, J. (1979). *Communication and the evolution of society.* Boston, MA: Beacon Press.
Habermas, J. (1984). *The theory of communicative action.* Volume 1: *Reason and the rationalization of society.* Boston, MA: Beacon Press.
Habermas, J. (1987). *The theory of communicative action.* Volume 2: *A critique of functionalist reason.* Boston, MA: Beacon Press.
Habermas, J. (1989). *The structural transformation of the public sphere: An inquiry into a category of bourgeois society.* Cambridge, MA: The MIT Press.
Habermas, J. (1990). *Moral consciousness and communicative action.* Cambridge, MA: MIT Press.
Habermas, J. (1992). *Autonomy and solidarity.* London, UK: Verso.
Habermas, J. (1993). *Justification and application: Remarks on discourse ethics.* Cambridge, MA: The MIT Press.
Habermas, J. (1994). *Past as future.* Lincoln, NB: University of Nebraska Press.
Habermas, J. (1996). *Between facts and norms.* Cambridge, MA: The MIT Press.
Habermas, J. (1998). *The inclusion of the other: Studies in political theory.* Cambridge, MA: The MIT Press.
Hall, S. (1996). When was "the post-colonial"? Thinking at the limit. In I. Chambers & L. Curti, (Eds.), *The post-colonial question: Common skies, divided horizons* (pp. 242–260). London, UK: Routledge.
Holub, R. C. (1991). *Jurgen Habermas: Critic in the public sphere.* London, UK: Routledge.
Horkheimer, M. & Adorno, T. (1972). *The dialectic of enlightenment.* New York, NY: Herder and Herder.
Jay, M. (1973). *The dialectical imagination: A history of the Frankfurt School and the Institute of Social Research 1923–1950.* Boston, MA: Little, Brown and Company.
Lyotard, J. (1984). *The postmodern condition.* Minneapolis, MN: University of Minnesota Press.
Masolo, D. (1994). *African philosophy in search of identity.* Bloomington, IN: Indiana University Press.

Mattelart, A. (1979). *Multinational corporations and the control of culture.* Brighton, MA: Harvester Press.
Mudimbe, V. (1992). *The surreptitious speech: Présence Africaine and the politics of otherness, 1947–1987.* Chicago, IL: University of Chicago Press.
Offe, C. (1996). *Modernity and the state: East, west.* Cambridge, MA: The MIT Press.
Passerin d'Entréves, M. & Benhabib, S. (Eds.) (1997). *Habermas and the unfinished project of modernity: Critical essays on the "Philosophical discourse of modernity."* Cambridge, MA: The MIT Press.
Piaget, J. (1970). *Genetic Epistemology.* New York, NY: Columbia University Press.
Pierterse, J. N. (1995). Globalization and hybridization, In M. Featherstone, S. Lash, & R. Robertson (Eds.), *Global modernities* (pp. 45–68). London, UK: Sage Publications.
Rasmussen, D. (1982). Communicative action and philosophy: Reflections on Habermas' *Theorie des kommunikativen Handelns. Philosophy and Social Criticism,* 9, 1–29.
Read, W. H. (1976). *America's mass media merchants.* Baltimore, MD: Johns Hopkins University Press.
Said, E. W. (1978). *Orientalism.* New York, NY: Vintage Books.
Schiller, H. I. (1976). *Communication and cultural domination.* White Plains, NY: M. E. Sharpe, Inc.
Servaes, J. (1989). *One world, multiple cultures: A new paradigm on communication for development.* Leuven, Belgium: Acco.
Shohat, E. (1992). Notes on the postcolonial. *Social Text,* 31/32, 99–113.
Spivak, G. C. (1995). Can the subaltern speak? In B. Ascroft, G. Griffiths, & H. Tiffin (Eds.), *The post-colonial studies reader* (pp. 24–28). London, UK: Routledge.
Tomlinson, J. (1991). *Cultural imperialism.* Baltimore, MD: Johns Hopkins University Press.
Waters, M. (1995). *Globalization.* London, UK: Routledge.
Wilson, R. & Dissanayake, W. (1996). *Global/local: Cultural production and the transnational imaginary.* Durham, NC: Duke University Press.

Part II

Reconsidering Development Communication Practice

6

Communication for Social Change among Mexican Factory Workers on the Mexico–United States Border

Robert Huesca

The field of development communication has undergone significant transformation in its relatively brief history, moving from a fairly straightforward, if oversimplified, prescriptive science of modernization, to a more problematic process involving nuances of power and gender. Painted in broad strokes, development communication has evolved through three major phases: the Dominant Paradigm of modernization, the Third World critique of the Dominant Paradigm, and various initiatives to create alternative approaches to communication for development (Melkote, 1991; Tehranian, 1991). This final, contemporary stage in the history of development communication is of central interest to this chapter. This stage has been marked by theoretical and methodological pluralism that stands in stark contrast to the singular focus of the Dominant Paradigm.

While this pluralism has generated many positive consequences, it has not advanced the study of development communication with either the speed or clarity of earlier approaches. Indeed, the search for alternative paradigms of development communication has functioned as a heuristically rich period generating diverse theoretical frameworks and practical applications, ranging from reconceptualized mass media campaigns to newly directed grassroots movements. Furthermore, the search for alternative approaches has replaced the arrogance of certainty in the Dominant Paradigm with the humility of limitations that has resulted in more self–reflexive scholarship overall. Nevertheless, the search for alternative paradigms seems to be recycling familiar themes, plowing through well-worn terrain. The lack of theoretical advance among scholars of alternative approaches to development communication threatens to undermine the importance of issues of gender and power so central to the critique of the Dominant Paradigm. It also opens the way for a reversion to earlier approaches to development, especially in the context of the rapid innovation of new communication and information technologies (Lent, 1987).

This chapter explores a theoretical avenue that might advance alternative approaches to development communication by explicitly linking participatory communication models with research into new social movements. The new social movements literature that has been developing in political science and sociology since the 1970s offers a robust framework for examining structures of power and social change. Yet it is a framework that attends to communication only in a cursory, peripheral fashion. The key notions of both participatory communication and new social movements demonstrate how the two literatures can inform one another. Data collected from the Mexico–United States border illustrate the utility of this conceptual framework to both theory and practice of development communication.

PARTICIPATORY COMMUNICATION

As noted above, the passing of the Dominant Paradigm of communication for development has been followed by a period of pluralism in terms of alternative theories and practices of development. Amid this diversity, the call for participatory approaches to communication in development is potentially the most radical and significant turn away from the Dominant Paradigm, and it has generated a robust body of theoretical and empirical research. Indeed, recent overviews of the development field have hailed participatory approaches as a "new paradigm" guiding development communication theory and practice (Melkote, 1993; Midgley, 1986; Moemeka, 1994; Nair & White, 1993a; Servaes, 1996; White, 1994). While this proclamation is undoubtedly premature, the participatory turn does represent a potentially rich new direction for the study and practice of development communication—one that maintains a focus on issues of power and gender that were ignored for the most part in early development research.

The philosophical rationale and basic tenets of the participatory approach to development communication are located in the critique of the Dominant Paradigm that emerged from Latin America largely in the 1970s (Beltrán, 1975, 1980; Díaz Bordenave, 1985; Freire, 1970, 1973; Pasquali, 1963). This group of scholars rejected on fundamental grounds the modernization development model and the linear effects theories of communication that accompanied it. First, the Dominant Paradigm of development communication was rejected for introducing false premises and alien ideologies into Latin America through the training of communication scholars and practitioners and through the financing of development communication projects (Beltrán, 1975, 1980). The modernization model and sender–receiver theories of communication simply were unresponsive to the social and political context of most Latin American countries. Second, a more appropriate alternative, founded on models of dialogue, was advanced (Freire, 1970, 1973). This alternative focused attention on the grassroots of society as necessary participants in development projects, not as targets of communication, but as partners engaged through dialogic processes. Finally, the movement toward participation and dialogue was conceptualized not only as a pragmatic step, but more importantly, as a fundamental human right (Díaz Bordenave, 1985, 1994).

The critique of the Dominant Paradigm of development was successful in stimulating an intense stream of research into theoretical and applied questions concerning participatory approaches to persistent problems in development (Servaes, 1996; Thomas, 1994; White, 1994). The evolution of participatory approaches, however, has not been uniform or linear, but pluralistic and multidirectional (Melkote, 1993). In fact, some scholars view this pluralism as an essential component of this approach:

> rigid and general strategies for participation are neither possible nor desirable. It is a process that unfolds in each unique situation. (Servaes, 1996, p. 23)

While this theoretical openness is based on the important intention of avoiding the creation of a rigid, authoritarian approach to communication and development, an approach associated with the Dominant Paradigm, it has also resulted in conceptual fuzziness that actually has undermined the initial rationale of the move toward participation. Indeed, participation has been embraced by development scholars who have incorporated this notion into modernization practices, such as message development and social integration (Nair & White, 1993a, 1993b; Rogers, 1993). The pluralistic spirit of the participatory turn in development communication has had the ironic effect of redeeming the Dominant Paradigm from its critics (Lent, 1987).

At this juncture in the evolution of participatory communication approaches, scholars need to reclaim the moral and political dimensions that were implicit in the early critiques from Latin America. The field of development communication is in need of analytic tools that clarify the relationship of participatory approaches to larger social and political issues without rejecting the pluralistic spirit that is so important to avoiding the tyranny of any specific paradigm. Research into new social movements emerging from sociology and political science offers a potentially fruitful direction. The new social movements research provides a structural framework concerning the process of social change that is compatible with participatory approaches to development communication. By situating participatory communication theories within such a framework, scholars may begin to develop conceptual clarity without abandoning either the spirit of pluralism and tolerance or the commitment to social justice and equality.

NEW SOCIAL MOVEMENTS

Beginning in the late 1960s, scholars from sociology and political science started to examine the process of social change by looking at coordinated action occurring outside of formal institutions, such as political parties and labor unions. This focus on new social movements gained renewed momentum in the 1980s and 1990s, especially in Latin America, with the emergence of ethnic-, gender-, and issue-organizing initiatives that were not explained satisfactorily by traditional Marxist and/or liberal democratic theories of social change. This interest in new social movements has generated literally hundreds of studies that would be impossible to review. A sketch of the basic definitions, issues, and concepts of new social movements, with explicit attention given to notions of power in society, however, will demonstrate the compatibilities with and potential contributions of participatory communication approaches to development.

New social movements have been conceptualized as responding to major shifts in social, political, and economic relations that are occurring on a global scale. One of the earliest new social movements theorists describes this shift as being marked by a decline in the importance of material relations of production and a reduction, not elimination, of the role played by unions and parties in effecting change (Touraine, 1971). Since then, scholars in Latin America have agreed that new forms of organizing and acting for social change have occurred in the 1980s and 1990s (Alvarez, Dagnino, & Escobar, 1998; Escobar & Alvarez, 1992; Fals Borda, 1992; Hellman, 1997; Hopenhayn, 1993). Making sense of these new forms has evolved from early studies celebrating the profound impact of new social movements on political structures and policy agenda to current research that is more circumspect in assessing their consequences (Slater, 1994). Despite the changing sense of the overall impact of new social movements, this theoretical framework has always functioned to interpret social action in a broad social and historical context.

Defining new social movements and differentiating them from earlier theories of protest and collective mobilization has been contentious and inexact. In fact, several scholars have cautioned against defining new social movements at all, as such an external imposition would violate the self-determination, fluidity, heterogeneity, and openness that characterize them (Escobar & Alvarez, 1992; Melucci, 1998). Nevertheless, a number of shared general characteristics have emerged that distinguish this area of research from earlier approaches to collective behavior. First, new social movements are defined as heterogeneous, neither reducible to a single kind of action nor tied to a single set of strategies or demands (Melucci, 1989). This pluralistic aspect of new social movements is related to their origins; they arise outside of formal institutions, in the spheres of daily life (Hannigan, 1985, Hellman, 1997).

Second, new social movements are marked temporally by an ongoing yet cyclical orientation toward expressing collective identity and discontent (Downing, 1996). Again, the temporal ebb and flow of action is related to the inherent discontinuities of the invisible laboratories and submerged networks where new social movements are formed.

Finally, new social movements are oriented less toward instrumental aims of material concessions and more toward the construction of identities and meanings that give direction to collective behavior (Castells, 1983; Lowe, 1986; Melucci, 1998; Touraine, 1981). New social movements have been defined, then, as heterogeneous groups forming outside of formal institutions and operating in discontinuous cycles to forge collective meanings and identities that direct action.

Because new social movements form outside of institutions but are oriented toward social change, this literature has dealt specifically with gender and power. In Latin America, new social movements have often emerged from the household or the neighborhood, which has involved women at the center of organizing (Jelin, 1994; Schild, 1994). These and other studies have noted that women's organizing efforts include distinctive forms of participation that are often hidden or unseen by researchers. Attending to the conditions under which women become involved in movements and how their experiences in groups lead to specific organizing activities is important to understanding the shape and character of social movements in Latin America.

Because new social movements are directed toward rearticulating meanings and identities that serve as the basis for action, scholars have developed explicit conceptions of power as they relate to participation and social change. In general, whereas power may be asymmetrical, it generally is not conceptualized as transparent and one dimensional in the new social movements literature. Rather, power is viewed as a relationship that is diffused throughout the social system (Alvarez, Dagnino, & Escobar, 1998; Touraine, 1988). Furthermore, power is conceptualized as dynamic in nature, necessitating reproduction and subject to reinvention and change (Fals Borda, 1992). Therefore, new social movements are viewed as having a relationship to the general political culture through the questioning, contesting, and confirming of institutional definitions and boundaries.

This dynamic portrayal of the relationship between issues of power, gender, society, and collective action essentially has provided a theoretically rich framework for bridging the influences of both structure and agency on social change. Scholars have acknowledged that meanings and identities of social movements are not self-formed through collective action alone, but in interaction with powerful institutions (Scott, 1995). Hence, the examination of social movements entails an appreciation and understanding of both discursive-symbolic and material-structural factors that play a part in both the reproduction and transformation of the social system (Castells, 1983; Escobar & Alvarez, 1992). Nevertheless, researchers of new social movements have not treated these two factors as areas of independent investigation and analysis but as products of discourse and interpretation. In determining the characteristics of both symbolic and structural factors, researchers of new social movements have privileged the actual participants of collective action as sources of interpretation (Castells, 1983; Hellman, 1997; Melucci, 1998; Touraine, 1981). This turn toward the interpretive subjectivity of movement participants has created a prominent place for the process of communication in examining new social movements and analyzing their relationship to social change.

Indeed, the study of social movements is founded on an epistemology of action, whereby participation, mobilization, intervention, reproduction, and dissolution all emerge through interactions that create collective identities and visions for the future (Castells, 1983; Lowe, 1986; Touraine, 1981).

Empirical research into new social movements, therefore, has sought to understand how individuals become involved, sustained, and estranged from movements; how actors construct collective identity and action; and how the unity of various elements of action are produced (Melucci, 1989). Although all of these elements come about through communication, research into new social movements has proceeded without an explicit model of communication. In fact, when communication forms, such as popular mass media, are explicitly discussed, scholars appear especially naive regarding the communication process through references to "mass consumption" and the "manipulation of consciousness" (Melucci, 1998, p. 427). This paradox of elevating the place of interaction, while neglecting communication theory, opens a space for the contributions of participatory development communication research.

INTEGRATING COMMUNICATION AND MOVEMENTS

Current directions in participatory development communication research are not only compatible with studies of new social movements, but they also will contribute to theoretical advancements in this area. The evolution of participatory development communication research has been documented elsewhere as moving through a series of dualisms focusing on states and entities—the *whos* and *whats* of participation and development—toward attending to processes and dynamics—the *hows* of participation and development (Dervin & Huesca, 1997). Such an approach to participatory development communication is posited as most appropriate to the study of new social movements, because of its explicit interest in understanding *how* collective action is initiated, constructed, reproduced, and dissolved.

This approach conceptualizes communication as a verb or a procedure, instead of as a noun or an entity, in order to maintain a focus on processes (the *hows* of interaction), which has been difficult to achieve in the history of communication research (Dervin, 1993; Dervin and Clark, 1993). "Verbing" terms of communicating, such as observing, categorizing, defining, and the like, function in admittedly unconventional, awkward fashion as mental constructs with which to examine, describe, and analyze empirical phenomena. These somewhat awkward constructs serve as a reminder that process is often relegated to second place, while states and entities, such as identity, gender, and class, have received primary attention in much communication, as well as new social movements, research. Researching the communicating of and in social movements offers a promising way to document the "epistemology of action" that is central to their formation, mobilization, and operation.

A communication-as-procedure framework has been used productively in previous research focusing on communication projects for social change (Huesca, 1995, 1996). In this framework, communicating is embedded in context and consequence. That is, human communication actions are conceptualized as processes that are grounded in specific contexts (defined broadly to include social structures such as identity, gender norms, and material conditions) and that derive some sort of consequences (personal empowerment, transformation in consciousness, or improved living conditions). Holding onto this entire procedural chain, of context-action-consequence, is a way of centering on communication processes without losing touch with contextual particularities or real-world consequences. The focus of attention, however, is not on the entities of context or consequence, but on the dynamic communicating processes that confront, challenge, transform, and reproduce conditions and structures that give rise to new social movements. Such a framework has been used in an ongoing study of Mexican factory workers organizing for social change.

RESEARCH METHODS

For the past two years, I have been working on the Mexican border with a group of labor organizers who coordinate small-group meetings among workers in Mexico's assembly plants known as *maquiladoras.* The organizers belong to a group called the *Comité Fronterizo de Obreras* (CFO), or Border Committee of Working Women, a nonprofit organization formed in 1986 as a result of organizing efforts of the American Friends Service Committee's *Maquiladora* Project. The CFO is not a labor union or a formal, membership institution, but is a voluntary association of hundreds of factory workers and about six organizers (three in Matamoros, one in Río Bravo, and two in Ciudad Acuña) who receive a modest, weekly stipend. These organizers, referred to as *promotoras* (promoters, facilitators), conduct their organizing work for the most part in the homes of factory workers, who discuss workplace issues, problems, and solutions in a fashion commensurate with participatory development communication principles. This organization functions as an excellent exemplar of both a participatory communication project and an active social movement.

Furthermore, the conditions of the *maquiladoras* represent a compelling case for research into new social movements as the border industrial parks are, in effect, the laboratories and prototypes of global capitalism. *Maquiladoras,* or "twin plants" as some in the industry like to call them, are foreign-owned companies that perform assembly work in Mexico under special import–export arrangements that were drafted in the mid-1960s (Cravey, 1998; Kopinak, 1996; Sklair, 1989). Those arrangements allow a foreign company located in Mexico to import component parts duty-free, assemble them in the Mexican factories, and export the finished products back to the country of origin—again, duty-free. In Mexico, the plants pay taxes only on the "value added" or wages used to assemble the product. The major draw for companies to establish these plants are the low wages earned by Mexican workers coupled with logistical convenience. So a company like General Motors, which is the largest single employer in the *maquiladora* industry, sends components to its plants in Reynosa that assemble them into radios, air conditioners, brake assemblies, and alarm systems for Buicks, Cadillacs, and Oldsmobiles. Workers earn somewhere between $34.00 and $48.00 a week, or between $.75 and $1.17 an hour. The economic and logistical draw is so strong that Mexico now hosts corporations from Japan, China, and Taiwan. "Mexico ranks only behind China as global investors' favorite location in the developing world," declared *Business Week* magazine in a special report (Smith & Malkin, 1997, p. 65). As outsourcing, direct foreign investment, and "production sharing" increase as strategies for remaining competitive in the era of global economics, the challenges to organizing for increased wages and decent living conditions grow more difficult.

Over the past two years, I have lived for six to eight weeks each summer mainly in the cities of Reynosa and Río Bravo, working each day with *promotoras.* I have observed and participated in more than a hundred local meetings and have conducted in-depth interviews with twenty former and current CFO members. I conducted my interviews on the principles and assumptions of the Sense-Making methodology, which places the interview subject at the center of determining substantive content while providing a structure that allows for cross comparison of data (Dervin, 1989, 1992). Guided by Sense-Making questionnaires, participants discussed how they came to work in a *maquiladora,* how they came to be involved in the CFO, and how their participation in the CFO impacted their lives. All interviews were recorded and transcribed and were interpreted in conjunction with daily field notes. Because this research is still in process, the findings presented here are exploratory and tentative.

FINDINGS

A procedural approach to participatory communication for development generates rich portraits of how social movements operate and how participants conceptualize the process of social change. Because of space limitations, the full portrait emerging from this data set cannot be presented here. Instead, the most significant pattern in the data and some of its surrounding details demonstrate the value of both the new social movements analytic framework and the participatory communication approach outlined above.

The findings from the interviews and field notes reveal a dialectical relationship between collective behavior and individual action in effecting social change and in reproducing this particular social movement. The single most important pattern that has emerged from this project has been the identification of individual strategies as the route to effecting changes that will benefit workers in the *maquiladoras.* Across virtually all interviews, participants explained that "learning to defend oneself" and learning "not to take it" anymore were the most valuable strategies of this social movement. Nevertheless, these individualistic strategies were born of and energized by the collective process of workers' meetings organized by the CFO.

The individualistic strategies of "defending oneself" or "not taking it" emerged from a collective process that involved many workers across diverse settings. The CFO typically met with small groups of three to ten people who learned of the organization by word of mouth from coworkers or neighbors. The communication procedure *promotoras* typically used in initial meetings was to elicit the interests and concerns of workers through questioning about their jobs, problems, interests, and desires. This questioning resulted in collective agenda building of issues and topics that were then discussed in subsequent meetings. Once workers essentially constructed an agenda, the *promotoras* explained that many of the identified issues were addressed explicitly in the Mexican *Federal Labor Law,* which was used by all *promotoras* in cities visited during this study. Articles from this legal text were interwoven routinely with workers' discussions of problems and solutions. The identification of individual strategies for effecting social change seemed to be related to the use of *Federal Labor Law* in discussing workers' problems.

Indeed, when describing the need to defend oneself, workers often related this strategy to the rights that were spelled out in the federal law and that were unknown to most workers. A woman discussing the first time she attended a meeting organized by the CFO recalled learning that she had legal rights:

> The *promotora* began to show me the *Federal Labor Law* so that one could learn, so that one would know how to defend oneself, would know how to defend her job, would know her rights. This interested me quite a bit, and I continued going to the meetings. I began to organize meetings and I began hosting them here at my house. (Rosario A.)[1]

Learning to defend oneself on the basis of federal law translated into a practical action strategy on the factory floor, according to another woman:

> Here in my house we have discussed, we have studied the *Federal Labor Law.* Each person discussed, each person with their book began to learn various articles that we didn't even imagine existed. What this has done has been to help me be able to defend myself more. At any given time, if there is a problem, for example, I now have a little more ability to defend myself against the problems inside the factory, especially problems with the supervisors. (Tania E.)

In fact, this individualistic, self-defense strategy seemed to be related in part to the context of the factory, where collective actions could put one's job at risk. Several participants who had become volunteer organizers explained that collective strategies, such as work stoppages or the collective airing of grievances, were not desirable for two reasons. First, all factories seemed to include coworkers who had informed management of organizing efforts of workers. Invoking an individualistic action strategy was often described as a more discrete manner of working for change. Second, management in a number of factories seemed to pursue and punish more vigorously workers who were involved in collective organizing and mobilizing than those who individually claimed their rights regarding overtime, vacation pay, and other issues covered in the law. In fact, during my fieldwork in 1997, workers at General Motors's plants in Reynosa staged wildcat strikes to protest the lack of profit sharing, which is required by the Mexican law. After a settlement was reached with the company's union, the management of General Motors selectively fired more than twenty workers who were believed to be the leaders of the work stoppage. A number of participants who had experienced collective actions in the workplace mentioned cases of selective firing, intimidation, and rearrangement of schedule and work assignment.

Despite their individualistic nature, the strategies of self-defense and intolerance of abuse were energized in the collective atmosphere of CFO meetings. The ability to defend oneself in the workplace by responding to an abusive supervisor or questioning a manager about some irregularity required the cultivation of self-confidence among workers. Both gender and class factors hindered the development of such confidence, as both male and female factory workers occupy subordinate roles in their society and, in the case of women, in their households. Participating in group meetings contributed to the abilities of workers to defend themselves by modeling behavior and providing practical experience. A male worker described his surprise at hearing ordinary workers articulate their problems and responses during a regional meeting of the CFO:

> For me, the big meetings of the CFO had a big impact on me. The impact of getting to know people who came from different cities, and seeing their way of carrying themselves, how they explained their experiences, it leaves one, frankly, surprised. I didn't know that there were people, that there were workers who could speak so well about the law, who knew how to express themselves perfectly about the experiences that they have lived. (Jorge E.)

Aside from modeling poise and ability, group meetings provided a forum where workers could rehearse common scenarios to confront problems that had been identified. In one situation, a woman was suffering wrist pain related to her job of tying knots on the lassohandles of gift bags. Despite complaints to her supervisor, this woman was neither reassigned nor given a disability leave from work. In one group meeting, the participants rehearsed a confrontation with the supervisor as a response to her situation:

> So we enacted a sociodrama to see how to go about solving this problem. So some had the role of the workers, another the supervisor, others chose other roles. Since she had to confront the supervisor, she did it. I was another worker. And those who watched what we did also learned how to defend themselves. I think these help you, the sociodramas, because you learn how to speak up. (Carmen C.)

What these experiences demonstrate is that even a seemingly individualistic intervention strategy can be intimately intertwined with collective processes. Indeed, some participants in this study suggested that the individual nature of this strategy might be a misreading of its overall impact. While defending oneself is clearly explained as an individual action, it is often discussed in terms of a massive movement, as in this illustration by a female worker:

> Something that pleases me right now, and it pleased me when I was working in the plant, is that the people are no longer willing to take it. Anybody you ask defends herself on her

> own, in her own way, with her own words. Now it's not necessary that somebody else comes along to defend her. Now there are older people, older women who, before, you would look at them and they'd be closed, they'd take whatever they were told, whatever they were told. But with the talks that we have done, they have begun to defend themselves by themselves. I mean, they now defend their work, their being, so they won't be abused. (Rosario A.)

Therefore, even the dominant pattern of strategies that have emerged from a social movement is open to multiple and conflicting interpretations. In this case, the isolated approach to effecting change in the factories has been interpreted by some of the participants as a far wider, more systematic effort resulting from collective meetings.

CONCLUSION

This truncated presentation of field data in light of the theoretical issues preceding it serves as a starting place for illustrating the continued utility of participatory communication approaches to development. Furthermore, it demonstrates the utility of placing communication approaches within the larger framework of new social movements to examine power, gender, and social change more explicitly.

The major pattern that emerged from the interview and observational data presents a portrait of social change that is premised on individual action: self-defense and unwillingness to tolerate abuse. This pattern only started to become visible to the researcher after many in-depth interviews with participants in the CFO. It was not an explicit approach that was ever articulated by the *promotoras* who were the initial field guides in this project. Indeed, a rational analysis of workers' conditions, factory ownership patterns, union behavior, and legal and political resources had not lead the *promotoras* to describe their work as that of "teaching people to defend themselves." Rather, this strategy was allowed to emerge because of the participatory communication procedures, such as questioning and agenda building, which were a formal aspect of the work of the CFO. Development practitioners would benefit not only from enacting participatory communication procedures in the field but also from periodically examining more abstract interpretations of issues and themes that emerge in group activities.

Grassroots strategies, such as these individualistic approaches to social change, have been criticized in the abstract and in concrete cases as potentially reproducing harmful social norms or as leaving oppressive structural forces in place (Hellman, 1994; Wilkins, 1999). While these criticisms are important to bear in mind, participatory communication research is useful at teasing out the multiple layers of interpretations that exist with even the most seemingly straightforward phenomena. In the case of the Mexican factory workers, one could argue that even while women have begun to contest the abuse of individual supervisors in the workplace, this strategy is actually illusory, as it gives the appearance of influence while never questioning the structures of wealth and poverty governing international trade. Such conclusions in effect privilege the interpretations of scholars and rely on one-dimensional models of power.

The literature from new social movements is helpful here at providing a broader framework for examining participatory development projects. With its more diffuse theory of power in society, new social movements theory helps to move participatory communication research into more complex directions. In the abbreviated case presented above, for example, the new social movements approach draws attention to how legal structures, such as the *Federal Labor Law,* and social norms, such as gender expectations, become animated through human action. In this case, the legal structure both enabled and constrained workers, who adopted its explicit rights, but implemented them through limited, individualistic steps. Furthermore, the implementation of the individual act of defending oneself subverted gender expectations that women should not speak openly to authority. Rather than reducing the self-defense strategy to a singular meaning, the new social movements approach requires researchers to examine how such patterns empower and disempower social actors and alter larger social relations.

Drawing together the approaches from participatory development communication and new social movements has beneficial implications for future research. It positions both theory and practice, analysis and intervention in the terrain between structure and agency where development projects and social change efforts necessarily reside.

NOTES

1. Quotes from this research are cited by pseudonyms for informants in order to protect their confidentiality.

REFERENCES

Alvarez, S. E., Dagnino, E., & Escobar, A. (1998). Introduction: The cultural and the political in Latin American social movements. In S. E. Alvarez, E. Dagnino, & A. Escobar (Eds.), *Cultures of politics/politics of cultures: Re–visioning Latin American social movements* (pp. 1–29). Boulder, CO: Westview.

Beltrán, L. R. (1975). Research ideologies in conflict. *Journal of Communication,* 25, 187–193.

Beltrán, L. R. (1980). A farewell to Aristotle: 'Horizontal' communication. *Communication,* 5, 5–41.

Castells, M. (1983). *The city and the grassroots: A cross–cultural theory of urban social movements.* Berkeley, CA: University of California.

Cravey, A. J. (1998). *Women and work in Mexico's* maquiladoras. Lanham, MD: Rowman & Littlefield.

Dervin, B. (1989). Audience as listener and learner, teacher and confidante: The sense-making approach. In R. Rice & C. Atkin (Eds.), *Public communication campaigns* (2nd ed., pp. 67–86). Newbury Park, CA: Sage.

Dervin, B. (1992). From the mind's eye of the user: The sense-making qualitative–quantitative methodology. In J. D. Glazier & R. R. Powell (Eds.), *Qualitative research in information management* (pp. 61–84). Englewood, CO: Libraries Unlimited.
Dervin, B. (1993). Verbing communication: Mandate for disciplinary invention. *Journal of Communication, 43*, 45–54.
Dervin, B., & Clark, K. (1993). Communication and democracy: A mandate for procedural invention. In S. Splichal, & J. Wasko (Eds.), *Communication and democracy* (pp. 103–140). Norwood, NJ: Ablex.
Dervin, B., & Huesca, R. (1997). Reaching for the communicating in participatory communication. *The Journal of International Communication, 4*(2), 46–74.
Díaz Bordenave, J. E. (1985). *Comunicación y sociedad.* La Paz, Bolivia: CIMCA.
Díaz Bordenave, J. E. (1994). Participative communication as a part of building the participative society. In S. A. White, K. S. Nair, & J. Ascroft (Eds.), *Participatory communication: Working for change and development* (pp. 35–48). New Delhi, India: Sage.
Downing, J. (1996). *Internationalizing media theory: Transition, power, culture: Reflections on media in Russia, Poland and Hungary 1980–95.* London, UK: Sage.
Escobar, A. & Alvarez, S. E. (1992). Introduction: Theory and protest in Latin America today. In A. Escobar & S. E. Alvarez (Eds.), *The making of social movements in Latin America: Identity, strategy, and democracy* (pp. 1–15). Boulder, CO: Westview.
Fals Borda, O. (1992). Social movements and political power in Latin America. In A. Escobar & S. E. Alvarez (Eds.), *The making of social movements in Latin America: Identity, strategy, and democracy* (pp. 303–316). Boulder, CO: Westview.
Freire, P. (1970). *Pedagogy of the oppressed* (M. Bergman Ramos, Trans.). New York, NY: Herder and Herder.
Freire, P. (1973). *¿Extensión o comunicación?* (L. Ronzoni, Trans.). Buenos Aires, Argentina: Siglo XXI.
Hannigan, J. A. (1985). Alain Touraine, Manuel Castells and social movement theory: A critical appraisal. *The Sociological Quarterly, 26*(4), 435–454.
Hellman, J. A. (1994). Mexican popular movements, clientelism and the process of democratization. *Latin American Perspectives, 21*(2), 124–142.
Hellman, J. A. (1997). Social movements: Revolution, reform and reaction. *NACLA report on the Americas, 30*(6), 13–18.
Hopenhayn, M. (1993). Postmodernism and neoliberalism in Latin America. *Boundary 2, 20*(3), 93–109.
Huesca, R. (1995). Subject authored theories of media practice: The case of Bolivian tin miners' radio. *Communication Studies, 46*, 149–168.
Huesca, R. (1996). Participation for development in radio: An ethnography of the *Reporteros populares* of Bolivia. *Gazette, 57*, 29–52.
Jelin, E. (1994). The politics of memory: The human rights movement and the construction of democracy in Argentina. *Latin American Perspectives, 21*(2), 38–58.
Kopinak, K. (1996). *Desert capitalism:* Maquiladoras *in North America's western industrial corridor.* Tucson, AZ: University of Arizona.
Lent, J. (1987). Devcom: A view from the United States. In N. Jayaweera, & S. Amunugama (Eds.), *Rethinking development communication* (pp. 20–41). Singapore: Asian Mass Communication Research and Information Centre.
Lowe, S. (1986). *Urban social movements: The city after Castells.* New York, NY: St. Martin's Press.

Melkote, S. R. (1991). *Communication for development in the Third World: Theory and practice.* New Delhi, India: Sage.

Melkote, S. R. (1993). From Third World to First World: New roles and challenges for development communication. *Gazette,* 52(2), 145–158.

Melucci, A. (1989). *Nomads of the present.* Philadelphia, PA: Temple University.

Melucci, A. (1998). Third world or planetary conflicts? In S. E. Alvarez, E. Dagnino, & A. Escobar (Eds.), *Cultures of politics/politics of cultures: Re–visioning Latin American social movements* (pp. 422–436). Boulder, CO: Westview.

Midgley, J. (1986). Community participation: History, concepts and controversies. In J. Midgley (Ed.), *Community participation, social development and the state* (pp. 13–44). London, UK: Methuen.

Moemeka, A. (1994). Development communication: A historical and conceptual overview. In A. Moemeka (Ed.), *Communicating for development: A new pan–disciplinary perspective* (pp. 3–22). Albany, NY: State University of New York Press.

Nair, K. S. & White, S. A. (1993a). The development communication process. In K. S. Nair, & S. A. White (Eds.), *Perspectives on development communication* (pp. 47–70). New Delhi, India: Sage.

Nair, K. S. & White, S. A. (1993b). Introduction. In K. S. Nair, & S. A. White (Eds.), *Perspectives on development communication* (pp. 12–31). New Delhi, India: Sage.

Pasquali, A. (1963). *Comunicación y cultura de masas.* Caracas, Venezuela: Universidad Central de Venezuela.

Rogers, E. M. (1993). Perspectives on development communication. In K. S. Nair, & S. A. White (Eds.), *Perspectives on development communication* (pp. 35–46). New Delhi, India: Sage.

Schild, V. (1994). Recasting "popular" movements: Gender and political learning in neighborhood organizations in Chile. *Latin American Perspectives,* 21 (2), 59–80.

Scott, A. (1995). Culture or politics? Recent literature on social movements, class and politics. *Theory, Culture & Society,* 12, 169–178.

Servaes, J. (1996). Introduction: Participatory communication and research in development settings. In J. Servaes, T. L. Jacobson, & S. A. White (Eds.), *Participatory communication for social change* (pp. 13–25). New Delhi, India: Sage.

Sklair, L. (1989). *Assembling for development.* Boston, MA: Unwin Hyman.

Slater, D. (1994). Introduction. *Latin American Perspectives,* 21, 5–10.

Smith, G. & Malkin, E. (1997). The border: Special report. *Business Week,* May 12, 64–74.

Tehranian, M. (1991). Communication and theories of social change: A communitarian perspective. *Asian Journal of Communication,* 2(1), 1–30.

Thomas, P. (1994). Participatory development communication: Philosophical premises. In S. A. White, K. S. Nair, & J. Ascroft (Eds.), *Participatory communication: Working for change and development* (pp. 49–59). New Delhi, India: Sage.

Touraine, A. (1971). *The post–industrial society: Tomorrow's social history: Classes, conflicts and culture in the programmed society* (Leonard F. X. Mayhew, Trans.). New York, NY: Random House.

Touraine, A. (1981). *The voice and the eye.* Cambridge, UK: Cambridge University.

Touraine, A. (1988). *Return of the actor: Social theory in postindustrial society.* Minneapolis, MN: University of Minnesota.

White, S. A. (1994). Introduction—The concept of participation: Transforming rhetoric to reality. In S. A. White, K. S. Nair, & J. Ascroft (Eds.), *Participatory communication: working for change and development* (pp. 15–32). New Delhi, India: Sage.
Wilkins, K. G. (1999). Development discourse on gender and communication in strategies for social change. *Journal of Communication,* 49(1), 46–68.

7

Power and Praxis in Development Communication Discourse and Method

Jody Waters

While we struggle over better ways to use participatory methods and ideals in our applications of communication to development strategies, we tend to overlook the communicative actions and processes that occur in development. Similarly, we often fail to apply our skills as researchers to the systematic documentation of ways that power intervenes in our activities as practitioners, participants, analysts, and producers of discourse about development. Our knowledge and practices can be enhanced by blending aspects of ethnographic research methods with the ongoing and critical analysis of power.

This suggestion expands upon recent concepts of development as a discourse that mediates and expresses power through the construction of the Third World[1] as a problem requiring management and intervention (Crush, 1995; Escobar, 1995; Ferguson, 1994). An examination of the issues of power and praxis in the framework of development anthropology, ethnography, and recent anthropological perspectives on development discourses makes the case that, as communication researchers, we should be particularly well-positioned to address issues of representation and processes of communicating in the field.

Discourse, power, and praxis have emerged as vital issues in our field. In positioning these issues as central considerations, my concerns are not limited to proposing ways of building better participatory practice through communication. Rather, I acknowledge that communication is fundamental to participation and argue that we need to conceptualize and operationalize these processes in ways that foster a different emphasis in our research practices. One way begins with the systematic analysis of factors that mediate communication practices within development, such as power. Another involves the reflexive examination of how we engage in, interpret, and document the intertwined processes of reflection and action that comprise praxis. Seeking a methodological framework to support these assertions, this chapter explores the role of anthropological perspectives in development communications and the implications of a critical, engaged perspective that incorporates the analysis of power and praxis in communication.

POWER AND PRAXIS IN DEVELOPMENT COMMUNICATION

Over the last two decades, the concept of participation has become prominent in theories of development. Modernization-based approaches to development postulated top-down, economically driven views of development as growth and tended to be implemented with little regard for local context or culture. Recently, scholars and practitioners have turned away from these models and have embraced participatory approaches that focus on assisting local communities with defining and implementing their own solutions to development problems.

Participatory models of development are generally considered more responsive to the circumstances of the people and communities to whom development is supposed to bring the most benefits. But it is crucial that we explore these strategies with a critical perspective that dismantles the assumption that participation is "better" than orthodox approaches. The relationship between development and communication demonstrates that adherence to participatory ideals and practices has not necessarily brought us any closer to either affecting or understanding communicative praxis or power in development processes.

Participatory approaches stress the need to construct theory from practice, positing the researcher and his or her subjects as equally and collaboratively engaged in development processes, and stress the need to develop the link between theory and practice in a contextual framework of social transformation. As Huesca (1996) notes, however, discussions of participatory approaches to development communications generally confine themselves to the ethical, normative, and prescriptive aspects of participatory practice; such distinctions leave unexplored the communicative procedures that occur in project situations where external practitioners and researchers work with local communities to solve development problems. Consideration of these issues demands more focused analysis of how participation is actually produced, perceived, and represented, and of whether participatory processes live up to the promise of significantly transforming power structures.

These questions problematize our understanding of participation in development in two ways. First, participatory approaches fail to deal with the communicative or interactive praxis that takes place in project settings. Einsiedel (1992) conceptualizes praxis as "critically-informed practice" that is enacted on three levels: "the exact nature of the action as conducted (and as it was perceived and understood), the impact or consequences of the action, and its context. This reflection is meant to transform the knowledge base in order to guide further action" (Einsiedel, 1992, pp. 3–4). The tendency to focus on the consequences and contexts has left a significant gap in our understanding of how action and interaction take place in development work in general. In development communications, specifically, this gap is even more troublesome.

Participatory communication stipulates that reflection and action should be guided by dialogue, that is, communication that is democratic, collaborative, and open, geared toward the mutual engagement of social actors as equal subjects (see, for example, Servaes, Jacobson, and White, 1996). But while the ethical and normative aspects that undergird these assertions have been discussed at length, few researchers have provided systematic accounts of the practical and operational aspects of dialogue. In other words, the praxis remains unexplored.

A second problematic issue is not unique to development communications but extends to a more general understanding of development as a political enterprise in which First World development agencies and institutions engage in defining problems and designing interventions aimed at effecting change in the Third World. A growing body of literature develops this critique by exploring how knowledge about development is filtered through structures of power and control, then expressed in discourses shaped by these structures. Gardner and Lewis define the "discourse theory" that informs these perspectives:

> Based on the ideas of Michel Foucault, discourse theory refers to the idea that the terms in which we speak, write and think about the world are a reflection of wider relations of power and, since they are linked to practice, are themselves important in maintaining that power structure. (Gardner and Lewis, 1996, p. xiv)

Apthorpe depicts this type of inquiry as the "semiotic approach to the cultural analysis of policy," reminding us that discourse analysis is a three-fold endeavor involving texts, institutions, and communication processes (1985, pp. 91–92). These critiques foreground questions about the factors that mediate how we gather, interpret, and represent the knowledge that is generated in development practice. Many of these questions, such as who represents processes in textual discourse about development, are elided in most development models. Similarly unchallenged has been the authority of the written text as the dominant mode of documentation and representation within official discourses of development organizations, funding agencies, and academia. Frameworks that reflect the dominant institutional discourses of development determine who has the knowledge, skills, and power to observe, interpret, and represent processes of development. Increasingly, however, in both development and development communications, these frameworks are being challenged.

"Development" itself has become highly contested, though it is beyond the scope of this discussion to give full consideration to the varied meanings that surround this term.

Generally, however, where it was once sufficient to think in very broad terms of development as a set of practices and concepts referring to the effort to bring about growth and change in the "Third World" or the "developing world," many analyses now frame development according to its political, cultural, and ideological dimensions. Between the 1960s and the 1990s, a variety of perspectives have emerged, critiquing the failure of development to improve quality of life in the Third World, the reduction of change in marginalized countries and regions to economic terms, and the assumption that First World concepts and technologies could guide all regions of the world to a state of growth and progress (Goulet, 1971; Hirschmann, 1967; Korten, 1990; Sachs, 1992).

The critical realignment of the field of development has also demanded change in the role of communication in development theory and practice. Early development communications practitioners designed interventions according to the assumption that mass media could be used to propel individuals, communities, and nations to a more modern or developed stage (Lerner, 1958). But by the late 1970s and early 1980s, scholars and practitioners, many from the Third World themselves, grew increasingly dissatisfied with these models. Their concerns echoed critiques of the ethnocentrism inherent in attempting to transfer First World patterns of development, the cultural and political inappropriateness of development interventions using images and ideas from developed nations, the impacts of development projects on local areas, and the technological–economic imperative driving most development work (Beltrán, 1976; Díaz Bordenave, 1976; Rogers, 1976).

Critics of earlier development models attempted to dismantle objectifying constructs of people in the Third World as passive audiences. Similarly contested was the application of primarily quantitative social science methods to measure the extent to which the media could "cause" people to develop by, for example, adopting new technologies. Further, the cultural implications of repeated exposure to media content and technologies from the First World were weighed against the marginal gains made in quality of life (Beltrán, 1976). In the wake of these critiques, new models emerged, positing the need for the active participation of local communities, empowerment, collaboration, autonomy, and self-reliance (Fals Borda & Rahman, 1991).

New approaches emphasized how communication and information could be used by marginalized people to investigate and articulate their own needs, solutions and strategies and thus enhance their abilities to engage in social transformation (Freire, 1970). Some researchers investigated the role of indigenous forms of communication such as music, theater, and dance as culturally validating ways of stimulating dialogue and critical awareness (Kidd, 1984; Mlama, 1994). Other projects utilized mainstream technologies, such as video, computers, and radio, to provide channels for marginalized groups, such as women, to develop their roles as critical and engaged communicators (Taylor, 1994).

Participation in these approaches generally referred to the right to define and control the process of development. This right lent itself to the formation of new decision-making structures, respect for culture, norms, and values, and participation in the active production of meaning. But the discourse produced from these models seldom engages the question of power much beyond the level of personal or organizational transformation. While many participatory projects demonstrated that communications can be a powerful tool in helping actors find new ways to interpret and approach their realities (Alfaro, 1994; Taylor, 1994), few researchers have been able to make connections between personal transformation and broader social change.[2]

Further, the negotiation of power in the communicative processes that take place in development continues to be overlooked in favor of discussing results. The right to document and describe experiences for feedback, interpretation, and learning still largely corresponds to academic and institutional power. We continue to see development represented solely from the perspective of the researcher and seldom from the point of view of the local community. Moreover, we are rarely invited to learn about how the researcher interacts with the community and the ways that decisions and strategies are conceived, particularly those that concern the ways that the processes are represented and interpreted.

These questions about power and praxis resonate with those raised by authors concerned with the institutional construction of participation as an alternative approach. In this context, analysts allege that the embrace of participatory constructs by large aid organizations robs these approaches of their critical power (Fals Borda & Rahman, 1991; Rahnema, 1990). Further, some scholars feel that development approaches that are engineered and implemented by agencies, institutions, and academics represent an ongoing process of legitimation and reproduction of the economic and political power held by developed nations (Escobar, 1991, 1995).

Even though new approaches may speak a language of empowerment, they do little to foster the type of social and political change that links local agents with higher levels of policy and decision making. Assuming that participatory approaches are inherently more capable of generating social transformation is questionable, because we simply have not seen systematic analyses of how local agents engage with larger power structures, represented by researchers and practitioners.

THE ROLE OF ANTHROPOLOGICAL PERSPECTIVES IN DEVELOPMENT COMMUNICATIONS

A growing body of research within anthropology aims to reveal the discursive structures at work in development. Scholars working in this tradition have examined the construction of development as a type of knowledge that is mediated by power and ideology (Escobar, 1991, 1995; Ferguson, 1994), the functions of power in the textual representations of development (Crush, 1995), and the intersection of local knowledge, institutional ideology, and global systems in development projects (Pigg, 1992). Moreover, current debates within ethnography can be linked to the emergence of discourse as the basis for proposing new conceptual structures for the analysis of development as a framework for the representation of social reality. As a stream within anthropology, ethnography provides a firm critical perspective for the analysis of social transformation. It foregrounds the intersubjective construction of social reality, the role of power and authority in the creation of texts that represent social processes, and the communicative dynamics involved in the contact between researchers and local people.

The political, social, economic, and ideological domains upon which development anthropology is located have shifted considerably over the last several decades. The mid-1970s were generally seen as a "boom" period for anthropological involvement in development projects. The U.S. Agency for International Development's (USAID) "New Directions" policy, for example, introduced a discourse of "cultural translation" and "social soundness analysis" to development projects, opening up a wealth of opportunities for activist-minded anthropologists to do applied work in the Third World (Green, 1986). Growing concerns to incorporate more information about culture and context also may have created a space for ethnographers and other anthropologists whose skills were viewed as valuable for helping to foster "buy-in" of local populations and devising culturally congruent modes of action that would increase the efficiency of interventions (Gow, 1993). In the 1980s, enthusiasm for culturally specific, grassroots, participation-oriented programs waned within agencies such as USAID when, for example, President Reagan's "Accelerated Development" programs shifted thinking toward more traditional views of development as economic and policy reform. In a context that favored structural adjustment programs geared toward establishing neoliberal economic programs in Third World nations and privatization of state-owned enterprises, funding priorities in large agencies such as the World Bank and USAID shifted away from small-scale projects attempting to empower local communities.

At the same time, however, new research, focusing on the forms of social transformation enacted by social actors and groups at grassroots levels, gained prominence. This trend is linked, on one hand, to burgeoning social, political, and economic crises in the developing world and, on the other, to rejection of mainstream concepts of development. Authors working in this area profess a concern to explore social change outside the confines of development rather than to generate new approaches or paradigms (Escobar, 1995). Studies of new social movements involving, for example, women, urban and rural peasants, gays and lesbians, and workers in the informal economy exemplify the increasing importance of concepts and practices of social and political change that take place outside the framework of strategic interventions (Moran, 1996). These studies emphasize the analysis of local cultures and systems of meaning, popular practices of protest and mobilization, and resistance to entrenched discourses of growth and change within the framework of global capital (Escobar & Alvarez, 1992; Scott, 1985).

This brief history illustrates the contradictions and debates that relate to larger political, epistemological, and methodological tensions that arise in the study of social and cultural processes. In some contexts, development anthropology primarily refers to the study of development as a social, cultural, and political process, while in others it describes the engaged application of anthropological methods for studying culture in order to bring about change (Gardner & Lewis, 1996; Gow, 1993; Moran,

1996). The latter, often characterized as "activist" or "applied" anthropology, aims to reveal the ideological and political stakes in cultural practices, thus opening them up to contestation, resistance, and transformation (Moore, 1996). This perspective sharply contrasts with that of "traditional" anthropology, in which analysis of local cultures overshadows other concerns.

These tensions also concern the stance occupied by development anthropologists toward the cultures, people, and processes they study and the institutions they represent. Anthropologists negotiate the terrain between research and activism in their study of development. Moran (1996) notes that in a world increasingly interconnected by technology, politics, and capital, development anthropology struggles to define its place. On one hand, if development destroys local cultures, dilutes indigenous knowledge, and erodes traditional value systems, then development practitioners and anthropological researchers work at cross-purposes. The former group promotes social change in the interest of improving quality of life, whereas the latter resists it in the interest of cultural preservation. On the other hand, if anthropologists are seen as advocates or protectors of the cultures they study, their ethics and motives become suspect, due to similar questions about paternalism, ethnocentrism, power, and control that challenge development researchers.

Ethnographers, reflecting on the politics and practices of cultural analysis and representation, have produced some perceptive considerations of these issues. Ethnography conceives an epistemological standpoint based on knowledge generated through the intersection of observation, interpretation, and representation (Van Maanen, 1995). In practice, the three primary axes of ethnographic research include intensive knowledge of a culture or community produced through long-term immersion in the research setting, the continual generation and interpretation of data, and the production of written texts that serve to locate research within a larger theoretical framework.

In classic ethnography, participant observation, undertaken through extensive field study, serves as the dominant mode of inquiry (for example, Malinowski, 1922). The resulting texts sketch out cultural, social, and political patterns derived through the observation and analysis of rituals, traditions, daily activities, and social relations. The hallmark of this type of ethnography is the "deep" analysis of culture based on two propositions. Rabinow explains: "An experiential 'I was there' element establishes the unique authority of the anthropologist; its suppression in the text establishes the anthropologists' scientific authority" (Rabinow, 1986, p. 244).

Lately, however, enthusiasm for researchers' authority has waned in a series of much more self-referential and reflexive texts that attempt to dislocate the categories of researchers and subjects as "knowers and known" (Behar, 1993; Conquergood, 1991; Rabinow, 1986; Rosaldo, 1989). Positioning ethnography as a dialogic, political, and intersubjective form of inquiry has placed most of its main tenets under close scrutiny. First, ethnographic research often involves the assumption that certain facts comprise social reality and can be learned and analyzed through participation and observation. An important debate over whether this reality is fixed and objective or relative and subjective has been staged in the arenas of ethnography and cultural anthropology in general. Researchers most invested in this debate are willing to divest their authority and explore their role in constructing a view of reality that simultaneously reflects the community they study, their academic and political formation, and the audiences for whom they write.

The act of writing an ethnographic text simultaneously changes and fixes the culture under study and its meanings (Clifford & Marcus, 1986). Political implications of this condition are clear: some events and processes warrant many pages, while others never appear in written texts at all. Researchers commit descriptions of people, places, events, rituals, and relationships to written form in terms that are accessible, and in many cases convincing, to a community that is likely to be far removed from the actual event. Most often, this audience is an academic or institutional one. It is thus largely inescapable that ethnography involves an appropriation of culture and acknowledgment that its "facts" are socially constructed and relate to the authority and power of the voice that speaks them. These issues have been highlighted in a lively and productive debate, largely focusing on the issues of subjectivity and the authority of representational texts in ethnography. In a larger context, however, they speak to a growing concern in anthropology to account for the constructs and the processes that guide researchers. Abu-Lughod observes that "the so-called 'facts' we get in the field are constructed through our personal interactions with particular individuals in specific social and cultural contexts" (1990, p. 10).

A parallel trend characterizes recent attempts by development anthropologists to link larger questions related to structures of dominance and the interests served by development work with the act of studying cultures and communities in processes of transformation. The hallmark of these approaches is the application of the theories of Michel Foucault to the analysis of development as a set of power relations that operates through discourse.

Discourses function both tacitly and hierarchically. They provide the unwritten rules or "maps," according to which social structures and agents working within these structures orient themselves in regard to the social processes that they aim to analyze or affect. Thus, development discourses embody a system of meanings and practices that construct and justify the need for strategic institutional intervention into Third World problems (Escobar, 1995).

Critique of ideology figures prominently in the conceptual origins of these approaches, as noted by Porter, who observes that discourse analysis enfolds postmodern acknowledgment of the situated nature of knowledge and the "modernist concern" with "emancipation" through scholarship that aims to reveal and deconstruct hegemonic structures of organizing and understanding the world (1995, pp. 63–64).

Discourse analysis uncovers the underlying frameworks that guide the formation of policy, texts, and practices in development. Crush (1995), for instance, argues for closer attention to the issues at play in development texts, vocabularies, and practices, because all three aspects are bound to strategic and tactical concerns. An interest in how the texts of development represent the world is, by extension, an interest in how they interact with the strategies and tactics of their authors and of those who lend them authority (Crush, 1995). Others relate scholarly and professional texts to the routines and practices of development workers (Rew, 1985). Watts (1995) analyzes development as a form of performance that acknowledges and reinforces a set of political practices entrenched in dominant "institutional fields." He argues that development works as an interpretive system through which the Third World is made and remade in narratives and dramas that essentially support the same themes (Watts, 1995, p. 56). These themes correspond to the wider relations of power that dominate the global system. Roe's work on development narratives posits a similar premise by pointing out the epistemological limitations imposed by the entrenchment of the notion of development as a "folktale," in which governments and aid agencies are "potential hero[es] whose failures continually disappoint us" (Roe, 1989, p. 287).

Thus, these critiques reveal a basic assumption underpinning development practice: "The language of 'crisis' and disintegration creates a logical need for external intervention and management" (Crush, 1995, p. 10). These "images of crisis" guide the practice of development as a series of strategic interventions aimed at alleviating the "problem" of the Third World. Therefore, the paradigm of development as a strategic intervention continues to be perpetuated in practice and in theory. Within this critical framework few scholars are convinced that alternative models of development, such as participation, have much to do with challenging hegemonic discourses of development. But this does not necessarily mean that development researchers do not produce, nor are capable of producing, useful and appropriate knowledge about their work and the settings in which they do it.

The task at hand is to avoid the "attachment of the knowledge" to a development rationality (Escobar, 1995). This perspective establishes important areas for further research. Most fundamentally, if development functions as an intersubjective construct involving power and control, we need to investigate ways to counteract the structures and practices that drive these processes. Despite understanding more about how discourses function, we know relatively little about the actual processes through which these discourses are produced. Furthermore, many of the anthropological critiques grounded in the problems of discourse and interpretation invoke resistance through critical and engaged inquiry. They encourage researchers to use their analytic capacities to explore and generate "counternarratives" and "antinarratives" of development. Finally, analysts are also beginning to reveal possibilities for dismantling some of the terminologies and meaning systems that have governed development (Watts, 1995).

The key point here is that it is useful and, in fact, necessary for researchers in development to foreground the institutions and practices that intervene in their attempts to learn about and effect social transformation. Further, research methods and modes of representing need to be much more responsive to and reflective of processes of transformation and changes in social formations. Thus, more attention needs to be paid to the discursive and interpretive communities formed by situations in which researchers and local people work together to effect change (Escobar, 1995, p. 223).

The kind of inquiry that these points suggest requires the analysis of the social forms and practices that are produced in the encounter between local populations and external agents. Whether this involves the study of social movements engaged in the struggle to maintain control over local politics and resources or of the ways that outside researchers work with local populations to implement strategic interventions on behalf of a development agency, the main point is clear. It is no longer acceptable to overlook the fact that power is an intrinsic force in social transformation. With respect to participatory approaches, for example, we need to acknowledge that power structures do not cease to exist even when researchers work within a framework that promotes solidarity, dialogue, and empowerment.

DOCUMENTING DISCOURSE IN COMMUNICATIVE PRAXIS

The circumscribed patterns of knowing that dominate development as a strategic enterprise have inscribed our roles as researchers and practitioners of development. The critique of discourse has generally focused on how the dominant vocabularies, texts, and concepts of development are laden with meanings imposed by agents of development working with First World structures and concepts. Similarly, the political aspects of studying cultural change, as described by ethnographers, challenge us to foreground these structures and concepts in the practice, interpretation, and representation of our research.

These theoretical streams pose an important challenge to development communications researchers. First, we need to find ways of apprehending the local, day-to-day practice of development processes. Second, we need to appreciate the matrix of political, cultural, and institutional forces that form and shape practitioners' and others' frameworks of understanding and the interpretive site formed by their collaboration.

The nature of new models of development, such as participatory communication, hinges on an effort to construct knowledge through the reflexive interplay of action and reflection. This dialectical, process-oriented understanding is the hallmark of praxis. But, surprisingly few communications researchers have attempted to develop methodological tools to inform this practice. We may begin by attempting to understand the context of a particular project, including the power dynamics between and among the local community or stakeholders and local, national, and regional political structures. As communications researchers, then, our attention might be focused less on how to bring about better participation and more on the processes of social communication in development settings and who maintains power to direct and represent these processes.

As described earlier, ethnographic methods are well-positioned to contribute to some aspects of these tasks. Ethnographic fieldwork is a form of communicative praxis, involving acts of communication and interpretation, while simultaneously demanding the political implications of interaction with an "other" (Conquergood, 1991). Ethnographers have foregrounded power by questioning cultural research practices and interpretive texts. They have explored their own positions in relation to their subjects and their institutional accountability and how these contingencies relate to the processes of interpretation and discourse. These epistemological, political, and ethical reflections have led many analysts to again identify communication as an important issue.

The convergence of development communications and ethnography points us toward a new way of thinking about development and its practice. First, analysts and practitioners engaged in social inquiry construct reality in ways that are informed by attributes such as social status, political formation, institutional affiliation, gender, ethnicity, and education. Second, these attributes cannot be divorced from power, because relationships reflect patterns of power and control that occur in all social formations. Third, we need to be more attuned to these issues of power and more reflexive about them in our representation of social processes.

Huesca (1996) provides an important starting point for such considerations in his recent attempt to meld ethnographic method with an operational concept of communication as a dynamic process. Following Dervin and Clark (1993), he generates a communication "template" to explore the procedural questions surrounding participatory practice. This approach permits a closer examination of how interactions, situations, and strategies are linked in social transformation. Huesca also provides an instructive example of the "how's" of writing up field processes in a way that does not overpower the theoretical framework with pragmatic considerations. Einsiedel (1992) concurs, linking ethnographic methods to the exigencies of representing participatory processes by advising researchers to be particularly vigilant about documenting processes with an eye to the action–reflection–action spiral that characterizes praxis.

But beyond these suggestions, we need to go further in accounting for power in our practice. Huesca and Einsiedel correctly suggest we begin by understanding the ethnography of a particular project, including not only the local community or stakeholders, but also the relations and situations involved in the contact between an external agent (that is, researcher and/or agency), and local, national, and political structures. Further, ethnographic understanding is contingent on communicative processes that occur between researchers and the communities they study. As we have seen, praxis cannot be achieved simply by reporting how local communities engage in new interactive processes. It is fundamental that we acknowledge our roles in these processes and the procedures by which we carry them out.

Moreover, we must be more reflexive in our documentation and practice, by continually and systematically interrogating the types and the sources of knowledge that guide practice according to power. As researchers involved in the concepts, processes, and discourses of development, it is necessary to problematize practice as the production and use of knowledge generated through the process of communicating. We need to situate this knowledge and our own roles in its use and production by considering such questions as who produces it and why, in what form it appears and is disseminated, and how social actors gain access to it.

Development communications, as a field, has greatly benefited from the participatory turn taken over the past several decades. But it is also clear that we are not giving these processes their due in terms of analyzing how they actually take place, nor are we effectively embedding them in a context that simultaneously engages power and practice with the knowledge systems that inform our work as researchers, practitioners, and producers of discourse.

NOTES

1. The construction of terms such as "First" and "Third" Worlds, and "developing" and "developed" nations, has been contested. These terms demonstrate the dominance of certain ways of looking at and describing the world. Critics correctly note that the use of such terms to describe widely varied and heterogeneous nations, cultures, and people is one way that the dominance of Western or Northern academic and institutional perspectives is reproduced. Satisfactory alternatives to these terms, however, still remain to be developed. Thus, I generally use the terms First and Third World in this chapter.

2. Alfaro describes the process undertaken by a women's collective in Peru to increase the voice and political power of marginalized women through the discourse of social maternity. The collective achieves a certain degree of success, but her analysis also demonstrates that individual empowerment and participation cannot themselves foster structural transformation at macrolevels. Empowered women in this project were prevented from achieving broad-based political change, because parallel transformations did not occur on a more general societal level. In Taylor's study, she speaks of the empowering process of communicating that her research subjects experienced in the context of sharing information with other marginalized women. Her own role, however, as facilitator and manager of this project, remains relatively unexplored.

REFERENCES

Abu–Lughod, L. (1990). Can There Be A Feminist Anthropology? *Women and Performance,* 5(1), 7–27.

Alfaro, R. (1994). Women As Social Agents: Social Maternity and Leadership. In P. Riaño (Ed.), *Women in Grassroots Communication: Furthering Social Change* (pp. 260–278). Thousand Oaks, CA: Sage.

Apthorpe, R. (1985). Pleading and Reading Agricultural Development Policy: Small Farm, Big State and the Case of Taiwan. In R. Grillo and A. Rew (Eds.), *Social Anthropology and Development Policy* (pp. 88–101). London, UK: Tavistock Publications.

Behar, R. (1993). *Translated Woman.* Boston, MA: Beacon Press.

Beltrán, L. R. (1976). Alien Promises, Objects and Methods in Latin American Communication Research. In E. Rogers, (Ed.), *Communication and Development* (pp. 15–42). Beverly Hills, CA: Sage.

Clifford, J. & Marcus, G. (Eds.). (1986). *Writing Culture: The Poetics and Politics of Ethnography.* Berkeley, CA: University of California Press.

Conquergood, D. (1991). Rethinking Ethnography: Toward a Critical Cultural Politics. *Communication Monographs,* 58(2), 179–195.

Crush, J. (1995). Introduction: Imagining Development. In J. Crush (Ed.), *Power of Development* (pp. 1–23). London, UK: Routledge.

Dervin, B. & Clark, K. (1993). Communication and Democracy: A Mandate for Procedural Invention. In S. Splichal and J. Wasko (Eds.), *Communication and Democracy* (pp. 103–140). Norwood, NJ: Ablex.

Díaz Bordenave, J. D. (1976). The Communication of Agricultural Innovation in Latin America. In E. Rogers, (Ed.), *Communication and Development* (pp. 43–62). Beverly Hills, CA: Sage.

Einsiedel, E. F. (1992). Action Research: Theoretical and Methodological Considerations for Development Communications. Paper presented to the International Association for Mass Communication Research, Sao Paolo, Brazil.

Escobar, A. (1991). Anthropology and the Development Encounter: The Making and Marketing of Development Anthropology. *American Ethnologist,* 18(4), 16–40.

Escobar, A. (1995). *Encountering Development: The Making and Unmaking of the Third World.* Princeton, NJ: Princeton University Press.

Escobar, A. & Alvarez, S. (Eds.). (1992). *The Making of Social Movements in Latin America: Strategy, Identity and Democracy.* Boulder, CO: Westview Press.

Fals Borda, O. & Rahman, M. A. (Eds.). (1991). *Action and Knowledge: Breaking the Monopoly with Participatory Action Research.* New York, NY: Apex.

Ferguson, J. (1994). *The Anti–Politics Machine: Development, Depoliticization and Bureaucratic Power in Lesotho.* Minneapolis, MN: The University of Minnesota Press.

Freire, P. (1970). *Pedagogy of the Oppressed* (M. Bergman Ramos, Trans.). New York, NY: Continuum.

Gardner, K. & Lewis, D. (1996). *Anthropology, Development and the Post–Modern Challenge.* Chicago, IL: Pluto Press.

Goulet, D. (1971). *The Cruel Choice: A New Concept in the Theory of Development.* New York, NY: Atheneum.

Gow, D. D. (1993). Doubly Damned: Dealing with Power and Praxis in Development Anthropology. *Human Organization,* 52(4), 380–397.

Green, E. C. (Ed.). (1986). *Practicing Development Anthropology.* Boulder, CO: Westview Press.

Hirschmann, O. A. (1967). *Development Projects Observed.* Washington, DC: The Brookings Institution.

Huesca, R. (1996). Participation for Development in Radio: An Ethnography of the Reporteros Populares of Bolivia. *Gazette,* 57(1), 29–52.

Kidd, R. (1984). The Performing Arts and Development in India: Three Case Studies and a Comparative Analysis. In G. Wang and W. Dissanayake (Eds.), *Continuity and Change in Communication Systems* (pp. 95–125). Norwood, NJ: Ablex.

Korten, D. (1990). *Getting to the 21st Century: Voluntary Action and the Global Agenda.* West Hartford, CT: Kumarian.

Lerner, D. (1958). *The Passing of Traditional Society: Modernizing the Middle East.* New York, NY: Free Press.

Malinowski, B. (1922). *Argonauts of the Western Pacific.* New York, NY: E. P. Dutton.

Mlama, P. (1994). Reinforcing Existing Indigenous Communications Skills: The Use of Dance in Tanzania. In P. Riaño (Ed), *Women In Grassroots Communication: Furthering Social Change* (pp. 51–64). Thousand Oaks, CA: Sage.

Moore, H. L. (1996). The Changing Nature of Anthropological Knowledge: An Introduction. In H. L. Moore (Ed.), *The Future of Anthropological Knowledge* (pp. 1–15). London, UK: Routledge.

Moran, E. F. (1996). *Transforming Societies: Transforming Anthropology.* Ann Arbor, MI: University of Michigan Press.

Pigg, S. L. (1992). Inventing Social Categories Through Place: Social Representations and Development in Nepal. *Comparative Studies in Society and History,* 34(3), 491–513.

Porter, D. (1995). Scenes From Childhood: The Homesickness of Development Discourses. In J. Crush (Ed.), *Power of Development* (pp. 63–86). London, UK: Routledge.
Rabinow, P. (1986). Representations Are Social Facts: Modernity and Post–Modernity in Anthropology. In J. Clifford and G. Marcus (Eds.), *Writing Culture: The Poetics and Politics of Ethnography* (pp. 234–261). Berkeley, CA: University of California Press.
Rahnema, M. (1990). Participatory Action Research: The "Last Temptation of Saint" Development. *Alternatives,* xv, 199–266.
Rew, A. (1985). The Organizational Connection: Multi–disciplinary practice and anthropological theory. In R. Grillo and A. Rew (Eds.), *Social Anthropology and Development Policy* (pp. 185–197). London, UK: Tavistock Publications.
Riaño, P. (Ed.) (1994). *Women in Grassroots Communication: Furthering Social Change.* Newbury Park, CA: Sage.
Roe, E. M. (1989). Folktale Development. *The American Journal of Semiotics,* 6(2/3), 277–290.
Rogers, E. M. (1976). Communication and Development: The Passing of the Dominant Paradigm. *Communication Research,* 3(2), 121–133.
Rosaldo, R. (1989). *Culture and Truth: The Remaking of Social Analysis.* Boston, MA: Beacon.
Sachs, W. (1992). *The Development Dictionary: A Guide to Knowledge as Power.* London, UK: Zed Books.
Scott, J. (1985). *Weapons of the Weak: Everyday Forms of Peasant Resistance.* New Haven, CT: Yale University Press.
Servaes, J., Jacobson, T. L., & White, S. A. (Eds.). (1996). *Participatory Communication for Social Change.* New Delhi, India: Sage.
Taylor, S. (1994). Communicating for Empowerment: Women's Initiatives to Overcome Poverty in Rural Thailand and Newfoundland. In P. Riaño (Ed.), *Women in Grassroots Communication: Furthering Social Change* (pp. 235–250). Newbury Park, CA: Sage.
Van Maanen, J. (1995). *Representation in Ethnography.* Beverly Hills, CA: Sage.
Watts, M. (1995). 'A New Deal in Emotions': Theory and Practice and the Crisis of Development. In J. Crush (Ed.), *Power of Development* (pp. 44–62). London, UK: Routledge.

8

A Discursive Perspective on Development Theory and Practice

Reconceptualizing the Role of Donor Agencies

Douglas Storey

In the late 1980s, McAnany and Storey (1989) assessed the field of development communication and reached the conclusion that as a domain of theory and practice old labels no longer applied. Beginning in the 1960s, rhetorically charged attacks from both the left and the right of the ideological spectrum gradually drove many scholars, applied researchers, and practitioners away from development per se. As a result, scholars largely (and for the most part, appropriately) abandoned the grand "modernization project" in favor of attention to a long list of factors—some structural, some behavioral—which were thought to impede or facilitate people and social systems in achieving their aspirations.

Donor agencies, such as the World Bank and the United States Agency for International Development (USAID), have often been portrayed as the villains of development, defining the nature of change, prescribing paths to achieve change (and limiting alternative paths), and perpetuating through their institutional discourse and practices inequitable global power relationships (Escobar, 1995) including gender constructions (Wilkins, 1999). However, while USAID, for example, is undeniably an institutional arm of U.S. foreign and economic policy, it is at the same time an extremely diverse social system composed of individuals with all imaginable political orientations, serving both the apparatus of the state and the expressed needs of people around the world. Attacked by some as paternalistic and manipulative and by others (most notably right-of-center critics in the U.S. Congress) as socialistic and immoral, USAID sometimes satisfies no one. Yet, donor agencies like USAID are engaged in discourse on many levels and are not unresponsive to grassroots initiatives and progressive voices for change.

It is true that USAID and other donor agencies typically engage in a discourse of (rather than about) power and regularly overlook assumptions about power implicit in that discourse. As in any institution or social system, the group culture and norms within USAID affect the circulation and negotiation of meanings. However, USAID and its programs are not self-contained; they are only one part of a much large discursive system.

DISCOURSE

Discursive or dialogic theories emerging from the humanities have had enormous impact on mass communication scholarship in the past ten years or so, but so far they have been used very little to illuminate problems faced by applied communication researchers, theorists, and practitioners in development, although the terms have been used with regard to development. For example, Escobar defines discourse as "a rule-governed system held together by a set of statements that the discursive process continues to reproduce" (1995, p. 154) and uses that definition to describe the creation and continued subjugation of Third World countries by global commercial and political interests. Wilkins (1999) uses the term to refer to the ways in which knowledge about women is generated and processed into institutional justifications for development intervention strategies by international aid agencies.

Such versions of the discourse concept draw on political–economic theories of structuration and the construction of social reality by transnational forces. While these forces are undeniably at work, other theories and close analyses of several development projects indicate that a structuralist perspective tells only part of the story. One such perspective is that of van Dijk, who describes discourse as "social action . . . engaged in within a framework of understanding, communication, and interaction which is in turn part of broader sociocultural structures and processes" (van Dijk, 1997, p. 21).

An even broader and less deterministic perspective has its origins in studies of literature and popular culture, such as the work of the Russian literary theorist, Mikhail Bakhtin (1895–1975). Bakhtin gradually has become known to communication theorists (far less so to communication practitioners, except novelists) through a growing number of translations of his work on a theory of the novel, through his views of authorship/readership/text in social context, in particular, and through interpretation of his work by cultural studies theorists who apply it to the analysis of media systems, media texts, and audiences. Voluminous and complex, an extended discussion of his work is far beyond the scope of this chapter. However, certain concepts from Bakhtin and his interpreters can indicate how they might inform perspectives on development theory and practice.

Bakhtin recognizes that language is inscribed within political, economic, and ideological systems, but it is also "in constant transformation, according to the history and evolution of subjectivity" (Mattelart & Mattelart, 1998, p. 119). For Bakhtin, dialogue is the process by which an utterance (defined broadly to include speech acts as well as words, messages, images, and texts) interacts with the greater social and ideological whole. An utterance,

> having taken meaning and shape at a particular historical moment in a socially specific environment, cannot fail to brush up against thousands of living dialogic threads, woven by socio-ideological consciousness around the given object of [the] utterance; it cannot fail to become an active participant in social dialogue. After all, the utterance arises out of this dialogue as a continuation of it and as a rejoinder to it—it does not approach the object from the sidelines. (Bakhtin, 1981, p. 277)

The pre-existence of a language world from which the utterance emerges ensures that the utterance will be relativized or juxtaposed against other competing definitions for the same things (Bakhtin, 1981, p. 427), thereby changing itself *as well as* the competing definitions. Furthermore, the language world is what Bakhtin calls *heteroglottic:* it encompasses multiple languages each of which is informed by histories of experience and socioideological contradiction that predate and survive any particular users of the language. Language, as a "matrix of forces practically impossible to recoup and therefore impossible to resolve" (Bakhtin, 1981, p. 428), causes every word, message, and image to be constantly reworked through dialogue.

According to Bakhtin (Morson & Emerson, 1990), dialogue is an open-ended, undominated, unfinalizable web of communicative (i.e., symbolic) interaction. As Bakhtin uses the term, dialogue cannot be trivialized as mere interaction or conversation between individuals. People (as well as social groups and social institutions) are not regarded as bounded selves or entities except in a physical sense. The historical reality of each entity is better regarded as a cultural field of richly intersecting temporalities and identities. People cannot be said to *enter into* dialogue because existence cannot be separated from the ongoing process of communication (Morson & Emerson, 1990, p. 50). Dialogue involves "the constant redefinition of its participants, develops and creates numerous potentials in each of them separately and between them interactively and dialogically" (Morson & Emerson, 1990, p. 52).

Bakhtin's image of the novel as an open system of interacting meanings is evocative. As his work became more widely available, cultural studies scholars were quick to pick up on its implications for the study of media systems and media texts. Newcomb (1980) argues that dialogue can be seen among audiences, community formations, governmental bodies, and media, with each entity generating texts (e.g., conversations, behavioral norms, policy statements, program offerings, social activities, value assertions, and so on) that reveal the unfinished and unfinishable nature of social change.

However, following Hall and colleagues (1980) and Morley (1980, 1993), cultural studies scholars have preferred to use the term discourse rather than dialogue to avoid some of the latter term's associations with speech and rhetorical studies. For Bakhtin, discourse has a narrower sense (meaning forms of speech—literally, *word*—including mediated and direct or unmediated, passive and active, unidirectional and varidirectional) (Morson & Emerson, 1990, p. 147) than dialogue (meaning the process of interaction), while cultural studies tend to inscribe *discourse* with the broader Bakhtinian sense of *dialogue.*

For example, in his book on audience interpretation of a popular British television show, Morley (1980) refers to the locus of dialogue as a *discourse system,* by which he means the system of interactions among readers (audience members), texts (words, images, and utterances), and social forms (media systems, a circle of friends, one's workplace, and the commercial market) of which both readers/audiences and texts are parts. A discursive system is defined "by reference to the area of social experience that it makes sense of, to the social location from which that sense is made, and to the linguistic or signifying systems by which that sense is both made and circulated" (Fiske, 1987, p. 268; see also Morley, 1993; Newcomb, 1980). From this perspective, mass communication begins to take on a new more interactive or participatory character.

If discourse is, by definition, uncontained (Newcomb, 1980), it is not, therefore, amenable to manipulation. Domination of discourse, such as occurs in persuasive attempts by authoritative media, involves the creation of boundaries or limits ("Buy this!" [Not that.] "Vote for me!" [Not for her.]). To try to create such boundaries in discourse is to deny discursive opportunities. It is in the nature of discourse that when powerful voices (e.g., government media or donor agencies) attempt to dominate, the discourse either shifts to other sites or the attempt at domination itself becomes a subject of discourse, is deconstructed, and defused (Hall et al., 1980).

Furthermore, discourse informs all of its participants. Therefore, it is antithetical to suppose that only some participants (e.g., powerful donor agencies) influence others without being influenced themselves. Because any element in a discursive system can only be known *in relation to* other elements, a change in *any* element changes the relative position of every other element. Discourse is rarely equable, because tensions and disagreements inevitably arise over values and meanings. Vested interests in one position or another cause participants in the discourse to attempt manipulation, obfuscation, avoidance, and coercion. But the Bakhtinian version of discourse asserts that such tactics can never be completely successful. To optimize discourse in development communication, then, all parties to the communication must be committed to engaging (rather than dominating) each other.

DEVELOPMENT

Development has been defined in a variety of ways and from many perspectives. However it is defined, development has always involved a complex set of interactions among people, technologies, and sociopolitical institutions struggling to articulate visions of the future and find paths toward those ends (for an example of how traditional communication systems can play a role in this process, see Storey, 1993). At the risk of oversimplification, development will be considered as the systemic improvement in the quality of life, as defined by those participating in the process. In other words, development is an inherently discursive process, although it has not always been seen in this light.

Improvement can be defined externally (e.g., by using the material prosperity of developed market economies or optimal levels of women's participation in decision making as referents) or internally (e.g., by using one's own aspirations as referent). "Quality" is similarly diverse, shifting, and temporal in nature. Quality of what and from whose perspective? Health? Freedom of expression? Freedom from hunger? Security? Power? In development, all of these priorities and many others contend with each other for validation and with the social institutions that facilitate or constrain their attainment. The complex interactions of institutions, issues, and actors is, at heart, a discursive process. Therefore, development can be seen as an ongoing process of negotiation among people, institutions, technologies, historical precedents, and power relationships.

EXAMPLES

Four examples of discourse in development, each occurring at a particular level of analysis (individual, interpersonal, media systems, and political–institutional), involve discursive links with other levels. The examples are drawn from different family health communication projects in Asia, all of which received funding from USAID and technical assistance from Johns Hopkins University Population Communication Services (JHU/PCS). Each example illustrates in different ways the complex discursive relationships involved in doing development communication work, how a discursive perspective can help illuminate the process, and establish a focal point for future development communication theorizing.

Several of these examples involve attempts to tap popular culture as a form of communication. Popular culture (and entertainment–education as a form of popular culture) may be the ideal venue for discursive engagement, because it is largely beyond the control of any particular party and is the site of ongoing construction, deconstruction, and reconstruction of social realities. According to Newcomb (1980), Morley (1980), Fiske (1994), and others, popular culture is inherently

1. *discursive* (because it represents an intersection of popular thought, media institutions, and marketplace economics);
2. *participatory* (because it engages popular imagination and grows in part from that imagination, even though it simultaneously has an institutional, commercial aspect); and

3. *uncontained* (because popular culture has life of its own, interacting with but not being entirely shaped by global commercial culture).

Mounting a social change drama, particularly if it is a serial, for example, involves a complex series of discursive negotiations among commercial, political, aesthetic, bureaucratic, and individual forces.

Discourse in the Home: Television Dramas in Pakistan

An important discursive system in its own right is spousal interaction. In health promotion programs, the degree of interaction between husband and wife often is associated positively with knowledge of health issues and healthy behavior. Especially in the area of reproductive health, husbands and wives influence each other's fertility choices (sometimes positively, sometimes negatively), so understanding the nature of this process is crucial to the study of community and family health. At the same time, interpersonal interaction is an important site of inquiry into the communication process itself.

Prior to 1990, population communication efforts in Pakistan had been limited to indirect paeans to the small family norm. Such indirect approaches (no explicit reference to contraception was made) were considered necessary to avoid provoking conservative religious opposition. Yet, maternal and infant mortality in Pakistan are among the highest in Asia. According to a national survey in 1991 (PDHS, 1992), the maternal mortality rate is 500 maternal deaths per 100,000 live births, while infant mortality is 100 per 1000 live births. The same survey showed that 58 percent of married women not using some form of contraceptive want to do so. Research indicated that reasons for this gap between desire and action stem from gender inequality: Half the women in a project baseline survey said the husband was the sole decision maker in household matters and fewer than half said they had ever discussed contraception with their husband. Many women reported fear of their husband's disapproval but said they lacked the skills to negotiate successfully for approval.

In response to these expressed needs, Pakistan Television (PTV) produced and aired three television sociodramas on reproductive health between May 1990 and October 1993. *Aahat* (An Approaching Sound) aired in October–November 1991. The six-episode drama aimed at fostering husband–wife communication regarding reproductive and family health issues, interest in birth spacing and family planning, clinic attendance, and adoption of some form of family planning. *Aahat* was followed by a single episode television film, *Aik Hi Rastha* (The Only Way) in July 1993, which focused on a father's growing appreciation of his daughter's right to self-determination on the eve of her marriage. The thirteen-part *Nijaat* (Deliverance), which aired from July–October 1993, ended the series.

Public response to all three dramas was positive and press coverage extensive: More than 50 articles about *Aahat* alone appeared in the national and regional press. Thus, at the macro level, the drama entered into and influenced public discourse on family planning. At the micro level, that of individuals and the family, research indicated substantial impact, as well: Twelve percent of *Aahat* viewers surveyed (n=2118) said the program had prompted them to do something to space their children, and 9 percent said they had visited a family planning clinic after viewing the drama (Lozare et al., 1993).

Consistent with the themes of the drama, spousal communication was closely linked with fertility decisions. Of the 9 percent of viewers who said they went to a clinic after watching the series, almost all of them (98 percent) had discussed family planning with his or her spouse.

At the political institutional level, the National Family Planning Program, especially its communication component, historically had been constrained by lack of political support. Yet, following the airing of *Aahat,* public and political support for televised population information led PTV to continue its participation in public discourse around population and family planning issues by developing and airing *Aik Hi Rastha* and *Nijaat.*

Nijaat was launched by PTV on July 19, 1993, amid highly favorable press reports and aired every Monday at 8:30 p.m. (prime time) through October 11. The story once more focused on husband–wife communication, but contained more representation of rural males. Hazoor Baksh, a financially stressed small businessman, his wife Sajida, their two sons, Kashi (age seven) and Tari (age five), and a baby daughter are the main characters. Zareena is a nurse at the understaffed hospital in their small town; she is Sajida's friend, having treated her through poor health and a series of miscarriages. Over time, Zareena convinces Sajida that she must talk to her husband about waiting to have another child. Hazoor, despite his softening attitude, fails to make a decision. Sajida discovers that she is again expecting, a condition that Zareena tells her is life threatening. When the time comes, the delivery is very difficult, the baby is lost, and Hazoor finally decides they should consider contraception. In the concluding episodes, Sajida and Hazoor struggle with the cultural and personal implications of that decision and try to bring their family together again.

A national television ratings service in Pakistan reported 60 to 75 percent viewership of *Nijaat* in the major cities of Karachi, Lahore, and Islamabad/Rawalpindi, making it the most popular program in its time slot by a wide margin. The impact of *Nijaat* was evaluated using qualitative methods (in-depth interviews with men, women, and female service providers) designed to explore how discourse functioned around the drama. This qualitative impact evaluation reveals discursive impact of the drama on husband–wife relationships, as in the following transcript from an interview with a thirty-year-old woman:

Q. Did you talk about the drama [while you watched]?

A. My husband watched [parts of the drama]. He doesn't normally talk much. Only sometimes while watching the play he would say, "What is A. C. doing to his wife?" or "What is Hazoor Baksh doing?" He would pass these short comments.

Q. Didn't you talk about the main subjects in the play?

A. No. We mostly talked about our own problems. Well, once he said that there was a cold war going on between A. C. and his wife: "[But] two people, [when] they live under one roof, develop some kind of relationship after all." And I said, "We had the same problem, didn't we?" And he said, "That was before, not now. It's something of the past; now we understand each other."

Clearly, the drama resonated with the life experience of this couple and provided a discursive opportunity for them to revisit and discuss their own concerns (IDRC, 1994). In terms of shifts in norms and values, witnessing the experience of a couple on television and hearing what they say to each other in the privacy of their bedroom altered the boundaries of what is thinkable, the limits of what is speakable.

Discourse in Health Systems:
The Radio Communication Project in Nepal

The second example comes from a radio drama project in Nepal. The first of many discursive elements in this project was that the Nepal Ministry of Health (MOH) came to grips with the fact that its own service delivery system was responsible for the poor performance of their family health program: poor interpersonal communication skills among health workers who treated clients insensitively, poor technical knowledge and skills among health workers who often misinformed clients or purposely misled them in order to meet predetermined targets, justifiably poor perception of services by clients, and lack of information on the part of clients about how to be an active seeker of services (Storey et al., in press).

The Radio Communication Project aimed to improve the technical capability and client orientation of health services and health workers. It did so through the coordinated use of a radio drama serial intended for the general public and a distance education serial (also dramatized) intended for remote health workers. Both dramas were based on extensive local research, qualitative and quantitative. Both were locally scripted, produced by Nepalese dramatists, and extensively pretested and monitored at the community level.

One of the most innovative monitoring techniques involved visits to every village in the project area during the first and second years of broadcasting by a field researcher, a program officer, and a recording technician. A village meeting was convened, sections of the dramas played, and an open discussion conducted. Village discussion was recorded and fed back to project planners and writers who incorporated it into their scripts. Excerpts of the discussions were also aired in special segments of the broadcast.

Effective discourse from the perspective of health workers means taking the client's perspective, that is, learning to engage on their own level the men and women seeking services. From the provider's perspective, this was expressed through the acronym GATHER:

G Greet clients and show respect.
A Ask clients about themselves and their concerns.
T Tell clients what they want and need to know.
H Help clients make their own decisions.
E Explain how to act on the decisions made.
R Refer or schedule a follow-up visit.

In Nepal, the acronym GATHER was translated into a Nepalese equivalent, *ABHIBADAN,* a respectful form of greeting.

From the client's perspective, optimal discourse means being an active participant in seeking adequate health care, expecting to be treated well, and actively engaging the health worker in his/her capacity to help. The client's perspective was expressed through the acronym VALUE:

V Value your own needs and concerns.
A Ask the provider what you want to know.
L Lead the conversation.
U Understand the benefits of services/treatments.
E Establish a personal action plan.

In Nepal, the acronym VALUE was translated into a Nepalese equivalent, *NAMASKAAR,* another form of mutually respectful greeting.

The effect of this effort to enhance the quality of discourse within the clinic system was clear from the evaluation: Interactions had more characteristics of two-way dialogue and less the character of one-way service delivery if either client or provider had listened to the radio dramas, but especially if both had listened. The mean number of observed positive interpersonal communication and counseling features in client–provider interactions increased over time and was significantly higher if either the client or the provider reported listening to the RCP programs. Client satisfaction with the services they received was also higher in proportion to the more interactive elements that were present (Storey et al., in press).

While it may seem that we are talking simply about interpersonal communication rather than discourse, I would argue that a much broader discursive process was at work: The project required full collaboration of the Nepal Ministry of Health and national training institutions to design and implement a coordinated public radio and distance education program; the Ministry's service delivery system and health workers countrywide had to be mobilized to implement distance education, in a country where highly didactic classroom-based training regimens had been the norm for many years; health workers listened to the distance education serial in groups at clinics, fostering opportunities for discourse among peers; in the main project areas, nearly as many members of the public listened to the distance education serial as listened to the other radio drama serial, suggesting the emergence of discourse about links between service delivery and service utilization; and a rethinking of the Ministry's training and certification system is beginning to take place, indicating internal self-reflective discourse about institutional practices. Both dramas are now in their third year of broadcasting with a fourth year of programming in development.

Discourse between Aesthetics and Influence: The Artist as Educator in Indonesia

Alang-Alang (Wild Grass), a three-part television drama promoting the education of female children, was a project of the Indonesian Family Planning Coordinating Board (BKKBN). The drama was directed by Teguh Karya, one of Indonesia's and Asia's most experienced and respected film directors. Broadcast in December 1994, the drama tells the story of Ipah, the young motherless daughter of a trash scavenger living on the margins of the great garbage dumps of Jakarta. Ipah's father, Pak Rengga, fails to understand Ipah's desire for education and a better life, and withholds the money she needs for her school fees, causing Ipah to seek odd jobs and to work long hours to pay for her own education. Through the help of neighbors and her own diligence, Ipah eventually sways her father's opinion, completes her schooling, and becomes a teacher herself.

The drama was seen by 25–30 percent of the Indonesian television audience in major cities in Java and was the subject of several dozen newspaper and magazine articles in the Jakarta area alone. The discourse that occurred among Ipah, her father, their neighbors, and her school, and the media coverage of the broadcast are only a few facets of the discursive quality of the entire project. Numerous other valuable and constructive discursive outcomes occurred as a result of this popular culture event.

Teguh Karya himself illustrated the intersection of or discourse among aesthetic priorities, commercial forces, social activism, government policy, health promotion, and foreign aid. As a renowned artist and activist (he has run a grassroots theater company, *Teater Populer,* for many years) and member of an ethnic minority group, Teguh struggled constantly with the tensions between self-expressive art and delivery of a message, reaching accommodation between his priorities as a filmmaker and social critic and the government's wish for him to use his art in support of its family welfare (*keluarga sejahtera*) program. He embraced the creative tension between artistic expression and social scientific health communication by participating in focus group research used to inform the story development process. He accommodated JHU/PCS requests for explicit population themes by adding a female character who dies as a result of repeated high-risk childbirth. Also, by following up on an earlier collaboration with BKKBN and JHU/PCS (*The Equatorial Trilogy*), Teguh continues to set an example as a socially active artist.

The television industry also played a role in the discourse surrounding *Alang-Alang.* Originally planned for broadcast on a state-owned television channel, a major commercial television station (SCTV) bought the series instead and aired it, knowing of its prosocial content and purpose, in part because they recognized the popularity of social dramas (drama with a message) and the artistic quality of the director's work. This was the first time that SCTV had aired such a program.

BKKBN was enthusiastic about female education as a subcomponent of its *keluarga sejahtera* program and saw Teguh Karya's interest in marginal group issues as an opportunity for collaboration. Through their involvement with and support for social dramas like *The Equatorial Trilogy* and *Alang-Alang,* BKKBN continues to build relations with the artistic community and to support popular culture as a site where health discourse can occur.

Public reaction to the drama was also discursive: Using focus groups, a qualitative evaluation of audience response to the drama revealed multiple interpretations of what the drama's main messages were (e.g., girl's education, problems of street children, community solidarity, parent–child communication, antismoking). This finding, in turn, generated discussion within JHU/PCS and between JHU/PCS and BKKBN about the specificity and relationships among BKKBN's *keluarga sejahtera* program goals and the clarity with which those goals were or could be represented in television drama. In addition, mother–daughter interaction was stimulated by the drama. References to characters in the narrative occurred in mother–daughter interactions following the broadcasts. For example, several mothers and daughters reported discussing how their own family relationships were similar to and different from that of Ipah and her father.

Discourse changed the institutions as well as the audiences that participated in it. JHU/PCS, while hoping to make the family planning and population themes as explicit as possible, supported the broad theme of girl–child education as consistent with its aims to expand reproductive health options for women in Indonesian society. This reflected a gradual shift within JHU/PCS, and within the larger structure of U.S. and international population programs following the Cairo and Beijing conferences in 1994–1995, away from a narrow focus on family planning and toward a broader conceptualization of population issues in terms of women's rights.

A further institutional change was revealed in the choice of evaluation methodology. *Alang-Alang* impact evaluation had a qualitative component aimed at discovering what viewers had to say about their understanding of and response to the story. This was in contrast to a historical preference (within the donor community in general) for quantitative assessment of program impact. Due to the usefulness and richness of findings from qualitative evaluations of *Alang-Alang* (and the aforementioned *Nijaat* in Pakistan), JHU/PCS recently has undertaken several additional qualitative evaluations of entertainment–education projects.

Discourse at the Institutional/Policy Level: USAID and its Institutional Partners in Asia

USAID is a discursively more open institution than is commonly recognized by those who consider merely its organizational image or examine programs disaggregated from its historical context. In terms of gender representation, published staff directories show that USAID/Washington's Population, Health, and Nutrition sector is 73 percent staffed by women, including 52 percent of the sectoral and divisional directors/chiefs. In addition, all three of the USAID Population, Health, and Nutrition country offices where aforementioned projects occurred (Pakistan, Nepal, and Indonesia) have been headed by women.

Reproductive health itself is a discursively rich area of development, intertwined with and strongly influenced by historical shifts in perspective since the first international population conference in Bucharest in 1974 (Jacobstein, 1998). In the late 1950s and early 1960s, USAID population programs focused mainly on family planning and the promotion of contraceptive use as a way to reduce population pressure and avoid food shortages. Medical models centered on hospital- and clinic-based delivery of services. By the time of the Mexico City conference in 1984, and as population programs matured, program perspectives looked more to the community as the context of health and development. A wider range of interrelated issues was addressed (e.g., child survival, maternal health, environmental quality, sexually transmitted disease, income generation, and gender relationships) in the recognition that fertility decisions were conditioned by a complex array of structural and cultural factors.

The International Conference on Population and Development in Cairo in 1994 and the Fourth United Nations World Conference on Women in Beijing in 1995 fostered this expanded view of reproductive health. Both conferences tried, not without controversy, to position population programs away from narrow technological perspectives on fertility control towards broader integrated perspectives on population growth, poverty, and patterns of consumption and production as they relate to comprehensive reproductive health, reproductive rights, and the status of women and children (Garcia-Moreno & Turmen, 1995).

The recognition that entrenched power structures and political bureaucracies do not easily change reinforces strategies that were more "consumer" oriented. The use of marketing language to describe these strategies, while appearing to reflect a commercial view of behavior change, obscures another rationale for the approach: If existing health delivery systems and government bureaucracies are hard to change in and of themselves, perhaps public awareness and demand for better treatment, coupled with pressure from the private sector, can drive structural changes in health care systems.

Following the Cairo conference, emphasis grew on the sustainability of population programs (meaning the growth of programs with popular support), the importance of community-based NGOs, and the breakdown of male biases against women's health and full participation in social change (Jacobstein, 1998). A recent example of this trend is support by USAID for the NGO Networks for Health Project, a loose international confederation of participatory development groups with an interest in community health issues, especially gender and women's access to health care.

More specifically, within the Asian health communication projects described in this chapter, a number of important discursive shifts can be observed on the part of USAID and other development institutions. In Indonesia, USAID increased its institutional support for the theme of women's education, where the historical emphasis had been on the more narrowly defined adoption of family planning. Seeking to broaden social and cultural perspectives on the rights of women represents a substantial discursive shift.

Again, in Indonesia, acceptance of commercial broadcasting by Government of Indonesia development broadcasters (i.e., the airing of *Alang-Alang* on commercial television, in spite of the fact that a government ministry had paid for the production and should have received credit for it) reflected a loosening of control over the development process. On the other side of the coin, a commercial broadcaster (SCTV) bought the rights to the prosocial television drama, even though the broadcaster had never done social broadcasting before and knew the advertising revenues would be lower for that programming. The decision was based in part on a desire to participate in a growing public reform movement.

The openness of government to the artistic community in the form of Teguh Karya, a well-known social critic, was unanticipated. The government of Indonesia accepted an unflattering picture of Indonesia (televised representations of poverty that had been routinely banned or "sanitized" in years past) in the interest of advancing its family welfare agenda. This may have been an early sign of increasing openness that has since lead to the downfall of the Suharto regime and the growth of a national reform movement.

With respect to research methodology, a source of concern to critics of empirical social science, there has been a growing acceptance of more interpretive qualitative approaches to research and evaluation as evinced by JHU/PCS's use of such techniques, including community interaction sessions to understand popular reaction and critical response to television and radio social dramas.

DEVELOPMENT FROM A DISCURSIVE PERSPECTIVE

To conclude, I have tried to develop a discursive perspective on development that I believe could bring some unity and focus back to a struggling, but still important field. Instead of devolving into endless debates over bipolar extremes (modernization/dependency, hegemony/resistance, top-down/bottom-up, local/global, power and powerlessness, determinism/free will), or retreating to subspecialties (health or media economics), a discursive perspective permits us to look at links within and across levels of social systems. Much of the discourse may involve struggles over power, representation, and access to resources, but it is no less discursive just because some actors have greater influence to begin with. The value of the discursive perspective is that it forces us to deal with the fluid nature of meaning and what falls in-between conceptual polarities rather than on reified concepts and the polar extremes themselves.

A Bakhtinian perspective encourages us to look critically at the language we use to describe what we do but not to jump to conclusions about what terms mean. Language has an important measure of autonomy, so the subtle distinctions between use of terms by critics and proponents of donor-supported development projects merit close inspection. Development is an unfinalizable process of negotiating social reality, i.e., *discourse.* Recognizing it as such is both a humbling and an enabling move. Powerful institutions, both domestic and international, must face the fact that their "truths" are negotiable and that many other actors are engaged in negotiation. Individuals, communities, and other "participants" in the development process must similarly face the fact that meanings can be contended and negotiated, but that there are many voices in the discourse, some of which are indeed loud and powerful.

Theories of discourse and cultural studies see the possibilities of popular participation in the negotiation of reality, even in the face of powerful transnational forces of production. Popular culture is the arena where this process plays out. Development goals and projects, for all their carefully reasoned, scientifically based underpinnings, will still be reworked, reinterpreted, adapted, or ignored in the arena of popular culture. Outcomes are not predetermined; development is always a work in progress.

REFERENCES

Bakhtin, M. (1981). *The dialogic imagination.* Austin, TX: University of Texas Press.

Escobar, A. (1995). *Encountering development: The making and unmaking of the third world.* Princeton, NJ: Princeton University Press.

Garcia-Moreno, C. & Turmen, T. (1995). International perspectives on women's reproductive health. *Science,* 269, 790–792.

Fiske, J. (1987). British Cultural Studies and Television. In B. Allen (Ed.), *Channels of discourse: Television and contemporary criticism* (pp. 254–289). Chapel Hill, NC: University of North Carolina Press.

Fiske, J. (1994). Audiencing: Cultural practice and cultural studies. In N. Denzin and E. Lincoln (Eds.), *Handbook of Qualitative Research* (pp. 189–198). Newbury Park, CA: Sage.

Hall, S., Hobson, D., Lowe, A., & Willis, P. (1980). *Culture, media, language.* London, UK: Hutchinson.

International Development Research Center (IDRC). (1994). A qualitative evaluation of the impact of *Nijaat* in the rural vicinity of Lahore, Pakistan. Karachi, Pakistan: Aftab Associates.

Jacobstein, R. (1998). Current and future priorities in funding development communication. Paper presented at the annual conference of the Association for Education in Journalism and Mass Communication, Baltimore, MD.

Lozare, B., Hess, R., Yun, S., Gill-Bailey, A., Valmadrid, C., Livesay, A., Khan, S., & Siddiqui, N. (1993). Husband–wife communication and family planning: Impact of a national television drama. Paper presented to the American Public Health Association annual conference, San Francisco, CA.

Mattelart, A. & Mattelart, M. (1998). *Theories of communication: A short introduction.* London, UK: Sage.

McAnany, E. & Storey, D. (1989). Communication and development: A reappraisal for the nineties. Paper presented at the 39th Annual Conference of the International Communication Association, San Francisco, CA.

Morley, D. (1980). *The nationwide audience.* London, UK: BFI.

Morley, D. (1993). *Television, audiences and cultural studies.* London, UK: Routledge.

Morson, G. & Emerson, C. (1990). *Mikhail Bakhtin: Creation of a prosaics.* Stanford, CA: Stanford University Press.

Newcomb, H. (1980). On the dialogic aspects of mass communication. *Critical Studies in Mass Communication,* 1(1), 34–50.

Pakistan Demographic & Health Survey (PDHS). (1992). *Pakistan demographic and health survey, 1990/1991.* Islamabad, Pakistan/Columbia, MD: National Institute of Population Studies/Macro International.

Storey, D. (1993). Mythology, narrative and discourse in Javanese *wayang:* Toward cross–level theories for the new development paradigm. *Asian Journal of Communication,* 3(2), 30–53.

Storey, D., Karki, Y., Heckert, K., Karmacharya, D., & Boulay, M. (In press). Integration and synergy: Impact of the Radio Communication Project in Nepal, 1994–1997. *Journal of Health Communication.*

van Dijk, T. (1997). The study of discourse. In T. van Dijk, (Ed.), *Discourse as structure and process* (pp. 1–34). London, UK: Sage.

Wilkins, K. (1999). Development discourse on gender and communication in strategies for social change. *Journal of Communication,* 49(1), 46–68.

9

Mexican Popular Culture and Development

An Intertextual History of Agustin Lara's *Aventurera*

Mark Pedelty

Modernity took hold of the Mexican popular imagination in the decades following the Revolution of 1910–1917. Throughout the 1920s and 1930s, various political camps—socialist, anarchist, and capitalist—did battle, finding agreement on little else but their shared modernity and a commitment to progress. Development, in its various guises, became the new religion. The Institutional Revolutionary Party (PRI), also a product of the postrevolutionary era, championed this utopian vision. The PRI proffered a clear, socialist vision of the future (promoted in didactic fashion by state-subsidized artists and intellectuals) while developing a formidable state–capitalist system.

As the century draws to a close, both the PRI and its development vision for the future show serious signs of stress. Successive waves of development paradigms and policies, including nationalization under Cardenas, oil speculation by the Lopez Portillo administration, and neoliberal privatization under Salinas, have all failed, shaking the faith of the Mexican people in the modern promise of development. By 1996, in a poll conducted by centrist *La Reforma* newspaper, 67 percent of Mexicans queried felt that Mexico had experienced "little or no success" with the North American Free Trade Agreement (NAFTA), the PRI's latest development solution (*La Reforma* poll cited by Public Citizen, 1999). Between 1993 and 1997, productivity increased under

NAFTA, yet wages declined by 29 percent (INEGI, 1998). According to sociologist James Petras (1997, p. 46), 60 percent of the Mexican labor force lived below the poverty line in 1997, a marked increase since NAFTA was instituted.

This century-long narrative of economic promise, failed development, and shattered faith has been reflected in Mexico's popular culture and mass media. Agustin Lara's *Aventurera* illustrates this textual transformation. Born as a *bolero* (a romantic musical style) in the days of postrevolutionary excess, *Aventurera* evolved into film soon thereafter and was recently transformed into musical theater. A history of this text, within its social contexts, looks at the ways *Aventurera* has reflected the political–economic fate and outlook of the Mexican nation during the twentieth century.

The *bolero* formed part of a postrevolutionary ritual complex, which effectively mediated the relationship between development ideology, as proffered by the state, and people's actual experiences. Postrevolutionary ritual was intertextual, connecting nascent mass media (cinema, radio, and phonograph), performance contexts (dance halls, bars, and cabarets), and people's lives within a cultural nexus that helped this new, modernizing Mexico make sense. Between development ideals and modern realities, there was *bolero.*

Eventually, however, the contradictions between the promise and experience of development became too great for any ritual, popular or otherwise, to mediate. The *bolero* lost its central ritual function. Yet, in doing so, the *bolero* gained a new set of cultural meanings. Today, as the tropes of modernity and development lose favor, *bolero* has been salvaged as a form of self-reflective nostalgia, and reinvented, as postmodern, postdevelopment politics.[1]

REVOLUTIONARY ORIGINS

The Mexican revolution of 1910–1917 is a good starting point for examining the origins of both the *bolero* and Mexican modernity. While the revolution was fought under the banner of agrarian and electoral reform, its results were largely antithetical to those goals. Instead of agrarian renewal, the rural devastation and dislocation of the revolution caused a radical increase in the pace and scale of urbanization. After the revolution, cities grew "like mushrooms after a rain" (Bonfil Batalla, 1996, p. 122). Mexico City grew "from 350,000 Christians at the turn of the century," until, "by the mid–20's, it had 1,750,000 unbelievers who had left their native soil, and in it they left behind their moral traditions for good" (Aura, 1990, p. 27). These people left their rural homelands to help construct what the great *bolerista,* Agustin Lara, lovingly referred to as "the capital of sin" (Kay, 1964, p. 144). Rather than rural collectivism, the revolution resulted in urban anomie and a new, modern Mexican culture.

The urban newcomers left behind most of their rural traditions, including the anonymous *corridos,* which told of a people's pride of place, great men, and moral tragedy. The *corridos* and municipal band music that formed the core of nineteenth-century community ritual life were replaced with new, nostalgia-soaked popular songs produced in the metropole. Lament (e.g., *Lamento Jarocho*), sadness (e.g.,

Triste Recuerdo), and soft betrayal (e.g., *Dos Palomas al Volar*) would be the new keywords for both musical and cultural life in the new city. Instead of the *corridos*' coarse stories of lives sacrificed and evil conquered, the velvet *bolero* offered bittersweet memories of love lost and evil enjoined, of moral ambivalence and moral relativism. In short, the "*bolero* functions as a genuine hymn to desperation" (Monsivais, 1993a, p. 114).

Boleros, like Lara's *Noche de Ronda,* gave popular voice to the strong sense of loss and longing felt by the urban neophytes, drawing idealized images of pre-Revolutionary Mexican life. Other *boleros,* including Lara's *Aventurera,* gave witness to the seductive forms of sin and corruption surrounding the former peasants in their new cosmopolitan contexts:

> Sell your love, dearly, Adventuress.
> Give the price of pain for your sin.
> And for those who desire the honey of your lips,
> That they would pay, with diamonds, for your sin. (Lara, 1999)

As evident in these initial lyrics of *Aventurera,* the most popular protagonists in both the song and film narratives of the *bolero* era were young, chaste woman who, by urban circumstances, were forced to leave their traditional rural values behind in order to survive.

The overwhelming popularity of the *bolero* demonstrates the fact that neither rural traditions nor the manufactured nationalism of government-sponsored public arts (e.g., *indigenista* muralism, music, theater, and literature), could truly represent, or offset, the revolutionary refugees' longing for rural paradise lost, their equally desperate faith in modernity, and their strong ambivalence regarding the pleasures and freedoms made possible in the city. Biographical texts from the era burst forth with that sense of heightened ambivalence. Moral condemnations of the cultural environment appear alongside joyful celebrations of urbanity's libertine pleasures, a life where there was

> now no one who watches you, who snoops on you, who judges what hour you arrive, what hour you leave, with whom you come or go, how long you wear your skirt, how high or low plunges your neckline, how long your hair is. (Aura, 1990, p. 27)

Bolero perfectly mirrored the new urbanites' ambivalent relationship with their adopted home.

Many of the new residents in the capital looked to the *bolero* and its close affine, *Danzón,* for an understanding of how they were to comport themselves in this new world. A vibrant ritual complex was developed around both musical styles which, in turn, served as a guide to urbane behavior.

The youth who had become socialized during the revolutionary violence were in particular need of this new cultural map. A range of public establishments came into being, most notably the dance salón, where young men and women could go to learn about and reinvent this urban sensibility. Salón signs asked the young men not to toss burning cigarettes on the floor, so as not to burn the ladies' feet. Rigid rules regarding the nature of the dance and dress were also enforced, signaling a more urbanized and "civilized" way of life for the former warriors. These "recent arrivals from the Revolution," explains Raymundo Ramos, "were looking for their place and equilibrium in the emergent middle class, their bravado calmed sexually in the amalgamation of *Salón México*" (Mendizabal & Mejia, 1993, p. 106).

Salón México also mirrored and instructed the postrevolutionary era's transformed class structure. Everyone "from workers to famous women" (Trejo, 1992, p. 67) came to dance at *Salón México,* filling the clothes check with maid's bread baskets, *rebozos,* and uniforms alongside the fur coats of glamorous film stars like María Felix. The mixing did not stop with the new working, middle, and upper classes of Mexico; foreign élites like President Ahmed Sukarno of Indonesia and U.S. musician Aaron Copland were also to be found enjoying the modern aesthetics and decadence of *Salón México.*

Yet, while *Salón México* provided a place where the feudal caste system might soften, the result was hardly a complete carnivalesque surrender to the subaltern. There were four rooms in the Salón, including three dance floors whose class affiliations were made evident in the culinary terminology by which they were known: "butter," for the oligarchs and stars, "lard," for the emerging middle class, and "fat," for the dance floor of the working class. Fittingly, the fourth and final room was the "hall of mirrors." Places like *Salón México* served as laboratories of social experimentation from which the *bolero*'s melodramatic tales of social climbing and moral decline would be derived, a trope that would follow through into the distorted cinematic mirror of the *Cabaretera* [cabaret] films of the 1930s and 1940s. The *bolero,* as a popular phenomenon, was partly an attempt by the lower and middle classes to approximate the sophisticated style of postrevolutionary élites who, despite their populist nods to *indigenismo,* retained inordinate control of the country's wealth and power.

In their hypercorrective attempt to appropriate the upper-class way of life, however, the popular classes invented something largely distinct from the object of their jealous affections. This popular modernity was neither a copy of élite cultures, nor a simple extension of Guillermo Bonfil Batalla's romanticized *México Profundo* (1996). What came out of this mix was a new Mexican popular culture. As such, the postrevolutionary *bolero* not only formed the core of a new culture, but also continued the centuries-old tradition of cultural *mestizaje* (Martin-Barbero, 1993, p. 149). *Bolero* narratives and style are highly melodramatic, extending a Mexican tradition that threads through precortesian ritual (e.g., Coyolxauhqui's myth and ritual complex), colonial Christian drama (e.g., Corpus Christi), and postindependence civic heroics (e.g., *corridos*).

If the main continuity was melodrama, the major break was in ritual focus. Rather than Huitzilopotchli or Christ, wine, blood, and profit were now offered up to the gods of industry. Whereas earlier rites mediated between mythic cosmologies and daily social practice, the *bolero*'s ritual complex mediated the relationship between modern state–capitalist development ideology and people's actual experiences. These were the disciplines of decadence. *Danzón,* for example, provided a cultural map befitting industrial discipline, and emphasizing urban sophistication and control, including the mandate to dance within a square without letting one's knees pass through the plane of one's partner's. Featuring suits, "smokings," and evening dresses, the new styles provided a costume for modernization that imitated the dress of Mexico's moneyed élite and their foreign capital associates. In music, people began imitating the sound and style of model sophisticates like Lara. Just as music was an integral tool in the missionaries' campaign to proselytize indigenous "neophytes" four hundred years before, acquisition of these new styles became an essential means for gaining cultural citizenship in postrevolutionary Mexico.

MEDIATING MODERNITY

The incipient entertainment media were central to this process of cultural modernization. While the *bolero* first flourished in live venues, the medium of radio came of age at the right moment to transport the style to all of Mexico and beyond. The first nationwide transmitter, XEW, "The Voice of Latin America from Mexico," began operation in 1930. Able to reach all of Mexico, the Caribbean, parts of the southern United States, and occasionally even further afield, XEW broadcast the seeds of modernity throughout Mexico and Latin America. Classical musician Manuel Ponce, along with most other *indigenista* artists and intellectuals, lamented the new medium's power:

> I have been in an hacienda that is very far from the railroads, yet a radio is there, and the boys sing these "sun–drunk palms" [*boleros*]; and just like that they have killed the vernacular music. (Pineda, 1990, p. 17)

A new breed of musician, neither classical nor traditional, came into being "just like that" as well. Bakers (Emilio Tuero), painters (Luis G. Roldán), mechanics (Fernando Fernández), and brothel entertainers (Agustin Lara) were suddenly elevated to the status of cultural icons, ritual interlocutors between the laboring classes and Mexico's adopted modernity.

The film industry was undergoing significant transformation at the turn of the decade as well. At about the same time as XEW's inauguration in 1930, Mexico's silent cinema gave way to sound with the release of the film *Santa.* Naturally, Lara wrote the soundtrack and theme song. The film, based on a novel by Federico Gamboa, is a cinematic inscription of the typical *bolero* narrative: a corrupted provincial girl–turned–prostitute who finds redemption in death. This melodramatic theme would dominate the Mexican film industry for decades as the *Cabaretera* films drew millions of Mexicans to the theaters. Through cinema, Mexico would continue learning about, and constructing, modern ways of life. The "myth-fabricating machine was put into movement" (Ramos, 1993, p. 93), teaching a distinctly cosmopolitan philosophy.

Film became "the most powerful influence" in this new urban curriculum (Monsivais, 1993b, p. 144), and "the first language of the popular urban culture" (Martin-Barbero, 1993, p. 166). *Bolero* era films featured the cabaret, a "moral hell and heaven of the senses" symbolic of Mexico City itself (Monsivais, 1993b, p. 144). *Cabaretera* films made loving display of the amoral pleasures possible in urban society, as well as the horrors which often accompany them. In both the cabaret and the city, "all that is forbidden is normal" (Monsivais, 1993b, p. 144). Moral absolutes were replaced by moral relativism, as cosmopolitan attitudes replaced the communitarian strictures of rural and Porfirian Mexico. Despite concerted campaigns by conservative critics, the market and media would make only minor moves toward moral containment (Rubenstein, 1998).

Whether film was the instructor or "great corrupter of the masses" during the postrevolutionary era, it was textually dependent on *bolero* music for its popularity (Dueñas, 1993, p. 11). Just as most of the earlier tent shows and reviews were based on *bolero* song titles, so too, most of *Cabaretera* films were based on *bolero* themes. Lara's film inspirations included *Aventurera, Palabras de Mujer, Pecadora,* and many others. These films were not only titled but also narratively patterned upon their namesake songs. Audiences would sing along when the title songs were played, turning cinema into a participatory ritual rather than a passive form of entertainment. By the time the song, *Aventurera,* was sung in the film, *Aventurera,* the audience was quite ready to join in the catharsis:

> And now that the infamy of your ruinous destiny
> Has wilted your admirable Spring,
> Make your path less difficult,
> Sell your love dearly, Adventuress. (Lara, 1999)

The 1942 film, *Aventurera,* would faithfully follow the song's narrative, resulting in a harsh story of a young woman's fall from grace at the hands of various urban underworld characters. This "most virulent of Sevilla's *Cabaretera* films" (Lopez, 1993, p. 158) features a much less ensconced misogyny and violence than most *Cabaretera* films. Yet, as is true of all the *Cabaretera* films, there is a thin moral narrative contesting the seductive aural and visual aesthetics, resulting in a highly ambivalent message regarding urban decadence.

CINEMATIC DECADENCE AND REDEMPTION

An analytical plot outline of the film, *Aventurera,* provides context for subsequent texts (a play, a playwright, several lives, and a city). The film begins with an idyllic view of family life. Elena, an innocent young dance student, is showered with affection from her father, while overly protected by her watchful mother. Yet—and this is the sin upon which the whole plot turns—the daughter catches her mother kissing a friend of the family. This cuckolding betrayal is a clear example of the time honored "terrible mother archetype" in Mexican popular fiction (Herrera-Sobek, 1990). This unnatural act by

Elena's mother sets off a tragic chain of events: the bad mother leaves, the good father kills himself, and innocent Elena is left with no means of making a living.

Fortunately, it would seem, Elena's underworld friend, Lucio, finds her secretarial employment at a club owned by the infamous Rosaura, a fading yet charismatic beauty. Smashing illusions of hope, Rosaura's henchman, Rango, serves Elena a drugged tea, rapes her and forces her at knifepoint to become both prostitute and cabaret dancer. She quickly "succeeds" at both, and soon rivals Rosaura in power, having derived cultural and financial capital from using her seductive stage presence, dancing skills, and siren-like voice. Elena finally goes too far, however, by directly challenging not only Rosaura, but customers and coworkers as well. Elena loses her position after clubbing a cabaret guest (the man whom she had earlier found kissing her mother) with a wine bottle.

Elena flees the scene with Lucio, becoming his lover and sidekick. While Lucio robs a bank, Elena waits in the getaway car. Rosaura discovers the plan, however, and tips off Comandante Treviño, who is both the police chief and a loyal client. Lucio is captured in the act, but Elena escapes unnoticed.

Elena then returns to dancing. While watching her perform, a wealthy, handsome, and kind young lawyer from "one of the best families in Guadalajara" falls in love with her and proposes marriage. While considering the proposal, Elena discovers that her new fiancée's mother is none other than Rosaura. She had been living a double life, financing her upstanding family in Guadalajara with ill-gotten gains from the Ciudad Juarez brothel. Rosaura had thus symbolically violated the soul of central Mexico, the Bajio, by posing as *gente de razón* when she was, in reality, nothing more than an invader from the borderland. Rosaura is thus exposed as the latest female facilitator of Mexico's rape, a *Malinche* who must be exposed and punished.

Yet, Elena has, by this point in the film, essentially become Rosaura in order to overcome her. The audience has been allowed voyeuristic delight in watching that transformation and thus can be certain Elena will indeed marry the son, seeking security, money, and most of all, revenge. Elena gets her revenge by seducing another of Rosaura's sons and exposing the bad mother to her good husband. Seemingly satiated, Elena returns to her dancing career at a rival cabaret.

In *Aventurera*'s complex collapse of victim and victimizer, the audience is drawn further into the decadence than they might prefer, both as voyeurs and saviors. As opposed to typical melodrama, the audience is not ceded a comfortable moral distance. There is no absolute incarnation of "innocence and virtue," no princess archetype whose "weakness calls out for protection and inspires the protective feelings of the public" (Martin-Barbero, 1993, p. 117). Elena goes too far into depravity, and with too great a volition, to gain such absolute empathy. Conversely, the antagonists are made much too comprehensible to provide the catharsis of unqualified loathing. Even evil Rosaura elicits some sympathy, having used her craven gains to raise, protect, and educate two good sons.

Yet Lopez and other film critics seem to have missed an important point in their critiques of this "virulent" narrative. Despite the violence, or perhaps because of it, redemption can be found in these urban (a)morality tales, a redemption made that much more satisfying by the depths of decadence through which the audience is dragged. The city is a pleasurable hell, but salvation is still possible in the end.

Elena's salvation springs from her own act of mercy. After Lucio springs her from Rosaura's grip, Elena stops him from killing the evil, knife-wielding Rango. This passing act of mercy on a mute, simple, and violent man results in Rango's passionate devotion to Elena from there on out. He later repays her by saving her life, facilitating her return to moral society.

The second step toward Elena's salvation is taken by Rosaura's son. Having discovered the truth about both his mother, Rosaura, and Elena, his wife, he forgives Elena and asks for her to return. Lucio overhears them, beats the son/husband, and takes Elena away at gunpoint, saying that he is going to force her to go the United States (that very center of sin). Elena begs him to let her go, confessing true love for her husband. Elena's *Malinchista* mask is thus removed to reveal the violated *Virgen* inside.

Lucio agrees to let her go, but pulls out his gun as she walks away. Before the tragedy can conclude, however, Rango intercedes, throwing a knife into Lucio's back. Elena's beaten husband runs toward her and they embrace, a surprisingly happy ending to the sordid tale. Elena, unlike the *femme fatales* played by Maria Felix's in *Cabaretera* films, like *La Devoradora* or *La Mujer Sin Alma,* not only survives the tragedy, but weathers Hell in good stead. The film is "virulent" perhaps, but also full of redemption, a feature found in many *caberatera* narratives, even those in which the *antagonista* is not herself saved. Despite its Dante-esque vision of urban Mexico, *Aventurera* demonstrated that there was room for mercy, forgiveness, and redemption in modern Mexico. Like the atheist muralists of the same era, filmmakers and songwriters were embedding elements of "Christian myth" (Martin-Barbero, 1993, p. 117) into their modernist narratives, adapting them to urban realities. The *Cabaretera* signaled that moral life was still possible amidst the overwhelming decadence of the city.

The surface message ("Elena as bad girl") provided traditional moral critique, whereas the sexual core of *Cabaretera* represented an amoral embrace of modernism. The theme of redemption, therefore, represented a ritual mediation between these poles. The traditional dichotomy of virgin versus prostitute was collapsed, combined, and reborn in the figure of the virginal prostitute, women like *Elena, Aventurera, Santa,* and *Pecadora,* as symbols of an ambivalent age.

Traditional dichotomies were collapsing in the realm of postrevolutionary political economy as well. The war between capitalists and socialists resulted in a mutually unsatisfying, yet politically effective, compromise, embodied in the state–capitalist development programs of the PRI (Krooth, 1995, pp. 186–215). Like the *Malinchista–Virgen* prostitutes of film fame, the state–capitalism of the PRI was recombinant, an unhappy marriage of neo-Porfirian policy and revolutionary rhetoric.

THE HYBRIDIZATION AND DECLINE OF *BOLERO* CULTURE

The *bolero,* through hybridization with traditional song styles and media-influenced *mariachi,* gave birth to *bolero–ranchero* and, eventually, modern *Ranchera* music.

Ranchera has since become closely identified, both domestically and abroad, with Mexican national identity. *Bolero* also spawned the string-based *trio* ensembles. *Ranchera* and *trio* competed throughout the 1950s for popularity. Also thrown into the mix were Mexican rock and pop music, the latter heavily influenced by the *bolero.*

With the advent of *Ranchera's* midcentury reign, the experimental days of postrevolutionary popular culture segued into an era of nationalistic cliché. *Ranchera* drew from the nostalgic element of the *bolero,* combining neotraditionalism with stereotypical nationalism to form a somewhat simplified sense of *Mexicanidad.* Rock and roll, conversely, represented a youthful embrace of modernity, urbanity, and transnationalism. In essence, the *bolero's* nostalgic modernity was split into two competing tendencies, transnational modernism for youth and nostalgic nationalism for their parents.

Charro films represented the conservative turn as well. No longer enamored with the city sounds and styles, the urbanites' angst-ridden desires for rural ways propelled the trend. Nostalgia, fueled by invented memories of rural life (by the 1950s the majority of Mexico City residents, or *Chilangos,* had never experienced life outside the city) and the surprisingly high export value of *Mexicanista* cultural products, led *Ranchera* music and *charro* films to be dominated by stereotypes. A plaque at a 1998 exhibit in the Mexican National Museum of Popular Culture clearly described this quality: "*Mariachi,* between tradition and stereotype." Indeed, just as the *bolero* represented modernity for the masses, the *charro* complex was an equally accessible form of mass nationalism. Perhaps for the first time, Mexico's collection of *Patrias Chicas* (Small Fatherlands) became a full nation, as all began to reference a shared stock of national cultural symbols. Mass media played no small role in this process (Sevilla, 1990, p. 45).

Other factors, beyond the popularity and conservative ethos of *Ranchera,* combined to undo the *bolero's* dominance. One was the government-led and popularly embraced attack on vice. Postrevolutionary nationalists, most of them atheist, found common cause with religious conservatives against what they saw as the corrosive influence of the *bolero.* Having reached an official détente between government and religion during his presidency, President Manuel Avila Camacho permitted Mexico City's archbishop to create the "League of Decency" in the mid–1940s, providing a united front of nationalist propagandists and religious conservatives versus the *boleristas.* Jesus Flores y Escalante described the censorship movement as a "neo-inquisition" (Dueñas, 1993, p. 30). Although initially not very effective, these moves signaled the counterrevolution that was to follow.

The conservative turn would triumph by the 1950s. Though perhaps not quite as violent nor extreme as the reactionary conservatism experienced in the United States during that decade, this trend marked the end of the *bolero's* postrevolutionary party. Mexico was headed toward a more sober form of popular modernity, less open to its cultural potential and more fearful of its moral effects.

This conservative consensus, and the chimera of the "Mexican Miracle" economy, were being widely challenged by the late 1960s. The very people who were to fulfill the PRI's future development plans, college students, became its major opposition.

Faith in the PRI has been continually diminished since then, due to failed development and modernization campaigns, from the oil boom speculation of the late seventies to the oil bust of 1982 on through to current widespread disillusionment with the North American Free Trade Agreement (NAFTA). Momentary periods of popular optimism notwithstanding (such as early optimism regarding NAFTA), the trend for three decades has been against the development vision of the PRI, if not "development" in general. Ethnographer Matthew Gutman found that by the early 1990s "cynicism was already widespread in Santo Domingo [a *barrio* of Mexico City] with regard to the government's and the ruling PRI party's providing any kind of democratic hope for the future" (1996, p. 259). This was true of nearly the entire city by 1997, when Cuauhtemoc Cardenas of the Democratic Revolution Party (PRD) easily won the city's first mayoral election. Unquestioning faith in the development solution has dissipated and may be nearing the point of complete exhaustion.

THE *BOLERO'S* REBIRTH AS POSTMODERN MELODRAMA FOR THE NAFTA AGE

Aventurera was resurrected in 1998 amidst this climate of popular disillusionment and apprehension. After evolving from song to film, it has recently been remade as live musical theater. Performed at Salón Los Angeles, *Aventurera* marshaled the talents of eight dancers and sixteen actors, most on contract with media giant *Televisa.*

The 1998 version has been greatly modified. The new *Aventurera* places greater emphasis on the role of Police Chief Comandante Treviño, for example, providing a very obvious, comical representation of governmental corruption and a not-so-thinly veiled critique of the PRI. It is a polysemic attack, however, critical but evasive as jokes concerning the conservative National Action Party (PAN) and left–reformist Democratic Revolution Party (PRD) are thrown in by the ad-libbing Rosaura (played brilliantly by *telenovela* staple, Carmen Salinas).

The PRI's development schemes are coming under severe scrutiny, on stage, on the streets, even in the traditionally supportive mass media. Seventy years of modernization programs proffered by the PRI have failed to convince the wider populace, even the urban middle class, that the answers to their problems lie in capitalist development (Krooth, 1995). When queried on their outlook for the next millennium, 43 percent of Mexican poll respondents stated that they are "pessimistic," compared with only 37 percent, who are optimistic (the remainder were "indifferent" or "did not know"; Notimex, 1999). For comparison, the same poll conducted in the United States found only 9 percent of United States' respondents pessimistic about the economic future. What is indicated, both in polls and popular culture, is not just a loss of faith in the PRI, NAFTA, and neoliberalism per se, but pessimism regarding the carrot-and-stick promises of development.

Olmos's *Aventurera,* therefore, is an attempt to look back and see what might be salvaged from the early days of Mexican modernity. In an interview, I asked Olmos

(1998) to explain the political elements and historical context of his *Aventurera.* "[W]e have not advanced sufficiently politically, due to corruption." Therefore, he decided "to adapt the argument of forties' life to the urban reality of today, including the corruption," in order to show how little things had changed in political terms in the interceding decades. "I am from Chiapas," he continued, "That [the EZLN uprising] is a preoccupation in everyone's mind," he explained, as are "the elections, the PRI—that they could fall—narcotraffic, political assassinations, etc." Olmos argues that Mexican "theaters and films are full of nostalgia, because the current reality is so violent," and that even amidst the uncertainty and violence, "still, we have to go to the theater and movies . . . still, we dance the *Danzón.*"

Olmos admits a love for melodrama, "because it is the genre that the people like best." Olmos, like many Mexican authors, artists, and composers, has enacted a cultural politics of engagement with popular media, embracing its inevitable contradictions and compromises. Olmos rejects the facile forms of distancing practiced by artists and intellectuals who see melodrama simply as "degrading" the sensibilities of the popular classes. Like Martin-Barbero (1993, p. 118), Olmos makes the case for political engagement with mass culture and artistic work within melodramatic forms.

Trying to work within, rather than in opposition to, mass culture, Olmos's *Aventurera* celebrates the "democratic" spirit of popular culture during the postrevolutionary era, and the fact that "people went out to dance and mixed with prostitutes, politicians, and with everyone." He places that democratic sensibility in contradistinction to the cultural and political exclusivity of NAFTA-era Mexico.

The fact that *Aventurera* is a distinctly Mexican text provides further political appeal in an age where the great majority of films, and a significant percentage of live theater, are foreign in origin. Olmos cited the currently popular *Beauty and the Beast, Fame,* and *A Chorus Line* as spectacles against which, on the technical level, the Mexican theater industry cannot compete. Therefore, Olmos has turned to cultural history and the "collective memory" of *Aventurera* for competitive advantage. Middle-class couples, dressed in their finest, paid the equivalent of US$10 per seat to revisit the modern past, escape the uncertain present, and take part in reinventing the future. Nearly everyone present sang along to the familiar songs chosen for the theatrical adaptation, led by familiar voices and personalities from Mexican television and film.

The *Aventurera* characters performed their melodramatic tale from amidst the customers' tables at Salón Los Angeles. As *telenovela* stars, the actors were familiar and more "real" than typical stage actors. *Aventurera,* for the couples that I sat with at the show, was nothing short of "a dramatic catharsis," just as Olmos intended.

The 1998 *Aventurera* is a highly polysemic text, befitting what is, once again, a highly ambivalent, confused, and liminal era, in which the political, cultural, and even sexual consensus of midcentury Mexico continues to dissolve. *Aventurera* provides both the comfort of nostalgia, as well as a means for reflective contemplation of the future. In Olmos's words: "We are reviewing ourselves. It [*Aventurera*] is like being in a church." Olmos softened certain elements of the film, including the violence, putting emphasis on others. Thus, the henchman, Rango, of the film is replaced by a transvestite, a (wo)man who is, at the same time, both ultrafeminine and macho. Just as the film dissolved the boundary between virgin and prostitute, Olmos's play violates the sacred limnus between masculine and feminine.

Aventurera—as equal parts ritual escape to the past, disturbing reflection on the present, and contemplative questioning of the future—provides textual insight into both the political and cultural moment, as Mexican employees/citizens/audiences decide how they will negotiate the current crisis. Ultimately, Olmos's *Aventurera* has succeeded because it is "narrating something that is important" to Mexican people, not simply as citizens or workers, but "as an audience." Like all popular culture, *Aventurera* is partly a political text, not despite its popular entertainment value, but because of it.

As indicated by the popularity of Olmos's *Aventurera, bolero* culture was not completely killed off by the rise of *Ranchera* and rock. Pablo Duenas points out that "in the Yucatan," for example, the *bolero* has continued "to be alive, very alive" (1993, p. 175). The *bolero* is still a living phenomena in the cities as well, experienced nightly at piano bars, nightclub shows, and, of course, on the radio. Likewise, thousands of taxi drivers, teachers, and clerks rush home on special nights of the week to dress up in their finest before going out for a night at their favorite dance hall. There they will continually relive the modern tradition of *Danzón* and, between sets, the *bolero.* As so well illustrated in Maria Novaro's film *Danzón,* this subculture has taken on a working class patina, layering nostalgia for postrevolutionary ways over the already romantic sensibilities of the music itself. The recent economic downturn appears to have strengthened this trend as other diversions become increasingly out of reach for all but the rich and emerging professional classes. Contemporary *Danzón* demonstrates a strong desire on the part of the urban working class to continue the modern traditions it developed in the postrevolutionary decades, a modernity of its own making, which is neither an extension of *México Profundo,* nor a capitulation to an imposed model of modernity.

In addition to being coded as urbane and sophisticated, *bolero* culture is experienced today as something intrinsically Mexican, thus romantic and sentimental. "The Americans are not so interested in love, right?" asked one of the *bolero* aficionados in my study, "They are more interested in practical things, true?" Having been officially inscribed as *Norteamericanos* through the signing of NAFTA, many Mexicans are seeking ways to reconstruct and reassert a distinct national identity, rather than being reduced to second-class citizens in a newly imagined regional community with Canada and the United States. Calling upon the traditional construction of Gringos as *frío* (cold) technocrats, they view themselves oppositionally as artful, passionate beings whose priorities lie more in spirit and aesthetics than material and logistics. The *bolero* is becoming an effective symbol in this intercultural dialectic of identity.

Yet, cultural dialectics rarely allow for such dichotomies—cold versus hot, spiritual versus technical—to remain salient, especially in an age more characterized by cultural flow and hybridization than coherence and exclusion (Appadurai, 1996; García Canclini, 1995). Along with the rebirth of *bolero* in contemporary Mexico City, one can witness scenes like the following: a Mexican *trova* ensemble at a sushi restaurant performing Alvaro Carrillo's *Sabor a Mí* to tables full of Mexican secretaries and Japanese businessmen, flanked by a large banner selling Jamaican Rum. The participants in this postmodern pastiche nevertheless manage to negotiate points of cultural stability, by reconstructing and reimagining past traditions. Recalling past Mexican hybrids, including French-inspired *Mariachi,* the *bolero* is being used to provide one such cultural anchor. Although this anchor will, in turn, be swept away by the continuing flow and hybridization of local, national, regional, and global cultures (Appadurai, 1996, p. 33), such reinvented traditions do provide at least momentary hold in the form of subcultural identification and community. *Bolero* has become the center of a working class community in Mexico City, surviving its popular past in order to become subcultural code in the present.

The local Mexico City dance hall is not the only venue where *bolero* lives on. Mexican pop stars will occasionally include *boleros* in their repertoires as well. These latter-day *boleristas* include Luis Miguel, Lucero, Ana Gabriel, Angela Carrasco, Daniela Romo, and many others. Miguel, for example, recently brought Lara's *Noche de Ronda* back to the charts with his 1997 release of a CD completely dedicated to the *bolero.* When Miguel and other contemporary stars include *boleros* on their CDs and in their performances, it is now experienced, ironically, as a nod to Mexican "tradition."

Others, more critically reflective, perform the *bolero* with a sense of ironic disdain for the present. There is an impoverished family band, for example, which plays on the street in Mexico City's perverse *Zona Rosa,* skillfully performing *Triste Recuerdo* (Sad Memory), fully cognizant that the private meaning of their music is being lost on the largely foreign and élite passerby. A boy passing around the hat cocks a wry smile, mouthing "sad memory" to no one in particular, because practically no one but he and his family understand the bittersweet meanings of their performance. In this case, *bolero* is transformed from romantic text into social–realist critique.

Probably the most interesting *bolero* subculture in contemporary Mexico, however, belongs to the avant–garde community of songwriters and musicians associated with *Bar Habito* and associated art houses. Eugenia Leon, Astrid Hadad, and a small clique of Bohemian neo–*boleristas* have used *bolero* and *Danzón* to craft a new political aesthetic. Combining the apoliticism, hypermodernity, and urbanity of *bolero* and *Danzón* with biting, satirical, and political lyrics, they have given new life to these aging styles. Lilliana Felipe's *Que Devuelvan*—sung by Eugenia Leon—provides a brilliant case in point. Indicting the Salinas administration and "the arrogance of their modernity" for Mexico's current predicament, the song repeatedly states that Mexicans are the "victims of Neoliberal sins."

As indicated in the example of *Que Devuelvan,* Felipe and other Mexico City performance artists are using a postmodern aesthetic—combining modern styles with discordant lyrical messages—to challenge directly the basic tenets of the PRI and its development schema. Much of the political pop and avant–garde music of the 1990s has taken on this postmodern tone. Although emphasizing political and cultural critique, many of these musicians demonstrate suspicion of any claims toward popular alliance, while absolutely rejecting any "totalizing" utopian, thus modern, alternatives. The neotraditional satires of musicians like Astrid Hadad, Lilliana Felipe, and Eugenia Leon, as well as popular rock anthems by El Tri, Tijuana No, and Café Tacuba, to name just a few, provide very scathing critiques of NAFTA, the PRI, the United States, neoliberalism and, at least by association, development discourse. Yet, all of these musicians remain conspicuously distant from any carefully articulated alternative vision for the future. They do not pretend to speak from outside the modern frame, but rather find ways to work through it. In doing so, these "cultural actors . . . transform their practices in the face of modernities' contradictions" (Escobar, 1995, p. 219), presaging the potential for a postdevelopment popular culture.

CONCLUSION

The *bolero* movement has come full circle. Born as a product of Mexican modernity, it is now, among other things, a recruit in the war against its worst ravages. The *bolero*'s polysemic simplicity has allowed the form to adapt and evolve while other modern artifacts, such as the *Ranchera* phenomenon, have become culturally fixed as "authentic" elements from a past Mexican tradition.

George Lewis reminds us that the "past, as encoded in popular music, is always with us in the present, waiting quietly to be loosed on the wings of some half forgotten song" (1993, p. 63). In other words, music is memory. And in the words of Eduardo, a *Bolero* aficionado, "to remember is to live." Yet, cultural memory is contested terrain, subject to a struggle over whose cultural desires and institutional designs whose memory will define social life. International development discourse, with its ideological overtones of *noblesse oblige*, has fit the propaganda needs of the PRI all too well. Many Mexicans have opposed that vision, however, remembering a different past and conceiving a better present, going beyond the negative and transitory social categories of development discourse (e.g., underdeveloped, neoliberal) in order to fashion a future more responsive to social needs and desires. Therefore, it serves us well not only to examine the cold demographics and prosaic rhetoric of technocrats when considering questions of development, but also the living memory of popular culture. It is in cultural texts like the *bolero* that dominated classes and subcultures instill some of their deepest passions and strongest desires.

NOTES

1. Like the cultural texts in question, my research has been conducted in intertextual fashion. The historical data are drawn from primary (media texts, letters, and autobiographies) and secondary sources (studies of genres and events, mainly by Mexican authors). The contemporary data are drawn from ongoing ethnographic research in Mexico City that formally began in 1997, albeit informed by previous research experiences in Mexico as well. By use of the term ethnographic, I refer to a method combining focused interviews and, most importantly, par-

ticipant observation in the homes, bars, dance salons, restaurants, and concerts where *boleros* are sung and experienced today. An extensive interview with playwright Carlos Olmos, in his home, and observation of *Aventurera,* the musical play in Salón Los Angeles, were particularly informative for the purposes of this chapter. However, dozens of formal, and hundreds of informal, interviews have been conducted, and a nearly equal number of days and nights have been spent studying the history, creation, production, performance, and consumption of the *bolero,* Mexico's most understudied musical form.

REFERENCES

Appadurai, A. (1996). *Modernity at large: Cultural dimensions of globalization.* Minneapolis, MN: University of Minnesota.

Aura, A. (1990). *La hora intima de Agustin Lara.* Mexico City, Mexico: Cal y Arena.

Bonfil Batalla, G. (1996). Mexico profundo*: Reclaiming a civilization.* Austin, TX: University of Texas.

Dueñas, P. (1993). *Bolero: Historia documental del bolero Mexicano.* Mexico City, Mexico: Asociación Mexicana de Estudios Fonográficos (AMEF).

Escobar, A. (1995). *Encountering development: The making and unmaking of the Third World.* Princeton, NJ: Princeton University Press.

García Canclini, N. (1995). *Hybrid cultures: Strategies for entering and leaving modernity.* Minneapolis, MN: University of Minnesota Press.

Gutman, M. (1996). *The Meanings of* macho*: Being a man in Mexico City.* Berkeley, CA: University of California.

Herrera-Sobek, M. (1990). *The Mexican* corrido*: A feminist analysis.* Bloomington, IN: Indiana University Press.

Kay, J. (1964). *Las siete vidas de Agustin Lara.* Mexico City, Mexico: El Universal Gráfico.

Krooth, R. (1995). *Mexico, NAFTA, and the hardships of progress: Historical patterns and shifting methods of oppression.* Jefferson, NC: Mcfarland.

Lara, A. (1999). *Aventurera.* September 3, 1999. Available: http://www.musica.org/letras/espa1/904.htm.

Lewis, G. (1993). Bringing it all back home: Uses of the past in the present (and the future) of American popular music. In R. Brown & R. Ambrosetti (Eds.), *Continuities in popular culture: The present in the past and the past in the present and future* (pp. 61–73). Bowling Green, OH: Bowling Green University Press.

Lopez, A. (1993). Tears and desire: Women and melodrama in the "old" Mexican cinema. In J. King, A. Lopez, and M. Alvarado (Eds.), *Mediating two worlds: Cinematic encounters in the Americas* (pp. 147–163). London, UK: BFI.

Martin-Barbero, J. (1993). *Communication, culture and hegemony.* Newbury Park, CA: Sage.

Mendizabal, G. & Mejia, E. (1993). *Todo lo que quería saber sobre Agustin Lara.* Mexico City, Mexico: Editorial Contenido.

Monsivais, C. (1993a). Serenata con *trio* en un cementerio de rockolas. In E. Mejia & G. Mendizabal (Eds.), *Todo lo que quería saber sobre Agustin Lara* (pp. 113–120). Mexico City, Mexico: Editorial Contenido.

Monsivais, C. (1993b). Mexican cinema: Of myths and demystifications. In J. King, A. Lopez, and M. Alvarado (Eds.), *Mediating two worlds: Cinematic encounters in the Americas* (pp. 139–146). London, UK: BFI.

Notimex (1999). *Realiza CEO encuesta en México y EU sobre próxima visita de Clinton.* February 10 (wire).

Olmos, C. (1998). Interview with author. February 10.

Petras, J. (1997). The political economy of early debt payment. *Z Magazine,* 10(4), April, 45–49.

Pineda, A. (1990). La evolución del *bolero* urbano en Agustin Lara. *Heterofonia XX,* January–December, 4–23.

Public Citizen (1999). *Global Trade Watch: The NAFTA Index.* Available: http://www.citizen.org/pctrade/nafta/naftaindex.htm#N_3_.

Ramos, R. (1993). Notas para una rapsodia. In E. Mejia & G. Mendizabal (Eds.), *Todo lo que quería saber sobre Agustin Lara* (pp. 85–111). Mexico City, Mexico: Editorial Contenido.

Rubenstein, A. (1998). *Bad language, naked ladies, and other threats to the nation: A political history of comic books in Mexico.* Durham, NC: Duke.

Sevilla, A. (1990). *Danza, cultura, y clases sociales.* Mexico: INBA.

Trejo, A. (1992). *Hey, familia, Dazón dedicado a . . . !* Mexico City, Mexico: Plaza y Valdes.

10

Same Language Subtitling on Indian Television

Harnessing the Power of Popular Culture for Literacy

Brij Kothari

"Gammat sathe gnan!" ("It's knowledge with entertainment")
—a woman from Aniyarigaon, Gujarat

As the year 2000 arrives, India still suffers under the weight of one-third the world's nonliterates.[1] Low levels of literacy, both in terms of rate and quality, are to a great degree maintained by frequent relapse into nonliteracy or stagnation of neoliterates' skills.[2] Thus, many short stints in school and adult literacy programs are considerably wasted, because they often fail to push their participants above the minimum threshold of learning.

A key factor responsible for India's slow progress with literacy is infrequent reading outside the classroom, sometimes due to a lack of opportunity or motivation, but more significantly due to the absence of a reading environment. Television, as a medium rapidly making inroads into rural and urban homes, could dramatically alter this bleak scenario by creating an inviting environment for reading. This environment might exist if written texts on television entertainment programming were creating more interest in reading and opportunities for practice.

Literacy and power are connected; individuals and collective groups gain social power by becoming literate. A strategic direction may still contribute to social transformation rather effectively. One operationalization of this direction is to modify certain popular television programs in the interest of national literacy development, through Same Language Subtitling (SLS). Since this suggestion has evoked a lukewarm response at best among top media and education policy makers, this chapter takes a close look at the institutional barriers confronting the implementation of such a project. These barriers are structured within the political power of policy makers.

LITERACY: A TOOL OF POWER

Power is a complex concept. The tools that attend to power are equally complex and inseparable from power itself. Latent in any tool in the service of power lies the potential for its various, often contradictory uses. On the one hand there is a capacity to reinforce power inequalities, and on the other to restructure the web of relationships in ways that make it more difficult to sustain or justify inequalities.

Since tools are never ideologically divorced from the hands of their users, they have and always will be used to sculpt a diversity of social expressions from multiple stakeholders. Unwittingly or otherwise, while some stakeholders may strive to maintain or exacerbate the inequities of the past, others may wage a struggle with the same tool for social justice and greater equality. A tool of powerful significance for the latter project is literacy.

In the hands of the powerful, literacy has often been used, explicitly or implicitly, to re-create the existing structural inequalities of society. An unequal society, in dialectical fashion, tends to work strategically to reproduce literacy asymmetries that mirror the structural power equations of society based on the complex intersections of caste, class, gender, religion, and language among other factors. For example, the Brahmins in India once strategized to maintain the powerful literate, namely, themselves.

However, industrialized nations, increasingly enmeshed in a global economy, need a literate workforce to compete. Modern nations have come to accept universal literacy, at the minimum level at least, as necessary for economic progress. For those supporting a transformational project, the potential of literacy in the hands of the masses cannot be underestimated. Yet, what are the conditions for a literacy movement to become transformatively critical? What kind of literacy, at what level, and what proportion of society? Where does India stand in terms of achieving these conditions?

LITERACY ACHIEVEMENTS AND CHALLENGES

The state of the educational situation in India, despite significant strides, leaves much to be desired. An indication of the road that has been traveled and still remains ahead can be found in raw numbers (Haq, 1997):

1. Between 1970 and 1993, the adult literacy rate increased from 34 to 51 percent, still leaving 291 million adults as nonliterate;

2. Although the gross primary enrollment has risen to almost universal coverage, in 1995 there were 45 million children out of primary school;
3. The mean years of schooling for those twenty-five years old and above had risen from 2.2 to 2.4 years during the 1980–1992 period;
4. Drop-outs from primary schooling (Class I–V) had been reduced from 62 percent in 1985 to 34 percent in 1993.

These figures cannot be seen in isolation from the underlying inequities of gender, caste, urbanity, and religion. Gender inequities cut across all categories (Ramachandran, 1998). For instance, the 1991 census reports a 64 percent male and 39 percent female rate of literacy (age 7 and over). In a 1993 survey cited by Haq (1997), in some rural areas, the rate of literacy in the 7 and over age group was 53 percent for males and 28 percent for females. The average schooling received by males was 3.5 years and females 1.2 years, even though female enrollment in primary schools had risen dramatically from 56 percent in 1970 to 90 percent in 1992.

These figures paint a picture of hope and challenge. The challenge is not only in terms of numbers, but of quality. Given the astoundingly low average number of years spent in school or in nonformal education, the vast number of neoliterates is not surprising. Relapse into illiteracy, a phenomenon much understudied and addressed even less at the policy level, is known to be a serious problem. According to the National Literacy Mission's (NLM)[3] own commissioned Report of the Expert Group to look at the literacy campaign in India critically, "it is clear that carrying out a successful post-literacy/continuing-education program remains the single most difficult problem confronting the NLM" (1994, p. 40).

From a gender standpoint, the report explains that women constitute "from two-thirds to three-fourths of adult illiterates" (Report of the Expert Group, 1994, p. 29) covered under many successful Total Literacy Campaigns (TLCs). Relapse would logically also affect women more. Hence, many literacy initiatives are temporary operations; nonliterates become neoliterate, only to be squeezed back into nonliteracy. What is then required, keeping a realistic perspective of scale and achievement, to promote the transformative potential of this literacy movement? Given the location of literacy campaigns in government structures, there is a need for realism in terms of the extent to which mass campaigns can and will attempt to develop a critical consciousness.

THE TWO FACES OF LITERACY: SCRIPTACY AND CRITICACY

From a social transformational perspective, it is difficult to argue with the Freirean approach that literacy skill development needs to be integrated within the development of a critical consciousness. However, in practice such an overtly transformational approach in a nonrevolutionary context is likely to be threatening to the establishment. Large-scale efforts toward this end can even be counterproductive, inciting debilitating reprisals from the powerful and ultimately preventing many people from becoming literate or critically aware. Besides, implementation of the Freirean model on an Indian landscape of over a half billion non- and neoliterates can assume proportions of a utopian challenge.

The scale of the literacy problem in India calls for a more strategically viable approach. Influenced by the pragmatics of numbers and social reality, the strategic approach suggested here requires a conceptual separation of an ideologically charged word such as "literacy" into "criticacy" and "scriptacy." "Criticacy" refers to the development of a Freirean critical consciousness and "scriptacy" implies, in a very narrow sense, the acquisition of skills related to reading, writing, and numeracy. If an integrated approach to the development of mass criticacy and scriptacy is difficult to achieve, a viable approach may be to aim for scriptacy levels that, once achieved, can be tapped by social movements to spawn wider criticacy.

Currently, the majority of those we label as "literate," for enumeration purposes, have extremely low scriptacy skills. But if these skills were developed enough for people to access information and literature at will, criticacy could then be promoted with greater effectiveness by forces fighting for equity and social justice. Adequately high scriptacy levels in the hands of a critical mass of people, even achieved with non-transformative ideological biases, will inevitably create a fertile ground for the unleashing of criticacy forces. Ultimately, the link between scriptacy and one's own experience in making sense of the world is far more potent than the ideological veneer under which scriptacy skills may be acquired. Scriptacy in the hands of the powerful will more likely be used to maintain the status quo, but in the hands of the disadvantaged it will eventually serve a transformational agenda.

A necessary condition for this is that sufficiently large numbers of people enjoy an adequate level of scriptacy. What constitutes an adequately high level of scriptacy and what constitutes a critical mass of people are thus central questions. Since the newly literate cannot be forced or persuaded easily to enter into scriptacy transactions, what kind of a scriptacy-rich environment will make the development of scriptacy skills inescapable?

EMPOWERMENT THROUGH MASS SCRIPTACY DEVELOPMENT: A ROLE FOR TELEVISION

Considering that India is home to the largest number of nonliterates and possibly neoliterates in the world, a creative use of the mass media, especially to aid the transition from neo- to irreversible literacy, holds promise. Although the NLM's efforts have concentrated on the creation of neoliterates, currently there is no large-scale effort in the country to create scriptacy transactions that would be accessible in everyday life.

The cornerstone strategy of the NLM for postliteracy and continuing education has been to open rural neighborhood libraries. Necessary as these are, their proliferation has been limited by resource constraints. But more fundamentally, even for those neoliterates for whom these reading spaces are accessible, they are used at best in short spurts, and rarely as an internally driven lifelong process. For people whose lives revolve around livelihood considerations, purchasing reading material or visiting libraries is understandably a low priority. Alternatively, a family may save enough for acquiring a television set and need not be persuaded to make time for watching it.

A scriptacy-rich environment that appeals to the majority can prevent relapse and help the movement from non- to neoliteracy. The role of television, specifically for the development of scriptacy skills, has been limited in India. Television's use has been confined to promoting interest and awareness for literacy. Our approach aims to achieve scriptacy development in an indirect and subliminal fashion. However, this does not rule out the possibility that greater interest and awareness in literacy may also result.

Mass scriptacy skill development of a critical mass and at an adequate level, it has been argued, will create amenable conditions for the unleashing of empowerment processes. The use of television makes it possible to provide lifelong scriptacy skill improvement for a critical mass and beyond. By creating an environment for individuals to further their own skills in an everyday context, this approach contributes to putting skill development within an individual's capacity and control. For unleashing forces of social change, questioning what should be the critical level of skill for a critical mass thus becomes redundant to some degree. A scriptacy-rich environment created by the media could potentially engage neoliterates in subconscious practice. Such an environment would also aid their skill development to reach higher levels, furthering lifelong improvement more by individual capacity than by opportunity.

In India, television has emerged as an entertainment medium, having mostly left behind the development mantle it once employed during the stages of early expansion.

Same Language Subtitling

Same Language Subtitling (SLS) is a technique that holds enormous potential to create a scriptacy-rich reading environment. Simply, it suggests subtitling motion media programs in the "same" language. Thus, Hindi programs would be subtitled in Hindi and likewise with all of the regional language programs in the country. The basic idea is that what you see (text) is what you hear (audio). The argument made presently is that SLS's strength lies in the incidental learning processes it would launch in the everyday lives of children as well as adults, across the nation. For SLS to contribute to literacy skill acquisition and improvement, there is no better context than film-song programs that already exist in most regional languages.

Film songs pervade the popular culture ethos in India like no other music (Arora, 1986). Film-song programs command regular and extremely high viewership. They attract people from all walks of life, including large numbers of school children and adults with developing or partially developed literacy skills. In everyday life many of these people will not be able to afford reading material and/or be motivated enough to find time for reading. However, watching television and film-song programs has become an integral part of people's lives in today's rural and urban India and will continue to dominate popular culture. The contention made is that SLS, when used in popular culture, can create entertainment, which invites reading. The technique is simple and inexpensive, and, according to audience feedback, promises to be generally popular.

The literature is replete with studies that have argued for the appropriate use of subtitling in language learning (Holobow et al., 1984; Lambert, 1986; Vanderplank, 1988, 1990). Few, however, have explored the possibility of merging subtitling with popular culture and not with educational programs specifically. Lambert suggests from experimental studies in language learning that adding English script to educational television programs that normally have English dialogue may help literacy:

> For those with English as their only language but who are poor readers, poor spellers or illiterate in English, this simple addition could become a valuable aid over time, not only for improving literacy and reading abilities, but also for enhancing and enriching listeners' general comprehension of verbal information. (1986, p. 499)

A plethora of studies on closed captioning,[4] originally implemented to aid the hearing impaired and deaf (Carney and Verlinde, 1987; Koskinen et al., 1986), have suggested how this could be useful in second-language acquisition, reading improvement (Bean, 1989; Koskinen et al., 1985), listening comprehension development (Froehlich, 1988), vocabulary enrichment (Neuman and Koskinen, 1992), and even speaking performance (Borras and Lafayette, 1994).

Context for Implementation

The proposed context for the implementation of SLS is the proliferation of vastly popular Indian language film-song programs on Doordarshan (National and State television) and other private television networks. For example, nationally, SLS could be used in popular Hindi film-song programs like *Chitrahaar* and *Rangoli* and statewide in the different regional languages (e.g., Gujarati-language Chitrageet and so on).[5] Such programs also enjoy higher viewership among women.

Access to and viewership of television is rapidly increasing. According to Doordarshan (1999), the network has an estimated viewership of 415 million people. In the last five years, a number of commercial satellite channels have made an entry into Indian homes through various cable television networks. The combined viewership of all the networks is estimated to be 448 million (220 million urban and 228 million rural viewers). Doordarshan, however, claims that it has maintained more than 85 percent of the total viewership. While these figures are debatable, this station does attract high viewership in rural areas, where literacy levels are low. Even in areas where reading opportunities exist, people are more inclined to make time for television than for reading.

Subliminal literacy skill development and enhanced entertainment (SLS), if done appropriately, is not likely to evoke significant resistance from viewers whether they be literate or partially literate.[6] Both categories of people will have something to gain, either in the form of entertainment or reading practice opportunity or both. The twofold rationale for the use of SLS is that it can "add" entertainment value to already popular song programs and, as a consequence, contribute to the development of literacy skills nationally.

Only when reading itself becomes part and parcel of everyday life, without necessarily becoming a consciously laborious effort, will many neoliterates graduate to irreversible literacy. SLS of film-song programs does that by making literacy skill development a subliminal process through the association of text and song lyrics. Songs have a natural advantage over dialogue in that people know them by heart to varying degrees and repeat them frequently. This is crucial in enabling people with even extremely low levels of literacy to benefit from SLS.

Will the neoliterates read SLS rather than watch the pictures? d'Ydewalle and colleagues (1991) have demonstrated, with an eye-movement registration method, that people are naturally drawn to read subtitles. Commenting on teletext, Vanderplank argues that "the presence of text does not reduce television watching to text reading + pictures, but that learners continue to try and match sound and text, and indeed try to monitor the correctness of their own match" (1988, p. 280). But to derive any measurable benefit in language learning, he cautions, "subjects who watched subtitled programs needed to take out language" (Vanderplank, 1990, p. 228). This is likely to occur given the pervasive interest in film songs. The high motivation among Indians to memorize song lyrics is well known, with song games like Antakshari having been around for generations and further popularized recently on television.

SLS may also benefit the already irreversibly literate, because they, as much as the neoliterate, may enjoy singing along or know the song lyrics. In viewing situations of poor sound, group, and/or ambiance noise, people would still be able to follow the songs. Therefore, it is crucial not to view SLS as an "educational" initiative alone. Learning promises to be a by-product of enhanced entertainment; therein lies a central aspect of the real potential of this simple technique.

Having argued for SLS's potential, we now turn our attention to a series of pilot studies conducted in Gujarat to explore audience reactions to the idea. The findings confirm that people actually do read the lyrics to varying degrees and at different times during the song. If this should occur regularly during the plethora of song-programs on television, one might expect progress in scriptacy skill development at the national level.

Field Tests

The main objective of the field tests, conducted over three months, was to investigate the following questions: Do people read or at least try to read subtitles on their own, i.e., without any prompting? Do they like the idea of SLS, and if so, what benefit do they see in it? What bothers viewers about SLS, either the idea itself and/or the format chosen? Should song programs on Doordarshan include SLS? Eight sites were selectively chosen for field testing, to include urban slums, rural villages, a school, and a general city area. Programs with SLS were shown, and then followed by a group discussion. Our results conclude that at least in an experimental setting, people enthusiastically supported the idea of SLS. Respondents found SLS to be entertaining, educational, relevant to those who are hearing challenged, and socially beneficial. While many could only articulate that they liked SLS, a significant number of people were able to provide reasons. Respondents pointed out on occasion that SLS should come on Doordarshan (rather than other channels since most rural people watch Doordarshan), it should be in Gujarati (even if it is not available in Hindi), and it should be available in villages (even if it is not available in the cities; see Kothari, 1998, for details).

These field tests strongly argue for implementing SLS in the context of songs. SLS should be marketed, not as an "educational" program, but as a strategy that enhances people's entertainment. This would be necessary precisely because one would not wish to undermine its literacy potential. SLS promises to provide enormous social returns on a relatively modest investment.

POLICY BARRIERS

Whether SLS can be implemented on national and state television is a policy decision. With Prasar Bharati (the new broadcasting act) advocating greater local autonomy, Doordarshan Kendras (State Television Centers) are supposedly in a better position in the present climate to experiment with ideas. At different times, policy makers in Gujarat state have expressed various hesitancies, effectively stalling, for the moment, any attempts at experimentation with SLS. This is not to say that all policy makers are averse to the idea; a few have been extremely enthusiastic.

Hesitancies expressed, thus far, include:

1. film songs may be an inappropriate (read "vulgar") medium to promote literacy;
2. video clips are often available at the last moment, cutting into the time necessary for subtitling;
3. song programs are revenue generating, making decision makers skeptical of experimentation;
4. subtitles may be a distraction for viewers;
5. who should take the responsibility for subtitling; and finally,
6. who will bear the cost of subtitling.

Is it a good idea to mix film culture and literacy? First, it needs to be made clear that film songs are a mixed bag, ranging from the poetic to the risqué. Not all are "vulgar." The concern for values may negate the use of some film songs in formal and even nonformal education (e.g., schools, adult learning centers, and so on).

However, SLS, as proposed, is designed for programs that are already being shown on television, in an informal entertainment context, and not an educational one. SLS on *Chitrahaar* and *Chitrageet* is not likely to increase or lower these programs' viewerships. Put another way, the fact of subtitling is not likely to make an individual watch more film songs. As mentioned earlier, the strength of SLS is that it creates a subliminal context for literacy skill improvement, a context whereby improvement is a by-product of entertainment. If people are going to watch certain programs anyway, it is argued that there is no harm if their viewing leads to better reading skills by just adding this component. Thus, objections to SLS of film-songs for literacy on grounds of deteriorating values are misdirected. The battle against the "cheap" influence of film culture has to do more with what should and should not be shown on television. Whether programs include SLS does not alter their cultural influence; if anything, it only suggests the possibility of improved scriptacy.

The availability of song clips with enough lead time (typically forty-eight hours would be sufficient) is a management issue and can be enforced with little effort. But even if this is not desirable, there is no harm in subtitling only the songs that do become available well in advance. In fact, it creates a good scenario for viewers to compare songs with SLS with other songs. Regarding the concern that sponsors may not support the subtitling idea, the answer lies in viewer feedback. It has been argued based on field tests that both the literate and the partially literate have something to gain from SLS. Knowing song lyrics and being able to sing along is a significant form of entertainment enhancement. Subtitling, if done appropriately, is not usually found to be a hindrance to viewing pleasure by both the literate and partially literate.

Finally, who will subtitle and bear the cost of subtitling are critical issues. During the experimental phase, SLS services for song programs can be arranged commercially, at no additional burden to Doordarshan. How does one make it sustainable? If the literacy gains are proven to be substantial, national and international organizations involved in adult education and literacy development may be persuaded to pursue the activity as a service to the television networks and Doordarshan centers, similar to the National Captioning Institute's noncommercial services to the networks in the United States (Jensema et al., 1996). Another option may be to persuade corporate sponsorship of subtitled film song programs. Companies pursuing a philosophy of corporate responsibility may gain both in terms of advertising and image. However, this may imply "educational" branding of the program, compromising its potential to some degree.

At the national level, approaching policy makers in New Delhi has itself proved to be a tremendous task, despite the proposal's originate in an institution of national repute. The prime policy makers approached so far have been the director of NLM, the director of Doordarshan, and the chief executive officer of the newly formed Prasar Bharati Board designed to oversee both television and radio in India.

The institutional hurdles faced in convincing prime policy makers to facilitate experimentation with such a minor change in television programming are difficult. The director of the NLM, after seeking a preliminary expression of interest, referred the proposal to an internal "expert." Somewhere in the exchange between the director and the "expert," the proposal seemingly dropped from active consideration, notwithstanding the volley of letters sent to resurrect the issue and a failed attempt to meet him personally. But since the proposal is yet to be accepted or rejected after over two years of persistent efforts, the stream of (unanswered) letters continues. Doordarshan finished the matter in a quick stroke. The director of Doordarshan and the CEO of Prasar Bharati both referred the matter to the deputy director general of Policy, who in turn rejected the proposal with no explanation.

Top-level policy makers on both the literacy and television sides have relatively unchallenged power to decide the fate of SLS for scriptacy. The fact that they have not been able to muster a well-argued rejection of the idea is testimony to the merit of the idea itself. It is unfortunate, therefore, that policy makers have chosen either to ignore the idea or reject it without expressing cause.

Although field tests and experimentation continue to strengthen the SLS case, the accumulation of academic evidence is overshadowed by the political context of the program's acceptance. It is here that one proffers an unhesitating criticism of people in bureaucratic power who have grown adept at squashing rather than nurturing creativity. There has been for much too long an utter vacuum of economically viable and otherwise interesting ideas to address the postliteracy challenge at a national level. Ideas that show promise in this regard must be given a chance to succeed or fail in the field and not in the minds of a few people of position.

Media and education policy making in India create insufficient space to encourage the larger civil society's creativity. Equally missing is an openness to listen, let alone respond, to ideas that somehow reach policy makers through sheer persistence. A dismissive attitude even before a suggestion is voiced, an incapacity to respect the time, commitment, effort, expense, and experimentation by others, are major hurdles. Such experiences are recounted informally by many who try to make a difference, despite all the signals that ideas are likely to die an ignored death in the policy arena.

State financing for experimentation of ideas such as SLS has turned out to be another stumbling block. Policy makers tend to want ideas originating in civil society to be "proven" in pilot projects, with the help of donor agencies (usually multinational), before being seriously considered by the state. By being averse to risking support of new ideas, the state effectively squashes many initiatives that may not fall within the scope of donors but may still be in the national interest. Too much power is vested in policy makers, and as a consequence their ideas predominate the playing field of practice. A significant part of the process of empowering people through literacy is disempowering or decentralizing policy making.

If there was once a link between education and media during the 1970s, for example in the Satellite Instructional Television Experiment (SITE), presently this connection is extremely weak at best. The enormity of the challenges in India makes it imperative to re-establish the connection between social development and the media. However, this reforged connection may not be consonant with people's expectations of a given medium. Today, television is primarily seen as an entertainment medium. For development communication to succeed on television, the message must necessarily not be overtly educational. Since the SITE days, India has produced a plethora of well meaning but sparsely watched "development" programs. Now we should examine what people enjoy watching, in order to establish how development communication can be subtly integrated into popular culture.

To conclude, policy makers thus far have used their power to constrain the use of SLS on television. Using the political power vested in their administrative positions, these decision makers prevent individuals from achieving social empowerment possible through scriptacy skills, learned through SLS. Their lack of interest in experimenting with SLS may be due to a perception that the program is flawed or ineffective. However, the SLS approach has the potential to succeed, with important consequences. Programs such as this, lacking political support, may need to be implemented where powerful policy makers have the least interest or impact.

NOTES

1. "Nonliterate" is preferred over the term "illiterate" due to the pejorative connotations acquired by the latter.
2. A "neoliterate" person is defined here as one who is not irreversibly literate.
3. The National Literacy Mission (NLM) is the apex body created in 1989 for overall national literacy planning, implementation and funding.
4. Closed captioning is an option implemented in technology whereby all television sets thirteen inches or larger sold in the United States after July 1993 have the ability to decode captions. Closed captioning is conducted on network, cable, and syndicated programming by The National Captioning Institute, a nonprofit corporation. About 100 hours of captioned television programs are shown on national television each day in the United States (Jensema et al., 1996, p. 285). Closed captioning is "closed" when the viewer has control over whether it should be displayed or not; SLS is therefore open captioning with emphasis on the text matching the audio word for word.
5. *Chitrahaar* and *Rangoli* are both programs of Hindi film songs, shown weekly. Many states with a thriving vernacular language film industry show *Chitrageet,* similar in format to the other two programs.
6. Guidelines on subtitling were developed.

REFERENCES

Arora, V. N. (1986). Popular Songs in Hindi Films. *Journal of Popular Culture,* 20(2), 143–166.

Bean, R. M. (1989). Using Closed Captioned Television to Teach Reading to Adults. *Reading Research and Instruction,* 28(4), 27–37.

Borras, I. & Lafayette, R. C. (1994). Effects of Multimedia Courseware Subtitling on the Speaking Performance of College Students of French. *The Modern Language Journal,* 78(1), 61–75.

Carney, E. & Verlinde, R. (1987). Caption Decoders: Expanding Options for Hearing Impaired Children and Adults. *American Annals of the Deaf,* 132(2), 73–77.

Doordarshan (1999). Viewers and Viewership. September 9, 1999. Available: http://www.nfdcindia.com/view.html.

d'Ydewalle, G., Praet, C., Verfaillie, K., & Van Rensbergen, J. (1991). Watching Subtitled Television. *Communication Research,* 18(5), 650–666.

Froehlich, J. (1988). German Videos with German Subtitles: A New Approach to Listening Comprehension Development. *Die Unterrichtspraxis / Teaching German,* 21(2), 199–203.

Haq, M. (1997). *Human Development in South Asia.* Karachi, Pakistan: Oxford University Press.

Holobow, N. E., Lambert, W. E., & Sayegh, L. (1984). Pairing Script and Dialogue: Combinations that Show Promise for Second or Foreign Language Learning. *Language Learning,* 34(4), 59–76.

Jensema, C., McCann, R., & Ramsey, S. (1996). Closed–Captioned Television Presentation Speed and Vocabulary. *American Annals of the Deaf,* 141(4), 284–292.

Koskinen, P. S., Wilson, R. M., & Jensema, C. J. (1985). Closed–Captioned Television: A New Tool for Reading Instruction. *Reading World,* 24(4), 1–7.

Koskinen, P. S., Wilson, R. M., & Jensema, C. J. (1986). Using Closed–Captioned Television in the Teaching of Reading to Deaf Students. *American Annals of the Deaf,* 131(1), 43–46.

Kothari, B. (1998). Film Songs as Continuing Education: Same Language Subtitling for Literacy. *Economic and Political Weekly,* 33(39), 2507–2510.

Lambert, W. E. (1986). Dialogue in One Language, Sub–Titles in Another: Some Alternatives for Learning Languages. In J. A. Fishman, A. Tabouret–Keller, M. Clyne, B. Krishnamurti, and M. Abdulaziz (Eds.), *The Fergusonian Impact, Vol. 1, From Phonology to Society* (pp. 479–516). Berlin, Germany: Walter de Gruyter & Co.

Neuman, S. B. & Koskinen, P. (1992). Captioned Television as Comprehensible Input: Effects of Incidental Word Learning from Context for Language Minority Students. *Reading Research Quarterly,* 27(1), 94–106.

Peters, F. J. (1979). Printed Messages in American Commercial Television and the Reading Teacher. *Journal of Reading,* 22(5), 408–415.

Report of Expert Group (1994). *Evaluation of literacy campaign in India.* New Delhi, India: National Literacy Mission.

Ramachandran, V. (1998). The Indian experience. In Vimala Ramachandran (Ed.), *Bridging the gap between intention and action* (pp. 67–156). New Delhi, India: Asian–South Pacific Bureau of Adult Education UNESCO–PROAP.

Vanderplank, R. (1988). The Value of Teletext Sub-titles in Language Learning. *ELT Journal,* 42(4), 272–281.

Vanderplank, R. (1990). Paying Attention to the Words: Practical and Theoretical Problems in Watching Television Programs with Uni–Lingual (CEEFAX) Sub–Titles. *System,* 18(2), 221–234.

11

Civil Society and Citizens' Media

Peace Architects for the New Millennium

Clemencia Rodríguez

In the words of Andrew Arno, "Conflict . . . is created, maintained, and abolished through the exchange of messages" (Arno, 1984, p. 1); and, I would add, the same can be said about peace. Indeed, peace building is a process of message exchange among parties in conflict that escalates into tolerance, acceptance of difference, and negotiation. Without communication peace is unthinkable; communication is the raw material of peace.

Although social change is at the core of both development communication and peace studies, these two fields traditionally have been foreign to each other. Articulating development communication and peace studies can facilitate the involvement of civil society in peacemaking efforts worldwide. The knowledge accumulated by development communication on community media, alternative media, and participatory media, or "citizens' media"[1] (Rodríguez, 1996; forthcoming), is one way in which our field can make an important contribution to peace studies' current attempts to engage communities in projects of peace construction.

During the 1970s and 1980s, the field of development communication went through a long, and some times excruciating, journey toward humility. Based on a formula in which experts designed lifestyles for passive communities, the field has reinvented itself as a more interactive venture in which development communicators and communities collaborate in shaping their future (Jacobson, 1993; Servaes, 1986, 1989, 1992). This journey has pressured the field of development communication through two important moves toward the decentralization of power: first, a move away from imposition and toward collaboration; and second, a move away from the mass media and toward citizens' media. These two lessons learned by development communication can offer important contributions to peace studies.

LESSON ONE: FROM IMPOSITION TO COLLABORATION

The traditional development communication model (i.e., development programs inspired by diffusion of innovations theories) assumed that communities in need of social change would follow the mandate of communication and development experts. According to this model and based on their expertise and research data, development communication scholars, international development agencies officials, and government officials devised a course of action for marginal, poor communities. The role of the community was limited to accepting and implementing the ideas and development plans of the experts. However, Third World scholars soon questioned this model, alluding to its overtone of dependency and colonization. This, plus a long series of failed development projects, unsettled the field and pushed it into a different direction. A new development paradigm emerged based on a more balanced relationship between experts, agencies, and communities. Conceived as a collaborative enterprise, development is now thought to be a joint attempt to shape the future of marginal communities. The empowerment of communities evolved into a fundamental goal of development communication.

Similarly, since the end of the Cold War, peace studies have acknowledged a need to rethink processes of peace construction in contemporary societies in conflict (Holguin, 1998c). From peacekeeping operations led by military, diplomatic, and United Nations leaders, peacekeeping is now thought of more as an undertaking for civil society. Attesting to these changes, Holguin observes:

> In the last seven years peacekeeping has developed from a mere security function to a broad spectrum of activities involved in the prevention, mitigation and termination of conflicts, as well as post-conflict reconstruction. (1998c, 2nd paragraph)

In 1988, a group of almost thirty intellectuals, artists, and development activists from eight African countries and Canada met with the goal of identifying the obstacles to peace in Africa. One of their main conclusions was that "peace efforts should come from the people, since imposed peace is fragile and elusive" (Barsalira & Nyambura, 1988, p. 37). In 1984, a similar group of academics and activists had met in the United States in order to pool their resources toward world peace; the resulting project, known as the Exploratory Project on the Conditions of Peace (EXPRO), adopted a mandate to involve the people. This goal follows the group's belief that "ordinary people are much more likely to make peace than policymakers" (Roach, 1993a, p. xviii). In the same vein, Smoker defends the need to diversify the social subjects involved in peacemaking ventures. He stresses that strong and lasting peace will only be attained with the participation of "the people of the world" (Smoker, 1992, p. 105). Drawing from successful experiences in the field of peace education, Ashford argues for a new approach to peace building carried out by nongovernmental organizations (NGOs) instead of military and governmental entities. She argues for this new direction, saying that

> this approach is based on the conviction that in the end, it is the local citizens, not the military or the government, who must work out how they will live together, using their traditions and strengths to build a just society. (Ashford, 1996, 3rd paragraph)

Summing up, peace studies and development communication have reached the same conclusions: Only when citizens take their destiny in their own hands and shape it using their own cultures and strengths will peace and social change be viable. In both cases power has diffused from being concentrated in a few experts into the everyday lives and cultures of civil society.

LESSON TWO: FROM THE MASS MEDIA TO CITIZENS' MEDIA

For development communication, the 1950s and 1960s are remembered by a hopeful fascination with the mass media. The role of the mass media, particularly in Third World countries, was to propel "backward" societies into modernization and the use of new technologies. However, history showed otherwise. The disastrous consequences of the introduction of mass media culture and modern technologies in Third World societies has been well documented. What was once called the "unanticipated consequences" (Rogers, 1983, p. 388) of the use of mass media for development range from whole generations of mothers shifting from breastfeeding to baby formula and the ecological devastation brought by the introduction of modern pesticides, to the frustrating combination of consumerism and poverty.

Again, Third World scholars and activists, this time led by Brazilian pedagogue Paulo Freire (1983), challenged the belief that mass media were the most appropriate communication means in processes of social change. Branded with ownership issues, the mass media privilege agendas that have little to do with the well-being of most people in the Third World. This conviction catapulted communication scholars and activists throughout the world into exploring different possibilities. The result has been a worldwide movement toward the use of citizens' media in processes of social change.

Today, thirty years after the first publication of Freire's classic *Educação como Prática da Liberdade* [Education as Practice for Liberation, 1967], the literature on citizens' media is vast. From diverse angles and perspectives, communication scholars have succeeded in articulating the potential of citizens' media in facilitating processes of social change toward more democratic societies.

First, citizens' media can give voice to the voiceless. By gaining access to the media, previously silenced communities can break the culture of silence and regain their own voices. Second, citizens' media can foster empowerment. Social structures of inequality and injustice result in entire communities feeling disempowered and paralyzed. Involvement in citizens' media projects strengthens people's sense of self and their confidence in their own potential to act in the world. Third, citizens' media can connect isolated communities. Facilitating alternative communication networks, citizens' media link communities and people who have much to gain from joining forces in projects for collective action. Fourth, citizens' media can foster *conscientization.* Citizens' media participants encode their own realities in their own terms, through processes of *conscientization* in the Freirean sense (Freire, 1980). And finally, citizens' media can serve as alternative sources of information. Unlike most mass media, which are normally restricted by either economic or political forces, citizens' media are able to maintain an independent position when gathering, processing, and distributing information.[2]

If disillusionment with the mass media upsets the field of development communication, the same can be said about peace studies. As development communication scholars have found that the mass media are not good allies in processes of social change toward democratic societies, peace studies scholars question the mass media's potential to advance peace and conflict resolution.[3]

Values deeply embedded in the mass media, such as conflict and objectivity, can easily become instigators of hostility. The assumption that conflict is news leads journalists and reporters to focus on social events and interactions that revolve around parties in conflict. As Arno states,

> the dramatic formula of A versus B is manifested in a thousand different versions, but the structure is there, nearer or further from the surface of the story. Disasters and accidents are portrayed as examples of the primordial conflict of the human struggle against nature and, perhaps just as ancient, against the malfunctioning of human inventions. (1984, p. 2)

The belief that there is a "human disposition" (Arno, 1984, p. 2) toward conflict stories, as opposed to stories of peacemaking or harmony, results in the news media industry being obsessed with finding and documenting social conflict. In the words of Colleen Roach, "not only do the media have this perverse fascination with war and violence; they also neglect the peace forces at work" (1993a, p. xi).

Labeled by Johan Galtung as "the bipolar disorder" (cited in Schechter, 1998, 3rd paragraph), this pervasive format to articulate social reality in terms of binary oppositions excludes alternative interpretations such as multiple versions of the same events, multiple causes, or multiparty interactions. The inclination to frame stories in terms of good versus evil, self versus other, or light versus dark has led Galtung to declare that "journalism does not only legitimize violence but is violent in and of itself" (cited in Schechter, 1998, 3rd paragraph).

Also, the fixation with a narrative structured around conflict directs mass media professionals toward formats, storylines, characters, and events that intensify the sense of conflict. Thus, "loud" and dramatic war events are privileged over usually quiet, patient, and long-term peacemaking efforts (Roach, 1993a). As Bruck and Roach observe:

> the tendency of the media to pick up on the sensational, dramatic, disastrous and dangerous, and on the negative in general, leads many peace activists to become generally skeptical if not hostile toward the media. The media are consequently seen as one of the main, if not *the* main, obstacle to the creation of a peace culture. (1993, p. 88, emphasis in the original)

Journalists persistently seek visible characters that embody social conflict as information sources (Bruck & Roach, 1993). Grassroots organizations and peace activists, generally working in collectives that tend to erase conspicuous personalities and operating at the margins of the official discourse, are then frequently neglected. The international media's role during the crisis in Somalia, for example, has been criticized for beginning coverage with the arrival of United Nations (UN) and United States (U.S.) military personnel, when the worst of the famine was over, and for abandoning Somalia as soon as the troops were pulled out, just as grassroots peace initiatives were being developed (Holguin, 1998a).

Objectivity shapes the performance of mass media reporters and journalists into a justified aloofness within contexts of conflict and war. The reporter's supposed adherence to only factual information legitimates detachment from the social events covered, even in cases where the survival of an entire community is at stake (Roach, 1993b). As a result, a conscious attempt on the part of mass media reporters or journalists to focus on peacemaking efforts or conflict resolution initiatives would be suspicious of bias. After the Gulf War, for example, a Fairness and Accuracy in Reporting (FAIR) study concluded that

> usually missing from the news was analysis from a perspective critical to the U.S. policy. The media's rule of thumb seemed to be that to support the war was to be objective, while to be anti-war was to carry a bias. (cited in Roach, 1993b, p. 23)

Given this state of affairs, an investigation of alternatives builds on what we have learned about citizens' media in processes of democratization, toward understanding processes of conflict resolution, and the construction of peace.

CITIZENS' MEDIA FOR PEACE

A conceptual bridge can be built between development communication and peace studies. Development communication's cumulative knowledge of citizens' media is a useful springboard into the exploration of their potential in processes of peacemaking and peacekeeping. In rethinking the role of citizens' media in peace processes I address the following issues: citizens' media as alternative sources of information; citizens' media as facilitators of communication among parties in conflict; citizens' media as seekers of peace initiatives; citizens' media as architects of peace genres; citizens' media as catalysts of forgiveness; citizens' media as sites of empathic communication and; citizens' media as sites to reclaim the experience of violence.

Citizens' Media as Alternative Sources of Information

Katharine Larsen, a volunteer with Conflict Resolution Catalyst (CRC)[4] working in Bosnia, observes that the local youth have developed a defeatist attitude toward the mainstream media. According to Larsen, young Bosnians are fed up with the conflicting reports, and worse yet, they believe "that there is nothing that they can do" (1997, 4th paragraph). To address this, several NGOs have launched citizens' media projects that "provide youth with the opportunity to speak out, to voice their own 'truths,' feelings and opinions" (Larsen, 1997, 5th paragraph). Publications, such as *Balkanski Omladinski Most* (Balkan Youth Bridge), *Nepitani* (Those who were not asked), and *Mirko,* entirely produced by local youth, serve as alternative sources of information where youth can voice their own perspectives. Through their work with these citizens' media, young Bosnians are taking control of their society's media content as they learn that media should be accountable to local communities (Stubbs, 1997, 8th paragraph).

Development communication scholars and activists have most praised citizens' media for their autonomy from large agencies and their close engagement in local communities; these attributes become, in war contexts, invaluable resources. While the mainstream media are driven by large economic and political parties, citizens' media can be used by local communities to make sense of their social reality and, in the process, to construct "new social meanings" (Stubbs, 1997, 9th paragraph).

Citizens' Media as Facilitators of Communication Among Parties in Conflict

Search for Common Ground (SCG), an NGO whose main philosophy is to "understand the differences and act on the commonalties" (SCG, n.d.a), has some of the most interesting projects using media to promote peace. In Burundi, SCG has established a radio production facility called Studio Ijambo (Wise Words); here, a combined staff of Tutsis and Hutus work together producing about fifteen hours a week of news, public affairs, and cultural programming. Among its most successful programs is *Our Neighbors, Ourselves,* "a radio drama featuring a Hutu family and a Tutsi family who live next door to each other. . . . The show describes the trials and tribulations of these neighbors and how, in the end, they reconcile their differences" (SCG, n.d.a, p. 2).

In Thokosa township, one of the most violence-ridden communities in South Africa, two commanders who have traditionally been mortal enemies, one from the Self Defense Unit aligned with the African National Congress, and the other one from the Self Protection Unit connected with Inkatha, were given access to two video cameras. Their assignment was to produce a documentary on the local killings; after six months, these two warriors have produced a collaborative film in which they attempt to find answers to the madness in their community (SCG, n.d.b).

In Angola, musicians have been divided by the civil war for years; there are National Union for the Total Independence of Angola (UNITA) musicians and Government musicians. "For someone on one side to hum a song from the music of the other was sometimes seen as a sign of disloyalty" (SCG, n.d.b, p. 3). SCG has invited musicians from both sides to produce a record and a video entitled *The Peace Song;* the video takes us behind the scenes where we can see "people who have been separated for decades come together, work together, and create together" (SCG, n.d.b, p. 3).

Elsewhere I have concluded that citizens' media can generate communication where previously communities have been excluded from the public realm. My research has documented how, through their use of citizens' media, Nicaraguan peasants (Rodríguez, 1994a), Catalonian citizens (Rodríguez, 1995), and poor Colombian women (Rodríguez, 1994b) have reclaimed their own public voices. The work of SCG shows that in situations of war, where parties in conflict have closed all communication channels, citizens' media can also re-establish dialogue. That is, if development communication articulated citizens' media as givers of a voice to the voiceless, peace communication could then envision citizens' media as facilitators of dialogue between antagonists.

Citizens' Media as Seekers of Peace Initiatives

One of the lessons to be learned from the work of SCG is that if media are to contribute to the construction of more peaceful societies, they will have to privilege peace initiatives. Even those societies imbued in extreme situations of conflict produce instances where conflict is resolved peacefully, where enemies come to an accord, or where collaboration succeeds over confrontation. Hamid Mowlana (1984) has proposed a code of ethics that makes the media responsible for giving exposure and prestige to peace initiatives and to peacemakers. Mowlana's code calls for the media to "increase the amount of information available on peaceful solutions to conflict; . . . to remind opponents of peaceful solutions to conflicts; and to confer prestige on the peacemaker" (1984, p. 34). However, it has been well documented how the mainstream media, particularly news genres, tend to select and focus on situations of conflict. Given their autonomy and their freedom to include traditionally excluded aspects of social reality, citizens' media have an immense potential to become media for peace. By attentively seeking out and exposing existing experiences of peaceful conflict resolution, by giving a voice and a platform to the individuals who have made them possible, citizens' media can bring these forms of resolution to the realm of the imaginable.

My research on women, culture, and violence in Colombia (Rodríguez, 1997) has shown that communities with long histories of violence engendered by specific material conditions breed cultural codes that naturalize violence and legitimize violent behavior as not only normal, but also effective. Such circulating cultural codes create a cultural climate in which other options are marginalized to the realm of what is unimaginable, unthinkable, or ineffective. In such cases, citizens' media can play a crucial role in retrieving those other options, such as peace initiatives, cases of conflict resolution, and negotiation through dialogue, from the margins to the center of civil society's dialogues.

Citizens' Media as Architects of Peace Genres

If the media are to contribute to the construction of peace, they will have to break away from the traditional genres, where conflict and opposition are taken for granted as necessary conditions for good drama. However, the mainstream media persistently cling to the unquestioned belief that only conflict produces marketable stories. On the other hand, citizens' media initiatives, such as those undertaken by SCG, have begun experimenting with other options to structure a narrative. In the words of SCG producers, each of their video episodes "demonstrates that good storytelling does not have to glorify conflict for its own sake—that a search for agreement can be as dramatic as a soap opera" (SCG, n.d.b, p. 1).

This becomes even clearer in SCG's *Resolutions Radio* project, a call-in talk show produced from Sarajevo and broadcast nationally. The hosts of *Resolutions Radio* are trained in conflict resolution techniques. Once the lines are open, Bosnians of all factions are invited to engage in participatory dialogue, with the host continually guiding guests toward listening to others, engaging in dialogue, and finding common solutions.

Overall, talk shows have tended to fall in the exclusive niche of polarized media narratives. In a typical Jerry Springer-style talk show, the host's role is to inspire as much conflict as possible with the guests, audience, and viewers. In contrast, Kenneth Clark, production director of *Resolutions Radio,* offers an alternative talk-show format, moving toward the use of citizens' media as a vehicle for peace.

Citizens' Media as Catalysts of Forgiveness

Could citizens' media play a role in cultivating feelings of forgiveness among communities and subjects attempting to overcome past experiences of intense violence? Some of the most interesting recent anthropological studies of violence emphasize the dehumanization of both perpetrators and victims of violence as one of the crucial outcomes of violent conflict. Victims lose their humanity as we articulate them as entirely passive recipients of a fate they cannot control. Victimizers, on the other hand, are stripped of their humanity because the social discourse within which we interpret violence has established "humanity" and "brutality" as mutually exclusive categories. Based on his work in Argentina, anthropologist Antonious Robben (1995) reminds us that the construction of peace is conditioned upon the humanization of both survivors and victimizers.

The Media Peace Centre, an NGO working toward peace and reconciliation in postapartheid South Africa, has developed a project called Video Dialogues, in which communities in conflict engage in processes of communication, understanding, and humanization (Holguin, 1998b). Produced in 1993, the first video dialogue, entitled *Abuntu Bayakhala* (The People Cry Out), encouraged members of estranged communities to begin speaking to each other; "in the video-making process people who previously did not communicate spoke out, and to each other through the camera" (Holguin, 1998b, p. 1). This type of dialogue in which, at the grassroots, communities in conflict learn to know each other and to understand each other, lays the foundations for a new social fabric that embraces forgiveness.

In communities at war, people from opposite camps commonly share the same human experiences of loss, displacement, and pain. At least this shared experience is common ground; however, by stressing difference and strengthening polarization, the mainstream media generally become instigators of conflict. Conversely, other media experiments are probing into different options, focusing more on the commonalties experienced by opposing parties as they endure war. Darko Popovic, a reporter for the Voice of America's Conflict Resolution Initiative,[5] recounts his experience in war-torn Croatia, where displaced Serbs make frequent trips to their old homes in the city of Drvar; here, though, their homes are now occupied by Croatian refugees from central Bosnia. Popovic recounts:

> Surprisingly, when the Serbs arrive, they are welcomed by the same Croats who now live in the homes of the Serbs. They offered them coffee and a local brandy, slivovitz, and invited them to stay overnight when they come the next time. . . . All of them are in somebody else's homes and in somebody else's towns and villages. They understand each other's problems and feel each other's pains. (Voice of America, 1997, p. 45)

By focusing on this type of story, the Conflict Resolution Initiative emphasizes the commonalties experienced by antagonistic communities in situations of war and conflict.

An important component of the lived experience of war revolves around feelings of empathy and understanding for the pain and loss experienced by self and others. Yet, the mainstream media systematically overlook all this as they favor one side while the other side becomes lifeless, as "a thing" incapable of communication or feelings (Galtung & Vincent, 1992, p. 127). On the contrary, by emphasizing that violent conflict immerses both parties into similar experiences of loss, pain, and grief, citizens' media can play an important role in humanizing the other, the enemy, the opponent.

Citizens' Media as Sites of Empathic Communication

From soap operas to *telenovelas* and *radionovelas,* dramatic genres have been traditionally a common staple of citizens' media. Throughout the world citizens of all ethnicities, creeds, and genders become involved in processes of video and radio production where they create their own fictional pieces, develop their own characters, and script their own storylines. Indeed, elsewhere I have shown how participating in the production of fictional video dramas engages women in intense transformative processes (Rodríguez, 1994b). As women perform fictional characters they find themselves redefining their opinion of such characters, their relationships with the characters, and, finally, their whole self-perceptions.

From the field of performance theory, Luis Valdez and Anna Deavere Smith offer valuable clues to reflect on the role of citizens' media drama in societies in conflict. On the basis of their vast experience working with politically committed theater, Valdez (National Latino Communications Center, 1996) and Smith (1993) reveal how, in situations of conflict, performing a role of the enemy has profound transformative effects in the performing subject. Smith explains: "If we were to inhabit the speech pattern of the other, and walk in the speech of another, we could find the individuality of the other and experience that individuality viscerally" (1993, p. xxvii).

Throughout the world, communities ravaged by violence are developing their own fictional dramas using citizens' media. Examples include the fictional radio drama *Our Neighbors, Ourselves* sponsored by SCG in Burundi; also, as part of the Civic Education for Peace and Good Governance, the United Nations Education, Scientific and Cultural Organization (UNESCO) supports the production of radio soap operas in Somalia (Holguin, 1998a).[6] We need to conduct ethnographic research that can assist in understanding the transformative processes of citizens engaging in media dramas where members of one party have to perform fictional characters from the opposing party. I believe this to be of great potential, as citizens' media are in a position to open a dramatic space where communities in conflict can "experience the other" (Smith, 1993, p. xxvii).

Citizens' Media as Sites to Reclaim the Experience of Violence

My final point revolves around the use of citizens' media to assist survivors of violence in processing their past experiences of violence. Anthropological studies of the lived experience of violence suggest that isolation, silence, and loneliness are primary components of the terror of violence (Nordstrom & Robben, 1995; Robben, 1995; Winkler, 1995; Zulaika, 1995). The experience of violence on one's own body and self and/or the selves of our loved ones pushes the survivor to a place where language frequently becomes inaccessible. The languages that we use to shape and to articulate our everyday life become insufficient and weak in attempting to capture the experience of violence. When a suitable language escapes us, sharing the experience with another becomes an impossibility. Citizens' media can be used to reclaim the experience of violence for the realm of human languages. Here, development communication has still a long journey toward exploring other disciplinary approaches to this subject matter, such as the anthropology of memory, the study of testimonial literature, and oral history.

CONCLUSION

Although it has taken several decades, development communication has learned that social change without the active inclusion of local communities, local social movements, and citizens rarely prevails. In this learning process, our field has had to relinquish power, resources, institutions, technology, knowledge, and skills to the people of the world. In what has proved to be a sometimes agonizing journey, development communication has succeeded in realizing important moves toward a healthy decentralization of power.

An important step of this journey has been the move away from an unconditional belief in the mass media and toward appreciating citizens' media. Through this move, we have learned to believe in the power of the people to establish and develop their own communication outlets, to weave their own communication networks, and to effect social change in their own communicative and cultural terms.

Now, a new learning journey begins as we, communication scholars as well as peace scholars and activists, come to accept that peace without the active and respectful inclusion of the peoples of the world will not happen.

NOTES

I am grateful to Lina Holguin for her generosity in sharing key information, resources, and ideas with me. Her unselfish attitude is as exemplary as it is exceptional.

1. In Rodríguez (1996 & forthcoming), I coin the term "citizens' media" as a more appropriate concept to refer to community media, participatory media, and/or alternative media. The concept emerges from the need to overcome oppositional frameworks and binary categories traditionally used to theorize alternative media. I suggest two moves to accomplish this goal: first, that instead of defining alternative media as nonmainstream media, we define them in terms of the transformative processes they bring about within participants and their communities; and second, that we break away from a binary and essentializing definition of power, whereby the mediascape is inhabited by the powerful (mainstream media) and the powerless (alternative media). This type of binary thinking limits the potential of alternative media to their ability to resist other media, and of our understanding of other instances of social change facilitated by alternative media. Instead, "citizens' media" articulates the metamorphic transformation of alternative media participants into active citizens. That is, "citizens' media" is a concept that accounts for the processes of empowerment, *conscientization,* and fragmentation of power that result when men and women gain access to and reclaim their own media. As they disrupt established power relationships and cultural codes, citizens' media participants gain power that is in turn reinvested in shaping their lives, future, and cultures. Citizens' media is a novel concep-

tual label, inspired by Chantal Mouffe's theory of radical democracy and citizenship; it is not founded on the notion of citizenship as defined by the liberal tradition.

2. For theoretical approaches as well as case studies of citizens' media, see Calandria, 1989; Downing, 1984, 1991; Downing et al., 1999; Festa & Santoro, 1987; Huesca, 1996, 1997; Huesca & Dervin, 1994; Lewis, 1984; Michaels, 1994; O'Connor, 1990; Reyes Matta, 1983; Rodríguez, 1987, 1994a, 1994b, 1995; Simpson Grinberg, 1981; Thede & Ambrosi, 1991.

3. Although mass media have very limited potential to advance peace processes, I do not want to suggest a monolithic understanding as if they have no fissures and fractures within their structures. Indeed, the existence of numerous journalists' associations and other media professionals' efforts toward peace attests to the contrary. Some such efforts include: The International Centre for Humanitarian Reporting (Switzerland), The Mediation Project for Journalists (The Media Peace Center, South Africa), The Initiative for Peace and Cooperation in the Middle East (Search for Common Ground, USA), The Pew Center for Civic Journalism (USA), The Carnegie Commission on Preventing Deadly Conflict (USA), and the Center for War, Peace, and the News Media (USA).

4. The CRC is a private nonprofit international organization and network whose mission is to facilitate the role of citizens as local and international peacemakers and to promote the education and use of nonviolent conflict resolution skills and processes (http://www.crcvt.org).

5. I hesitate to categorize Voice of America's media projects as citizens' media. VOA's persistent defense of United States elitist economic and political agenda worldwide is well known. From this perspective, VOA's communication projects can be considered far from promoting active citizenship, empowerment, and processes of power fragmentation. On the other hand, I mention their experimenting with media and the humanization of victimizers to be considered as an exceptional case.

6. This project is entirely based on participatory media production and action research.

REFERENCES

Arno, A. (1984). Communication, conflict, and storylines: The news media as actors in a cultural context. In A. Arno & W. Dissanayake (Eds.), *The news media in national and international conflict* (pp. 1–15). Boulder, CO: Westview Press.

Ashford, M. W. (1996). Peace education after the cold war. *Canadian Social Studies* [Online} , 30, 14 paragraphs. Available: http://vweb.hwwilsonweb.com/ [1999, March 2].

Barsalira, C. & Nyambura, G. (1988). Proceedings of the Seminar on African perspectives and issues on peace education and action in Africa. Lusaka, Zambia, 3–7 October.

Bruck, P. & Roach, C. (1993). Dealing with reality: The news media and the promotion of peace. In C. Roach (Ed.), *Communication and culture in war and peace* (pp. 71–96). Newbury Park, CA: Sage.

Calandria (1989). *La videodramatización popular: Retos para la comunicación participativa.* Calandria, Lima, Peru. Unpublished document.

Downing, J. (1984). *Radical media. The political experience of alternative communication.* Boston, MA: South End Press.

Downing, J. (1991). Community access television: Past, present and future. *Community Television Review,* 14(3), 6–8.

Downing, J. et al. (Forthcoming 1999). *Radical media and oppositional cultures.* Thousand Oaks, CA: Sage.

Festa, R. & Santoro, L. (1987). Policies from below. Alternative video in Brazil. *Media Development,* 34(1), 27–30.
Freire, P. (1967). *Educação como Pratica de la Liberdad. Rio de Janeiro, Brazil: Paz e Terra.*
Freire, P. (1980). *Educación como Práctica de la Libertad.* Mexico D. F., Mexico: Siglo XXI.
Freire, P. (1983). *Pedagogy of the Oppressed* (M. B. Ramos, Trans.). New York, NY: Continuum.
Galtung, J. & Vincent, R. C. (1992). *Global Glasnost. Toward a new world information and communication order?* Cresskill, NJ: Hampton Press.
Holguin, L. (1998a). Somalia. Unpublished document.
Holguin, L. (1998b). South Africa. Unpublished document.
Holguin, L. (1998c). The media in modern peacekeeping. *Peace Review* [Online], 10(4), 25 paragraphs, March 3 1999. Available: http://proquest.umi.com.
Huesca, R. (1996). Participation for development in radio: An ethnography of the *reporteros populares* of Bolivia. *Gazette,* 57, 29–52.
Huesca, R. (1997). Low–powered television in rural Bolivia: New directions for democratic practice. *Studies in Latin American Popular Culture,* 16, 69–90.
Huesca, R. & Dervin, B. (1994). Theory and practice in Latin American alternative communication research. *Journal of Communication,* 44(4), 53–73.
Jacobson, T. (1993). A pragmatist account of participatory communication research for national development. *Communication Theory,* 3(3), 214–230.
Larsen, K. (1997). Stories from the field. 12 paragraphs, March 23, 1999. Available: http://www.crcvt.org/story.html.
Lewis, P. (Ed.). (1984). *Media for people in cities. A study of community media in the urban context.* Paris, France: United Nations Educational, Scientific and Cultural Organization.
Michaels, E. (1994). *Bad Aboriginal art. Tradition, media, and technological horizons.* Minneapolis, MN: University of Minnesota Press.
Mowlana, H. (1984). Communication, world order, and the human potential: Toward an ethical framework. In A. Arno and W. Dissanayake (Eds.), *The news media in national and international conflict* (pp. 27–35). Boulder, CO: Westview Press.
National Latino Communications Center (1996). Chicano! *The struggle in the fields.* Los Angeles, CA: Author. Videotape.
Nordstrom, C. & Robben, A. (1995). *Fieldwork under fire. Contemporary studies of violence and survival.* Berkeley, CA: University of California Press.
O'Connor, A. (1990). The miners' radio stations in Bolivia: A culture of resistance. *Journal of Communication,* 40, 102–110.
Reyes Matta, F. (Ed.). (1983). *Comunicación alternativa y búsquedas democráticas.* Mexico: Fundación Friedrich Ebert & ILET (Instituto Latinoamericano de Estudios Transnacionales).
Roach, C. (1993a). Introduction. In C. Roach (Ed.), *Communication and culture in war and peace* (pp. xv–xxv). Newbury Park, CA: Sage.
Roach, C. (1993b). Information and culture in war and peace: Overview. In C. Roach (Ed.), *Communication and culture in war and peace* (pp. 1–40). Newbury Park, CA: Sage.
Robben, A. (1995). The politics of truth and emotion among victims and perpetrators of violence. In C. Nordstrom & A. Robben (Eds.), *Fieldwork under fire. Contemporary studies of violence and survival* (pp. 81–103). Berkeley, CA: University of California Press.
Rodríguez, C. (Ed.). (1987). *Contando historias, tejiendo identidades. Experiencias de comunicación popular.* Bogotá, Colombia: CINEP.

Rodríguez, C. (1994a). The rise and fall of the popular correspondents' movement in revolutionary Nicaragua, 1982–1990. *Media Culture and Society,* 16(3), 509–520.

Rodríguez, C. (1994b). A process of identity deconstruction: Latin American women producing video stories. In P. Riaño (Ed.), *Women in grassroots communication. Furthering social change* (pp. 149–160). Thousand Oaks, CA : Sage.

Rodríguez, C. (1995). Local television in Catalonia: A strategy of resistance. Paper presented at the International/development communication Division of the 45th Annual Conference of the International Communication Association, Albuquerque, NM.

Rodríguez, C. (1996). Shedding useless notions of alternative media. *Peace Review,* 8(1), 63–68.

Rodríguez, C. (1997). In the world of the father: Women gambling with death. A discourse analysis of life stories of Colombian women in violent contexts. Paper presented at the Feminist Scholarship Division, 47th Annual Conference of the International Communication Association, Montreal, Canada.

Rodríguez, C. (forthcoming). *Fissures in the mediascape. The transformative power of citizens' media.* Cresskill, NJ: Hampton Press.

Rogers, E. M. (1983). *Diffusion of innovations* (3rd ed.). New York, NY: The Free Press.

Schechter, D. (1998). Peace journalism 101. *The Nation* [Online], 267(15), 11 paragraphs. Available: http://proquest.umi.com/ [1999, March 3].

Search for Common Ground (SCG) (n.d.a). *Common Ground Productions.* Washington, DC: Author.

SCG (n.d.b). *Common Ground Productions. Videos with vision.* Washington, DC: Author.

Servaes, J. (1986). Development theory and communication policy: Power to the people! *European Journal of Communication,* 1, 203–229.

Servaes, J. (1989). *One world, multiple cultures. A new paradigm on communication for development.* Leuven, Belgium: Acco.

Servaes, J. (1992). Toward a new perspective for communication and development. In F. L. Casmir (Ed.), *Communication in Development* (pp. 51–85). Norwood, NJ: Ablex.

Simpson Grinberg, M. (Ed.). (1981). *Comunicación alternativa y cambio social: América Latina.* Mexico City, Mexico: Universidad Nacional Autónoma de Mexico.

Smith, A. D. (1993). *Fires in the mirror.* New York, NY: Doubleday.

Smoker, P. (1992). Possible roles for social movements. In K. Tehranian & M. Tehranian (Eds.), *Restructuring for world peace. On the threshold of the twenty-first century* (pp. 90–105). Cresskill, NJ: Hampton Press.

Stubbs, P. (1997). Peace building, community development and cultural change: Report on conflict resolution catalysts' work in Banja Luka, Bosnia–Herzegovina. [Online], 21 paragraphs. Available: http://wwwcrcvt.org/stubbs.html. [1999, March 23].

Thede, N. & Ambrosi, A. (1991). *Video the changing world.* Montréal, Canada: Black Rose Books.

Voice of America (1997). Conflict resolution project. Annual Report. Washington, DC: Author.

Winkler, C. (1995). Rape attack: The ethnography of the ethnographer. In C. Nordstrom & A. Robben (Eds.), *Fieldwork under fire. Contemporary studies of violence and survival* (pp. 155–184). Berkeley, CA: University of California Press.

Zulaika, J. (1995). The anthropologist as terrorist. In C. Nordstrom & A. Robben (Eds.), *Fieldwork under fire. Contemporary studies of violence and survival* (pp. 206–222). Berkeley, CA: University of California Press.

Part III

=

New Directions

12

Place, Power, and Networks in Globalization and Postdevelopment

Arturo Escobar

COMMUNICATION, PLACE, AND NETWORKS

Recent works in communication and development exhibit the richness of current debates in the field. As this volume suggests, it is time we examine the notion of power in the context of development communication. Although power has been discussed in development studies from various perspectives, from political economy to post-structuralist approaches, the link between power, development, and communication has not yet been built from critical development perspectives; hence the importance of attempts, such as those found in this chapter, to broach this task in a systematic fashion.

It is impossible currently to discuss development without referring to globalization. A particular relation between globalization, culture, and development might enable, in turn, an alternative perspective on development communication. I take as a point of departure two seemingly opposed and contradictory processes: the growing importance of technological networks and flows for the creation of the social, on the one hand; and, on the other, the defense of place against delocalizing and globalizing tendencies. I base my discussion of the importance of place, power, and networks on two projects with which I have been involved in recent years. The first involves a project sponsored by the United Nations Education, Scientific and Cultural Organization (UNESCO) and the Society for International Development (SID), "Women on the Net" (WoN), which links groups of women from all over the world through new information and communication technologies (NICTs). The second focuses on tropical rain forests in Colombia, considering current issues in understanding social movements, conservation, and development. These projects allow me to discuss contemporary concerns about using cyberspace and NICTs for the defense of place and place-based practices, with the concomitant implications for development communication.

Networks are "in" in our explanation of the world. For some, we are witnessing the rise of a new type of society, the network society, characterized by networks and flows (Castells, 1996). From the perspective of development communication, what is important is that these networks reflect the emergence of new actors, identities, and practices, such as "women on the net," indigenous peoples, environmentalists, and so on. It is important to consider, in this regard, the role of technological networks in the contemporary construction of social worlds. The Women on the Net project, for instance, highlights the ways in which women globally are using NICTs for crafting new identities. Beyond the hype and popular images, the project demonstrates concrete ways in which women from around the world can engage with these technologies as active agents, to create and build different worlds. And despite the risks of creating new barriers between those with access to the new technologies and those without it, the digital age, as the project shows, offers alternative forms of media through which women seek to achieve particular forms of gender equity (see Harcourt, 1999 for details on the project).

Similarly, rain forest political ecology highlights the defense of place and territory as an important site for the production of social worlds, the same social worlds that in many ways we are destroying. In both cases, there seems to be a paradox in the use of seemingly deterritorializing and delocalizing NICTs for the defense of place. Is it possible to use technological networks and cybercultures—the same technologies that connect places virtually while isolating them in the real world for the defense of place worlds? As it has been argued elsewhere (Escobar, 1999; Ribeiro, 1998), this paradox can be worked out, as far as social movements are concerned, only if this process is conceived as a double-sided struggle: over the character of the NICTs themselves, for their democratization in terms of design and access, and over the restructuring of the world by a type of capitalism that is fueled by the NICTs themselves. It is thus necessary and, as some groups are showing, possible to articulate cyberactivism with place-based activism in the "real" world. Strategies of communication are central to this double demand now faced by social movements. By building a bridge between cyberactivism on the one hand, and place-based activism or place-based political practice on the other, activists can integrate these different struggles in a significant and hopeful way.

In sum, with the new technological networks, we see very clearly the emergence of a set of new social actors, practices, and identities, among them women, indigenous peoples, and environmentalists. Communication questions are central to these processes, and essential to how we think about our hopes and future. Grassroots activists engaged in these networks and scholars alike concur on the importance of understanding these networks. As some even argue (Barlow, 1998; Negroponte, 1998), developing countries may leapfrog from agricultural development to cyberculture, jumping over industrial development altogether. This is a very daring but interesting proposition, and perhaps has some validity if we look at what some people are doing with electronic networks in Asia, Africa, and Latin America.

The second point involves the possibility of defending "place" in an increasingly globalized world. Let me start by defining place as the experience of a particular location that still maintains significant connection to everyday life, a certain degree of boundaries, however porous and permeable, and a certain degree of groundedness, however unstable.

"Place" thus refers to the particular site or location where people's lives and experiences are actually lived, becoming essential for thinking about identity, development, social movements, and the like. There are two features about place to emphasize. The first feature addresses what a number of people, including Turkish historian Arif Dirlik (1998, 1999) calls "the erasure of place" in globalization discourses: namely, how our theories of globalization, in equating the global with space, capital, and history and the local with place, labor, and tradition effect a veritable marginalization and erasure of place. The second feature suggests the assertion of place against that erasure, both at theoretical and social levels. The question that emerges is then: Is it possible to launch a defense of place in which place is constructed as the anchoring point for both theory construction and political action? What would be the role in such a defense of place-based practices of NICTs and technological networks, the same networks that also contribute, through their connection with technocapitalism, to the destruction of place?

Communication becomes central to enabling the link across this double-sided type of struggle. What connects place and networks is the question of power. We cannot talk about place, networks, and flows without talking about power. Many people now describe flows and networks, celebrating their potential. However, these discussions miss the importance of power, which becomes central to how we articulate a cultural politics of place, perhaps through technological networks.

POSTSTRUCTURALISM AND DEVELOPMENT

The question of development remains unresolved in any modern social or epistemological order. By this I mean the inability of development to bring lasting improvements in the social condition of much of Asia, Africa, and Latin America, on the one hand, and on the other, the epistemological crisis that seems to affect the field. After fifty years of development, including a number of years of critical development scholarship, we still have no better grasp of how to theorize or understand the reality of Asia, Africa, or Latin America in a way that leads to significant or lasting improvement. Unless we question the development model significantly, which has yet to be accomplished at the policy level, we will not be able to transcend this social and epistemological impasse.

It could be said that there have been three major paradigms for thinking about development, corresponding with three general social science paradigms. These paradigms include individual and market-based liberal theories, currently resulting in neoliberal development approaches that seem to dominate the policy field; production-based Marxist theories, which provided the foundation for dependency and world systems theories in the 1960s and 1970s, and which can be seen at play today in some neostructuralist approaches; and finally language and meaning-based poststructuralist theories, which have in recent years enabled a new type of critique of development discourses and practices. Poststructuralism is a social theory that starts by recognizing that language and discourse are constitutive of social reality; it highlights the shaping of social experience through meaning and representations, as do social facts with important power effects. Poststructuralist theory offers an important momentum to a set of pressing questions that are not satisfactorily addressed by other theories, particularly the production of subjectivity and identity through discourses and practices, the analysis of apparatuses that systematically link power and knowledge, and the construction of collective identities by social movements.

In the development arena, poststructuralism has yielded a productive set of inquiries. To begin with, this approach raises questions concerning development. Rather than asking whether development can be done differently or more efficiently, it asks: Why and through what processes were Asia, Africa, and Latin America constituted as realities for modern knowledge, and with what consequences? Second, the poststructuralist analysis of development shows the ways in which the discourse of development has produced an efficient apparatus that systematically organizes the production of forms of knowledge and types of power, linking one to the other, in the production of Third World social reality. Finally, these analyses also illuminate the dominant sites of knowledge production and this process as political, asserting at the same time the value of alternative experiences and forms of knowledge (see Escobar, 1995 and Ferguson, 1994, for a summary of this literature). In some ways, it could be said that a field of "critical development studies" of poststructuralist orientation has emerged out of the encounter between development and poststructuralism.

Poststructuralist theory, in other words, does not seek to provide mere grounds for doing development better, or even for producing a different view of development, but instead calls us to examine critically the grounds upon which development has been defined. By maintaining the instability of these grounds, we can continuously question the theories that are being produced and the shortcomings of development approaches. One of the important questions emerging from this inquiry is, of course, that of alternatives. This question has remained largely intractable. Many observers know what strategies no longer work, but very few seem to know what might work. A lot of experimentation is taking place at present with alternative approaches, especially among grassroots groups and social movements. Scholars, intellectuals, and at times policy makers are beginning to develop different forms of engagement with these groups in their efforts to promote alternative social theories and policy orientations. It is in this context that the issue of place becomes important.

FROM PLACE TO POSTDEVELOPMENT

The argument has been made recently, in a very general way, that place has been systematically marginalized in Western social theory (Casey, 1993, 1997; Dirlik, 1999). For philosopher Edward Casey, Western social theory has been overly space-centric and time-centric. Space is the absolute and universal, while place is contingent and secondary. Political economy has effected a similar marginalization of place. In recent works (e.g., Harvey, 1989), the space–time compression characteristic of contemporary capitalism entails the predominance of the space produced by capital over the place produced by labor. Places are rendered into a reservoir of cheap labor for capital to appropriate, and thus unable to ground a radical struggle.

Although interesting, this argument is problematic. In anthropology, concern with globalization has led scholars to problematize overly simplified conflations of place and culture, or place and identity (Gupta & Ferguson, 1997). In coming to terms with the dynamics of place, power, and identity, however, the field has come to highlight processes and metaphors of mobility—diaspora, deterritorialization, nomadology, displacement, traveling, border crossing, and the like—thus deemphasizing the importance of place. In globalization discourses, finally, an asymmetry exists between the global and the local, in which the global becomes associated with capital, space, history, agency, and the capacity to transform and change, while the local becomes associated with place, labor, and stagnation. These discourses take for granted a power structure in which the global always dominates over the local. This amounts, in essence, to an erasure of place.

Despite these tendencies, and perhaps as a reaction to them, there seems to be a renewed interest in place as a concept, and in the politics of place as a social process. This is happening in a number of fields and in ways that are beyond the scope of this paper, including poststructuralist political economy (Gibson-Graham, 1996), postmodern feminist geography (Chernaik, 1996; Massey, 1994), historical archaeology and the archaeology of landscape (Bender, 1998; Tilley, 1994), and ecological anthropology (Descola and Pálsson, 1996). Suffice it to say that what is emerging now from these minor but growing trends is a theoretical apparatus to articulate a defense of place as project. This apparatus is yet to be brought into development and communication.

Place has been central to the development experience, in that development projects are implemented in particular places or locations. Yet, at the same time, development has operated to erase anything that is particular to place in its application of allegedly universal and placeless interventions. In the name of progress and rationality, places have been rendered into a tabula rasa on which the universality of space and modern culture is to be inscribed. However, it has become clear by now that place-based practices and modes of consciousness continue to exist, even if hybridized with modern forms. Ecological anthropologists, for instance (Descola & Pálsson, 1996), demonstrate with growing eloquence how people construct their natural environments in strikingly different ways from modern forms. Many non-Western people exhibit or create local models of nature that retain significantly social, ecological, and political specificity. These differences are quite real and have important implications for questions of sustainability and conservation.

Confronted with this double situation of the erasure of place on the one hand, and its reassertion in certain fields on the other, the development questions thus become: Is it possible to launch a defense of place without removing places from their production by capital and modernity and without reducing them, conversely, to being the exclusive products of capital and modernity? Is it possible to see places as constructed and connected to global forces and yet avoid effacing what is specific to place, the place-based cultural, ecological, and economic practices that continue to be socially significant in the production of place? Finally, is it possible to advance this defense without feminizing or naturalizing place? For it is true that place has been feminized throughout history (Massey, 1994) and that body, home, and place have operated as sites of subordination for women and indigenous peoples. While this has been, and continues to be, true in many ways it is also important that we simultaneously visualize the continued vitality of local cultural, social, ecological, and economic practices that are still instances of difference because of their attachment to a particular place and signal how these practices may serve as an anchoring point for a different kind of development or view of the world.

To put the issue in the most general and abstract way, I would ask it in the form of a question of a utopian imagination. This is not strictly utopian, however, because the defense of place is always happening in every act of resistance and every act of cultural difference. From a utopian perspective, the question of place becomes: Can the world be reconceived and reconstructed from the perspective of the multiple, place-based cultural, ecological, economic, and social practices that still exist today in the world? How might we think about this project in social and theoretical terms? The first thing to realize is that, from the perspective of this question, postdevelopment is always under construction. We may understand postdevelopment as opening the possibility of reducing the role of development as a central organizing principle of social life in Asia, Africa, and Latin America, as a heuristic device for seeing local realities in Asia, Africa, and Latin America differently, and, finally, as a way to strive for other potential principles for thinking about and reconstructing the world. If we imagine postdevelopment in these ways, then we have to admit that postdevelopment already exists in what we have called here (placed-based) practices of difference.

THE SUPRAPLACE EFFECTS OF NETWORKS AND SOCIAL MOVEMENTS

The question that suggests itself out of this conceptualization is: While place-based struggles are not to be despised, will they amount to anything? Will they become significant beyond place itself? This is where the notion of networks offers an interesting set of ideas for thinking about the issue of "place beyond place," particularly in terms of creating place-to-place coalitions that produce supraplace or supralocal effects. The metaphor of networks is useful in this regard. In Castells's latest work (1996), for instance, he defines the fundamental feature of today's society as the networks and flows that arise out of the new technological paradigm based on information, computer, and biological technologies. These technologies transform the social, cultural, and spatial fabric of society, organizing it in new ways along networks and flows of bytes, information, commodities, media, and people. For Castells, the space of flows overtakes and overpowers the space of places, which themselves become subsumed in metanetworks. The fate of particular places depends on their capacity to insert themselves into the networks that count. Disconnection from these networks leads to instant deterioration and decline.

Similar conclusions are obtained by examining the impact of real-time technologies on everyday life, to the extent that they are seen as effacing the here and now of human activities (Virilio, 1997). History is no longer defined by the here and now but by processes that happen at a distance. This erosion of the here and now has been happening for centuries, especially in the last two centuries, grounded in a process of modernity that locates the quintessential aspect as the tearing apart of space from place by fostering relations with absent others. The norms that regulate social life come to be dictated by translocal and impersonal mechanisms of expert knowledge and administrative apparatuses linked to the state. With the advent of real-time technologies, the effacing of extension and duration that are characteristic of place-based social practice give way to a global delocalization of activity. For Latour (1993), what is most distinctive about modernity is the fact that "moderns" have invented longer and more powerful networks by enlisting the aid of nonhumans, particularly technologies, in the production of the social. If one were to contrast traditional and modern societies from this perspective, one would say that the traditional society maintains smaller local networks that mix nature and culture, whereas the modern society invents longer and more comprehensive networks based on a reputed separation of nature from culture. As Latour argues, however, what happens in reality is a proliferation of hybrids of nature and culture created by the networks linking one and the other.

The concept of network questions the dichotomy of the local and the global. Latour uses the metaphor of the railway to this end. The railroad is local at all points, but is global in that it goes to many places. It is, however, not universal because it does not go everywhere. As in the case of the railway, everything in the world today can be said to be global and local at the same time, only not in the same way. The very idea of networks thus complicates the arbitrary division between the global and the local. Used initially in social studies of science to explain the coproduction of technoscience and society, the concept of network is now used the explain the structure of society as a whole. A network is composed of a set of actors and sites that are very heterogeneous, including humans and nonhumans, organisms, people, machines, and more. Many different actors are linked through these networks. For example, in the case of the network of biodiversity production, the World Bank, the United Nations, and Northern environmental nongovernmental organizations (NGOs), along with national governments, local communities, and social movements, create a complex network through which the various actors struggle to define the discourse. Truths, discourses, objects, experts, and so on circulate and are translated, mediated, and appropriated through this network (Escobar, in press).

To the extent that networks involve a different way to understand the production of social reality, it also suggests a different theory of power. In this context, we need to see power as decentralized and disperse. Power does not reside in one particular site, even if there are of course powerful agencies, such as the World Bank, located in particular places. However, as poststructuralist theory emphasizes, power is dispersed throughout the social body and it is at once produced and contested. This understanding of power is essential for rethinking the dichotomy of the local and the global and the dominance of the global over the local. Instead, one might consider the production of "glocalities" (Dirlik, 1999), representing a type of configuration that is neither global nor local, but both global and local in particular ways. For instance, the networks of indigenous peoples of the Americas constitute an important case of network politics and identity. They have been able to construct very elaborate and effective social networks for political action. These networks rely, in part, on the Internet, being not entirely diasporic. Networks may have some diasporic component when they are committed to particular communities and territories. As geographer Sarah Radcliffe (1998) says, these networks are instances of nondiasporic transnational indigenous identities. They fit neither the identity model of diaspora, nor that of fixed identity linked to a place. They are transnationalized identities but ones with precisely the aim of defending place and culture.

For feminist political economists, instead of looking at globalization in terms of fragmentation, which is the standard view in political economy, perhaps we should think of the world in terms of coalitions. In this sense, coalitions can be defined more pertinently in terms of networks. Then we may ask: What are the kinds of politics that enable people to network and create powerful glocalities? The most important indication that these glocalities are increasingly becoming more pronounced is the fact that a number of social movements are moving beyond their immediate localities. Many indigenous movements, rain forest and women's movements for instance, have effects that go beyond their immediate localities through their connections with other movements.

Network politics of this kind are beginning to play an important role in particular struggles. For example, the infamous Multilateral Agreement on Investment (MAI) was actually defeated by very systematic, sustained work of coalitions from all over the world. Social movements in Asia, Africa, Latin America, Europe, and North America carried out both Internet and place-based campaigns in many parts of the world to oppose this proposal just before it was to be signed without consultation with civil society. There are a number of similar cases, such as that of the Zapatistas, already well known for its use of NICTs and for the creation of a worldwide set of sites of solidarity and movement support. Other examples include ecological and ethnic movements, which can be considered as movements of attachments to particular territories. The social movement of black communities of the Pacific rain forest region of Colombia, for example, defines itself as struggling both for territory and identity. This movement has articulated through its struggle an entire political ecology that entails an alternative vision of biodiversity conservation and sustainability as well as a precarious, yet important, defense of place (Escobar in press; Grueso, Rosero, & Escobar, 1998).

In these examples, it might be proper to speak of the creation of glocalities with original topological configurations, encompassing many different sites and actors across many different places. We need to be able to differentiate among the different glocalities that are coming into existence, particularly those created by the action of social movements. How are they produced? Through what combinations of actors, networks, and flows, and with what relation to places? From the perspective of postdevelopment, it is important to identify particularly those that enact a cultural politics for the defense of place (see Alvarez, Dagnino, & Escobar, 1998, for the notion of cultural politics of social movements). Movements of attachment to territory are exemplary in this regard. Although it is important not to idealize these cases, I do mean to suggest that these connections across groups merit our attention. In a general way, it could be said that these cases of social movements suggest the possibility of reorganizing social space from below rather than above. By creating supraplace effects and organizations, they might bring about a reorganization of space. As Dirlik (1999) points out, places need to project themselves into the spaces of capital and modernity to create new structures of power but in ways that incorporate places into the very constitution of these structures. It is a question of activating local knowledges and place-based practices against the imperializing tendencies of space, capital, and modernity. Social movements are pointing the way.

FROM PLACE TO DEVELOPMENT COMMUNICATION

I would like to conclude by trying to relate these concerns with place, flows, and power to issues of communication and development. First we might consider what kinds of communication might emanate from places that we can define as the sites of practices of ecological, cultural, social, and economic difference. To the extent that these practices of difference may serve as the anchoring point for a different construction of reality (and "development"), what kinds of communication might enable this process? Who may be important actors for communication in this respect? What kinds of communication tools and practices might be particularly effective in activating local knowledge and struggles for the defense of place-based cultures and identities? What kinds of networks might transform these practices of place toward becoming novel policies of development communication? We need to consider how a postdevelopment frame of communication practice may be linked with the idea of place as project, that is, with the potential to elevate local knowledges into different constellations of knowledge and power through enabling networks. This posture might also change significantly our view of development. We might ask, for example, what happens when we do not look at our clients in terms of a development agenda? How can we think about people with whom we are working in different terms?

The defense of place thus becomes a political construction that communication scholars, alternative development practitioners, ecologists, and feminists might articulate. If NICTs are fueling a type of technocapitalism that contributes to the erasure of place, then emergent practices of cyberactivism might also constitute both a struggle over the character of the new information and communication technologies, in terms of access, content, and democratization, and a struggle for the defense of place. We used to think that it was important to "think globally, act locally." At some point, we started to think that it was the other way around: "think locally, act globally." Certainly, a perspective on place seems to validate this position. However, to the extent that all global thinking contributes to the erasure of place, now we might have to conclude, with Esteva and Prakash (1997), that the aim of struggle against global delocalization should be to "think locally, act locally." We can conceive of localities as locally connecting with each other in terms of solidarity, in order to resist the global thinking that dominates imperialist and neoliberal approaches, because any type of global thinking, in sum, might may be too complacent with the same reconstruction of the world. This poses new challenges for development and development communication.

REFERENCES

Alvarez, S. E., Dagnino, E., & Escobar, A. (Eds.) (1998). *Cultures of Politics/Politics of Cultures: Re-visioning Latin American Social Movements.* Boulder, CO: Westview Press.

Barlow, J. P. (1998). Wiring Africa. *Wired,* http://wired.com/wired/archive/6.01/barlow.html.

Bender, B. (1998). *Stonehenge: Making Space.* Oxford, UK: Berg.

Casey, E. (1993). *Getting Back into Place: Toward a Renewed Understanding of the Place-World.* Bloomington, IN: Indiana University Press.

Casey, E. (1997). *The Fate of Place.* Berkeley, CA: University of California Press.

Castells, M. (1996). *The Rise of the Network Society.* Oxford, UK: Basil Blackwell.

Chernaik, L. (1996). Spatial Displacements: Transnationalism and the New Social Movements. *Gender, Place and Culture,* 3(3), 251–275.

Descola, P. & Pálsson, G. (Eds.). (1996). *Nature and Society. Anthropological Perspectives.* London, UK: Routledge.

Dirlik, A. (1998). Globalism and the Politics of Place. *Development,* 41(2), 7–13.

Dirlik, A. (1999). Place-based Imagination: Globalism and the Politics of Place. In A. Dirlik (Ed.), *Places and Politics in the Age of Global Capital.* New York, NY: Rowman and Littlefield (in press).

Escobar, A. (1995). *Encountering Development: The Making and Unmaking of the Third World.* Princeton, NJ: Princeton University Press.

Escobar, A. (1999). Gender, Place and Networks. A Political Ecology of Cyberculture. In W. Harcourt (Ed.), *Women@Internet. Creating New Cultures in Cyberspace* (pp. 31–54). London, UK: Zed Books.

Escobar, A. (In press). Whose Knowledge, Whose Nature? Biodiversity Conservation and Social Movements Political Ecology. *Journal of Political Ecology.*

Esteva, G. & Prakash, M. S. (1997). From Global Thinking to Local Thinking. In M. Rahnema & V. Bawtree (Eds.), *The Postdevelopment Reader* (pp. 277–289). London, UK: Zed Books.

Ferguson, J. (1994). *The Anti-Politics Machine.* Minneapolis, MN: University of Minnesota Press.

Gibson-Graham, J. K. (1996). *The End of Capitalism (as we knew it).* Oxford, UK: Basil Blackwell.

Grueso, L., Rosero, C., & Escobar, A. (1998). The Social Movement of Black Communities in the Southern Pacific Coast of Colombia. In S. Alvarez, E. Dagnino, & A. Escobar, (Eds.), *Cultures of Politics/Politics of Culture* (pp. 196–219). Boulder, CO: Westview Press.

Gupta, A., & Ferguson, J. (Eds.). (1997). *Culture, Power, Place.* Durham, NC: Duke University Press.

Harcourt, W. (Ed.). (1999). *Women@Internet: Creating New Cultures in Cyberspace.* London, UK: Zed Books.

Harvey, D. (1989). *The Condition of Postmodernity.* Oxford, UK: Blackwell.

Latour, B. (1993). *We Have Never Been Modern.* Cambridge, MA: Harvard University Press.

Massey, D. (1994). *Space, Place and Gender.* Minneapolis, MN: University of Minnesota Press.

Negroponte, N. (1998). The Third Shall be First. *Wired,* http://wired.com/wired/archive/6.01/negroponte.html.

Radcliffe, S. (1998). Unpublished Research Proposal.

Ribeiro, G. L. (1998). Cybercultural Politics: Political Activism at a Distance in a Transnational World. In S. Alvarez, E. Dagnino & A. Escobar, (Eds.), *Cultures of Politics/Politics of Culture* (pp. 325–352). Boulder, CO: Westview Press.

Tilley, C. (1994). *A Phenomenology of Landscape.* Oxford, UK: Berg.

Virilio, P. (1997). *Open Sky.* London, UK: Verso.

13

Border Crossings

Gender, Development, and Communication

Edna F. Einsiedel

A border is something one crosses; it is a boundary which demarcates one region from another. Things happen at borders. There is either a barrier designed to keep things in or out or a permeable edge, committed to maintaining life by promoting percolations across its borders. Cultural borders can show this vitality; the intermixing that results gives rise to hybrid cultures enriched by this exchange. So can intellectual borders.

I begin from a promontory where the field of development communications has been on one side and where it may be going on the other. Where Dominant Paradigms ruled on the one hand, pluralisms of frameworks now mark the terrain. Where to go from here? If I take the question of the place of gender in development and communications as illustrative, I propose that the metaphorical border of permeability, commensurability, and hybridity can serve us fruitfully.

How to make our way through the thickets of this varied terrain? In this chapter, I outline some of the shifts in feminist theorizing about gender and make the case for applying some of these lessons to theorizing about communications and development. In using the metaphor of hybrid cultures at the borders, I maintain that enriching our theoretical reflections will come not from erecting boundaries but by examining what emerges from the open interchange at the crossing.

THE DEVELOPMENT CONTEXT

Development is no longer what happens "over there," but is as much in our backyards. There is a "First World" in the so-called South as there is a "Third World" in our midst. Globalization has proceeded full speed with modernity's compression of time and space. Culture and identity have become the new arenas for engagement (Barber, 1996; Huntington, 1996), becoming the sites for expression and enrichment at the same time that they are also today's most vicious battlegrounds. Environmental challenges are made more intractable with their global impacts. In this context, the challenges for theorizing about development are immense. Development theorizing is a critical process that works in the spaces between the academy and the sites of policy and practice. In this sense, we do not have the luxury of mere philosophizing. Our work as development communicators puts us squarely in the midst of a commitment to and interest in questions of equity and equality, sustainability, and issues of social justice and social change. Given these challenges, there is much to learn from reflecting on the on-going work on gender and development.

GENDER ISSUES: WHAT HAVE WE LEARNED?

Understanding some of the key ideas and approaches in feminist theorizing and their connections with the development arena will help us examine the connections between theory, policy, and practice. It is not my intention to undertake an elaborate or exhaustive discussion of the many theoretical debates. In identifying some of the key ideas on gender that have had major impacts, I look at how these have expanded our understanding of development problems and processes. In turn, I argue that these sometimes seemingly disparate and incommensurable approaches have something to say to each other. Finding ways to accommodate their various strengths can, in fact, enrich our understanding of development and processes of social change.

Early theorizing on gender and development asked the questions "where are the women?" and "what are they doing?" The next question is essentially theoretical: Why are things as they are? This question, although theoretical, also suggests practical points of intervention with Boserup's (1970) seminal work on the absence of women in the development landscape, focusing attention on the importance of filling the gap of women's absence as an entry point to understanding the challenges of development. Here, policy shifts were notable as development agencies hurried to fill this gap. Further work, which disaggregated impacts of development by gender, demonstrated that development did not affect men and women in the same ways. In fact, many outcomes showed that as men gained from development interventions, women were often even more disadvantaged (see, for example, Jackson, 1985; Jain, 1984). This approach, focusing on redressing women's inequity, put its emphasis on making opportunities available to and accessible by women.

A second approach, a critique of this earlier modernist version of the status of women, suggested that women's subordination was in fact a result of systemic oppression. The change envisaged by this view requires transformation of structures of subordination that have been inimical to women, including changes in legal systems, civil codes, property rights, labor conditions, and reproductive rights (DAWN, 1985). Sen and Grown (1987) have articulated this position rather clearly: Equality for women is impossible within the existing economic, political, and cultural processes that reserve resources, power, and control for small groups of people. But neither is development possible without greater equity for, and participation by, women. Our vision of feminism has at its very core a process of economic and social development geared to human needs through wider control over and access to economic and political power (Sen & Grown, 1987, p. 20).

The shifts in conceptual and policy approaches to gender in the development arena are, of course, more nuanced than these two approaches (see, for example, Moser, 1993). I present these as a way of describing two very different (and often seen as competing) views of why things are as they are: In the first instance inequities arise from lack of opportunities and in the second inequities are among the outcomes of oppressive social and political structures. Both approaches, however, are attached to transformative agendas.

Underlying these approaches are practical questions of where the locus of change might be. Is it agency that matters? Is change going to come primarily from the individual? Or are we helpless in the face of structural forces? These questions suggest different arenas for intervention but are not mutually exclusive.

Two areas of policy and practice help to illustrate this problem. The history of fertility management policies illustrates the challenges and dilemmas of population intervention programs on women's lives. It is useful to remember the framework and context within which birth control programs were advocated. In the West, birth control proponents were advocating women's rights to reproductive choice as a basis for women's personal and political emancipation in the mid-nineteenth century. Not long after, the medical establishment and eugenicists took on the debate about reproduction and disseminated their perspectives to colonial regions.

In the first half of the twentieth century, many Southern countries began implementing fertility control policies. Many of these were based on the argument that population control was one of the factors that could undermine or promote economic development. In historical reconstructions of these policies, women's groups have demonstrated how fertility approaches have been influenced by political, cultural, ethnic, and racial factors (DAWN, 1994; Pyne, 1994). Some examples to illustrate:

In Puerto Rico, a government report admitted that by 1968, 35 percent of Puerto Rican women of child-bearing age had been sterilized as part of a policy that overpopulation strained resources. Many of the women who could not afford private health care were sterilized as they used the public health system, often without their knowledge (Correa, 1996, p. 30).

In Indonesia, targets were set for contraceptive adoption, specific to each method and imposed at all levels of the bureaucracy. This approach led to a high incidence of coercion, with officials at various administrative levels employing heavy-handed methods of persuasion in order to meet ambitious adoption targets, often infringing on human rights, a pattern also found in Indian, Bangladesh, and China (Correa, 1996, p. 26).

In Brazil, contraceptive approaches were restricted to the birth control pill and female sterilization. More than 80 percent of pills were supplied by drugstores (in contrast to NGO- or state-subsidized approaches in other countries). For many Brazilian women, recourse to sterilization (among the highest rates in the world) became a way out of the problems of poverty, lack of reproductive choice, and market conditions (Correa & Petchesky, 1994).

In Sri Lanka, the government made it a priority to invest in family planning but embedded this within broader considerations for universal education and primary health care. Its fertility drop (52 percent) surpassed many of its South Asian neighbors.

These snapshots point to the very different conditions within which women's reproductive opportunities and options operate.

In the economic or productive sphere, numerous gender interventions have targeted the poorest of the poor, many of whom were women. What has been the experience in this regard? If we take the example of microenterprise activities for women, some of the case studies relating to the extension of credit to poor women have yielded positive outcomes in terms of the empowerment of women (Carr, Chen, & Jhabvala, 1996). Understanding that "empowerment" has been an overused term, the various diverse indicators point to a positive story. They have demonstrated changes in such things as increased productive capital, increased assets for household consumption, increased credit worthiness, and a decrease in the gap between men's and women's wages (see Ray & Vasundhara, 1996; Selim, 1996). In turn, these changes have improved women's self-worth, enhanced their decision-making influence, and promoted greater community involvement. Many of these programs were operative at the microlevel and some demonstrated success despite inhibitory factors at the level of the state or the broader culture. In other instances, despite gaining some measure of economic independence in the household and in the community, many women remain limited by legal and cultural sanctions that minimize these gains. For example, marriage and kinship systems and laws still serve to keep women subordinated. In patrilineal communities, women continue to face restrictions on where they can live and whether they can inherit property. The net result is that in many places women's dependence on men is legally perpetuated. Unless changes can also be made at the structural level, economic independence will be limited at the local level. These illustrations serve to remind us that as local contingencies affect women, as do structural conditions, making the need to think at both levels critical.

Within the academy, broader conceptual shifts were occurring. In posing the earlier question "where are the women?" it was necessary to stake out a position that treated women as a class apart from men. It was an essentialist position, which faced substantial and substantive critique from women of color and Third World women, arguing that women's voices were not a monotone and that perspectives differed according to race, class, and ethnicity. Identity became the watchword, a position that also carried undertones of the essentialism it sought to criticize.

A variant on this position on identity was a social constructivist position, one that stressed that powerful social pressures produced identities that were constructed and were essentially mutable. Its underlying premise was that socialization processes and social structures could be changed.

More recently, there has been a shift to the postmodern position of emphasizing difference. This has found supporters among some feminists who have called for the recovery of women's voices and the development of knowledge from the standpoint of women's "lived experience." However, in philosophizing about difference in persuasive and sophisticated terms, postmodernists, some feminists charged that still demonstrated a blind spot when it came to advocacy for social change (Halberg, 1992).

A number of case studies, many done by women from the Third World, began showing the contingencies in women's lives. The particular experiences of the *maquiladora* in the textile plant in Mexico (Fernandez-Kelly, 1997), the computer chip worker in Malaysia (Arrifin, 1984), or the street vendor in India were in this vein, illustrating the particularities of women's lives at work.

Programs and practices are still extant reflecting these approaches. If systematic and cultural biases work to exclude girls from schooling opportunities open to boys, these can be changed with macrolevel legislative and cultural tools. In a recent assessment of the UN pledge in 1990 to make the education of girls universal by 2000, a report by the UN International Children's Emergency Fund (UNICEF) concluded that "all evidence points to a girl's enrollment rate as static" (Stackhouse, 1999, p. A1). However, the few success stories all pointed to combining grassroots efforts with cultural and policy initiatives (Stackhouse, 1999, p. A13).

IMPLICATIONS FOR DEVELOPMENT POLICY AND PRACTICE

As shifts in theoretical thinking have occurred, the links to policy and practice have also been evident. The examples I have used have demonstrated that if we think about extending credit to women or providing contraceptive services in the village, we cannot escape having to think about or relate to women in the context of their roles in the household or community (and neither can the women we work with on the ground). We cannot escape having to consider how overarching structures impede or enhance our activities within the home or in the community. This is the micro- and macrolinkage. By the same token, neither can those who make policy at the national or international levels escape thinking about how they conceptualize gender and gender relations (a so-called theoretical question).

For example, the Organization for Economic Cooperation and Development's (OECD) Development Assistance Committee on gender equality, in reflecting on past lessons learned, recognized that

- the problem is not women's integration in development, or their lack of skills, credit or resources, but the social processes and institutions that result in inequalities between women and men to the disadvantage of women.
- that inequalities between women and men are not only a cost to women but to development as a whole, and thus must be conceived as societal and development issues rather than a "woman's concern."
- there are political as well as technical aspects that must be taken into account in addressing inequalities: it is not only a matter of "adding women in" to the existing processes and programs, but of reshaping them to reflect the visions, interests and needs of women and to support gender equality (OECD, 1998, p. 13).

These statements recognize the limitations of the earlier approaches that focused almost entirely on redressing the absence of women in the development picture. They stress the importance of social and political contexts and focus on "social processes and institutions." It is an important institutional-level lesson. To put these into practice remains a significant challenge, as many international assistance agencies still remain uncomfortable with transformative agendas at the macrolevel (Marchand & Parpart, 1995).

The Communication Challenges

While the old communication question, posed in linear fashion, asked who was saying what to whom and with what effects, the questions on development issues tend to carry with them the richer undertones of complexity, difference, and historical specificities. We might ask whose voices are heard, what values are articulated, what representations are foregrounded, or what discursive practices are framed? We can ask these in both structural contexts as well as contexts at the microlevel (see Einsiedel, 1996). And always these are posed in terms of why these are as they are, what they would mean for women, and how we go about changing them if such transformations were warranted.

The View From the Borders

In drawing this landscape of conceptualizing women's conditions and strategies for change in theoretical and policy arenas, we find views that are often offered as THE way for redressing issues that women face. While some may offer strong (and important) rationales of fundamental philosophical commitments, this is insufficient justification, given the diversity and complexity of challenges for women. The particular goals at hand and the practicality of strategies required demand much more. Consider, for instance, the ten areas of critical concern for women articulated in the Beijing Platform for Action requiring concrete action by governments: unequal access to education and training; unequal access to health care and related services; violence against women; inequality in economic structures and policies, in all forms of productive activities, and in access to resources; inequality in the sharing of power and decision making; insufficient mechanisms to promote the advancement of women; inadequate protection and promotion of women's human rights; stereotyping of women and inequality in women's access to and participation in communication systems, especially in the media; gender inequalities in the management of natural resources and in safeguarding the environment; and persistent discrimination against girls and violations of their rights (Beijing Umbrella Network, 1996, p. 125).

To say these challenges are immense is an understatement. The question ought to be then: What kind of theorizing can pursue multiple approaches to development, using each approach to both inform and critique the others, questioning what they derive from each other, and respecting the differences between perspectives? This is the type of question that springs from viewing boundaries not as impermeable walls, but as sites for exchange and developing the vigor that can arise from hybridity.

When we focus on the issue of women's rights as human rights, this universalizing tendency can be balanced and enriched by some attention to the constitution of subjects and identity. At the same time, we recognize that within our local, multiply situated, historically constituted selves, we harbor desires for membership and participation in the human community.

What this means methodologically is also clear. We need the best and most diverse set of tools at our disposal. These can range from ethnographic approaches to economic indicators analysis. The quantitative–qualitative divide that has often plagued, and sometimes paralyzed us is something we have to leave behind. In commenting on this false dichotomy, Hammersley argues that

> what is involved is not a cross-roads where we have to go left or right. A better analogy is a complex maze where we are repeatedly faced with decisions, and where paths wind back on one another. (1992, p. 160)

The eclecticism of methods within the feminist big tent illustrates this view.

The challenge to our scholarship lies in understanding the needs for attunement to the historical and particularistic nature of knowledge, yet at the same time recognizing the premise of commonalities in the human condition—and in working to improve these conditions, which is, after all, what development work is all about. Indeed, these common understandings, across specificities, are the bases for communication. Many of these ideas exist or coexist with some tension. But tension can be a positive force for reflexive thinking and critical analysis, which can be the basis for informing one's self and the other. I want to inhabit a field of development and communications that occupies borders, between well-inhabited terrains of thoughtful paradigms, sometimes with tensions not fully resolved, frequently with syncretic moves. From such borders, the world looks richer and full of promise.

REFERENCES

Arrifin, J. (1984). Impact of modern electronics technology on women workers in Malaysia. In M. Aziz, C. Yip, & L. Ling (Eds.), *Technology, culture and development* (pp. 64–78). Kuala Lumpur, Malaysia: University of Malaya Press.

Barber, B. (1996). Jihad *versus McWorld: How globalism and tribalism are reshaping the world.* New York, NY: Random House.

Beijing Umbrella Network (1996). *Beijing and beyond: Summary of the platform for action.* Ottawa, Canada: Renouf.

Boserup, E. (1970). Women's role in economic development. London, UK: Allen and Unwin.

Carr, M., Chen, L., & Jhabvala, R. (Eds.). (1996). *Speaking out: Women's economic empowerment in South Asia.* London, UK: Intermediate technology publications.

Correa, S. (1996). *Population and reproductive rights: Feminist perspectives from the south.* London, UK: Zed books.

Correa, S. & Petchesky, R. (1994). Reproductive and sexual rights: A feminist perspective. In S. Gen, A. Germain, & L. Chen (Eds.), *Population policies reconsidered: Health empowerment and rights* (pp. 32–50). Boston, MA: Harvard School of Public Health.

Development Alternatives with Women for a New Era (DAWN) (1984). *Population and reproductive rights.* London, UK: Zed books.

DAWN (1994). Rethinking social development: DAWN's vision. *World Development,* 23(11), 2001–2004.

Einsiedel, E. F. (1996). Action research: Implications for gender, development and communications. In D. Allen, R. Rush, & S. Kaufman (Eds.), *Women transforming communications: Global intersections* (pp. 49–58). Thousand Oaks, CA: Sage.

Fernandez-Kelly, M. P. (1997). Maquiladoras: The view from the inside. In N. Visvanathan, L. Duggan, L. Nisonoff, & N. Wiegersma (Eds.), *The women, gender, and development reader* (pp. 148–156). London, UK: Zed books.

Halberg, M. (1992). Feminist epistemology: An impossible project. In S. Hall, D. Held, & D. McGrew (Eds.), *Modernity and its futures* (pp. 118–129). Cambridge, UK: Polity press.

Hammersley, M. (1992). *What's wrong with ethnography?* London, UK: Routledge.

Huntington, S. (1996). *The clash of civilizations and the remaking of world order.* New York, NY: Touchstone.

Jackson, C. (1985). *Women's roles and gender differences in development cases for planners.* West Hartford, CT: Kumarian Press.

Jain, L. C. (1984). *Grass without roots.* New Delhi, India: Institute of Social Studies Trust.

Marchand, M. & Parpart, J. (1995). *Feminism, post-modernism and development.* London, UK: Routledge.

Moser, C. (1993). *Gender, planning, and development.* London, UK: Routledge.

Organization for Economic Cooperation and Development (OECD) (1998). *Development assistance committee sourcebook on concepts and approaches linked with gender equality.* Paris, France: OECD Publications.

Pyne, H. H. (1994). Reproductive experiences of needs of Thai women: Where has development taken us? In G. Sen & R. Snow (Eds.), *Power and decision: The social control of reproduction* (pp. 89–101). Cambridge, MA: Harvard University Press.

Ray, N. & Vasundhara, D. P. (1996). Like my mother's house: Women's thrift and credit cooperatives in South India. In M. Carr, M. Chen, & R. Jhabvala (Eds.), *Speaking out: Women's economic empowerment in South Asia* (pp. 162–170). London, UK: Intermediate Technology Publications.

Selim, G. (1996). Transforming women's economies: Bangladesh Rural Advancement Committee (BRAC). In M. Carr, M. Chen, & R. Jhabvala (Eds.), *Speaking out: Women's economic empowerment in south Asia* (pp. 72–86). London, UK: Intermediate Technology Publications.

Sen, G. & Grown, C. (1987). *Development, crisis, and alternative visions: Third World women's perspectives.* New York, NY: Monthly Review Press.

Snyder, M. (1995). *Transforming development: Women, poverty, and politics.* London, UK: Intermediate Technology Publications.

Stackhouse, J. (1999). Education's greatest failure. *Globe and Mail,* January 12, A1.

14

The Contexts of Power and the Power of the Media

Bella Mody

The contexts of power in society are economic, political, cultural, and technological. Changes in the dominance of one group (be it based on gender, ethnicity, language, religion, region, or economic assets) are a result of the continuous struggle over resources, material (e.g., land) and cultural (e.g., how we live, speak, and behave). Dominant groups use all of the tools at their command, including power over the ownership, financing, management, professional values, equipment, programming, and media audiences, to influence subordinate groups' perceptions of a particular society.

Writing about communication technology in general (1983, 1988) and satellites in particular (1987, 1991), I intended to provide an alternative to the technological determinist framework for scholarly and policy discourse about media hardware. The notion that the characteristics of technology have an overwhelming influence on social effects, irrespective of who uses them and to what ends, was adopted by most communication scholars uneducated in social structural analysis or development praxis. I wanted national policy makers to analyze the power structure before they made technology adoption decisions. Little did I know that I was merely asking public policy analysts to do what those in the private sector already did: environmental analysis as the crux of strategic management of firms (Fahey & Narayanan, 1986).

The purpose of this chapter is historical, analytical and prospective. It describes U.S. research of the 1940s that established the limited effects of the media; shows how these findings were ignored when media were promoted as a panacea for developing countries in the 1950s and 1960s; and then documents the to-be-expected disappointment with media's contribution to national development in the subsequent decade. Shortcomings in program production and developing country dependence on foreign imports have culminated in the privatization of the ownership of domestic media systems, broadcasting from foreign satellites, and cosmetic program localization. The power of entrenched developing country power structures and the impotence of media-only interventions for social change are illustrated through a devastating experience from the Kheda Communication Project, initiated by India's space technology applications program in the mid-1970s. In the current context of developing countries, more than a billion people still live on less than one dollar a day.

The major global contextual power today is private capital. Foreign aid and the nation–state are in decline. Income gaps are widening between developed and developing countries and within developing countries. Many have written about media being only a complement to other inputs for social change (e.g., Hornik, 1988). This chapter agrees that a communication-only strategy for social change is doomed, but for very basic reasons: continuing limited media availability, in addition to the impotence of media alone to make an impact on the multidimensional complexity of social change. A new broad-based research agenda for communication in developing countries, rooted in the experiences of particular societies, is proposed.

THE RISE OF THE MEDIA FOR DEVELOPMENT FIELD

The power context that gave rise to the strategic use of print, radio, and television media for "national development" in Third World countries was the Cold War (Mody, 1997). The United States and the then Soviet Union were battling for global influence. While we know little about how the former Soviet Union used communication media to help it to win friends and influence nations, we do know a lot about U.S. policy and practice (Samarajiwa, 1987; Simpson, 1994). During World War II, many of the U.S. founders of the field of communication worked on the design and evaluation of media campaigns in support of the Allied war effort. Daniel Lerner wrote his doctoral dissertation, entitled *Sykewar,* on psychological warfare against Germany in 1949. Classical studies that gave birth to mass communication research in the United States (Lowery & DeFleur, 1995) also influenced the conceptualization of media-for-development. These include the World War II propaganda studies, the Yale attitude change experiments, Lazarsfeld's research at Columbia University, and the Iowa diffusion studies.

The U.S. War Department's Information and Education Division hired Nathan Maccoby, Carl Hovland, Irving Janis, and many other psychologists to evaluate the impact of the *Why We Fight* U.S. domestic propaganda films of World War II. Their experiments showed that films could teach facts, but that these were forgotten by viewers in a few weeks; their research also showed that films were even weaker at changing opinions and attitudes than they were at teaching facts.

Between 1946 and 1961, the Yale Program of Research on Communication and Attitude Change conducted more than fifty experiments with live speeches and illustrated lectures to understand how people's beliefs, attitudes and behaviors could be manipulated by modifying who said what (and how) to whom. Carl Hovland and his colleagues learned about the characteristics of an effective communicator, about how to "inoculate" audiences against subsequent propaganda, and how to bring about at least short-term (three to four weeks) changes in opinions and attitudes.

In the early 1940s, surveys conducted by Lazarsfeld and his doctoral students at Columbia University found that the power of radio and print media were limited by individual differences in personality, group affiliations, and interpersonal networks. Their study of the impact of the Roosevelt re-election campaign found only 8 percent had changed their opinion; for the majority, the primary effect of the media campaign was reinforcement of existing opinions, not opinion change. The most important influence on how people voted was interpersonal; the impact of media was filtered through social and cultural power structures, such as family and friends.

In rural Iowa, Ryan and Gross also found the diffusion of hybrid corn to farmers around Ames, Iowa, did not show that print and radio media were particularly powerful in either informing farmers or persuading them to adopt innovations. These findings from classical communication studies (Lowery & DeFleur, 1995) conducted around the 1940s in the United States showed particular media programs were not powerful manipulators of our hearts and minds in the short run. George Gerbner's significant demonstrations of the effects of media on the cultivation of social values over time were not conducted until the mid-1960s.

After World War II, some journalists and social scientists who worked for the U.S. government gravitated to the United Nations Scientific Educational and Cultural Organization (UNESCO), which the United States had helped to establish, while others went to universities. Wilbur Schramm and Daniel Lerner, who joined the faculties of U.S. universities, received funds from UNESCO, U.S. foreign aid agencies, and the Voice of America, giving the agencies old disproven ideas about media power for use in developing countries in return. It is conceivable (but unlikely) that they had scholarly reasons to think developing country populations would be more impressionable than U.S. audiences, or that power structures and agents of socialization more porous than in the U.S. With hindsight, it is easy for us to identify errors, baseless optimism, naiveté, or ignorance in earlier scholars, but these critiques advance scholarship.

Daniel Lerner (1958), who is credited with writing the first academic book on media and the modernization of developing societies, suggested that developing countries use the power of print, radio, and TV as syringes to inject empathy into the traditional personalities of their citizens to increase their social mobility. His communication model of economic growth and increased voting specified that people would need to migrate from villages to cities and, once there, literacy and mass media automatically would lead viewers to modern ways of living. The data he used on eight Middle Eastern countries (collected for a 1950 audience research contract from the Office of International Broadcasting that then ran the Voice of America) was not an adequate test of his media-for-modernization proposition. Nevertheless, Lerner's idea of using media for modernization acquired power in an intellectual climate and political context characterized by Walter Rostow's (1960) work on the West-to-East diffusion of modern science and technology as part of the non-Communist alternative for developing countries, and by David McClelland's (1961) work on the need for injecting achievement into fatalistic traditional personalities.

Wilbur Schramm, an alumnus of the U.S. Office of War Information, wrote *Mass Media and National Development* (1964) while a consultant to UNESCO. This very readable book diffused Lerner's unsupported notion of powerful media effects to developing countries. Young rural sociologist Everett Rogers exported Ryan and Gross's conceptualization of the process of the adoption of innovations, and the role of media in this process, to support the diffusion of Western scientific attitudes and technology as recommended by Rostow. UNESCO awarded research grants to Rogers and his doctoral students at Michigan State University, including Luis Ramiro Beltrán from Bolivia, Juan Díaz Bordenave from Paraguay, and Joseph Ascroft from Malawi, to understand how they could use media to support the process of the diffusion of innovations in their own countries.

Beyond the Hardware

When Lerner and Schramm advocated media pipelines, they did not pay attention to the following:

1. media content,
2. the high cost of program production,
3. ownership and administration of media systems (to ensure prosocial content),
4. access to production skills (limited in many countries),
5. middle- and upper-class preferences for entertainment programming rather than agricultural, health, and educational programming,
6. the advertising industry's desire to use media to carry commercials (thus limiting educational programming in order to maximize audiences), and
7. the limited diffusion of media technologies (such as radios, televisions, and Internet-ready personal computers).

Developing countries discovered that harnessing even the limited information-transmission power of media required professional expertise in message design. The content of the message had to be locally usable, credible and presented in an attention-getting format for the intended audience. In the 1970s and 1980s, the U.S. Agency for International Development (USAID) sought to remedy the lack of this expertise in developing countries by funding projects in Nicaragua, Kenya and Thailand, among other sites, which focused on designing instructional content through curriculum development and systematic formative research.

External Dependency

It was only a matter of time before resource-constrained print media, radio, and TV stations turned to importing Anglo-American news and entertainment. Writing only a couple of years after Schramm's advocacy of media for national development, Dizard (1966) highlighted aspects of the international context that should have been factored in, such as the unidirectional nature of television program flowing between industrialized and developing countries and the Hollywood dominance of TV program production (see Guback, 1969 for a similar argument about film). Schiller (1969, 1973) drew attention to the general process of cultural imperialism, particularly in terms of satellites, while Tunstall (1977) declared the media were American. Fifteen years after Schramm's initial advocacy, Boyd-Barrett (1977) drew attention to what he called the media imperialism process, whereby the ownership, structure, distribution, and content of media in one country were subject to external pressures from more powerful media interests of other countries, without proportionate reciprocation. This focus on externally dominated communication media complemented national economic and cultural dependency perspectives on Third World development that Boyd-Barrett had encountered in his work in Latin America (e.g., Cardoso, 1979). Third World countries had less political, economic, and cultural power than their former colonizers and the United States to determine and implement their own national agendas.

The Fall of Media for Development

Third World countries eagerly sought these magical multipliers of information diffusion, such as printing presses, film projectors, and radio stations, from USAID and U.S.-influenced UNESCO. However, within a decade Schramm (1976) and Rogers (1976) were independently writing about the disappointing performance of media power in producing change. On a visit to India, Rogers invited my senior colleague, Prakash Shingi at the Indian Institute of Management in Ahmedabad India, and me to contribute to his 1976 volume. One of our findings addressed the power of the urban middle class (agricultural scientists and TV producers) over TV program topics and scripting. This resulted in the development of agricultural TV programs that did not address the information needs and vocabulary range of small and medium farmers and even less, those of landless laborers. Those who could adopt the Western scientific practices featured in these agricultural TV broadcasts were those who had capital (land), education, and purchasing power. U.S.-based media advocates who had ignored United States findings on the limited effects of the media solutions found that the populations of developing countries were not any more malleable than U.S. audiences. In addition, they had not factored in the mediating influences of distinct economic, political, and social contexts of power in developing societies.

How Context Qualifies Media Influence

In the early 1970s, I worked as a social researcher on the first major direct broadcast satellite TV project in the world, the NASA–India Satellite Instructional TV Experiment (SITE) (Mody, 1979). I was appalled on my initial visits to villages when I encountered men and women telling me living conditions had not improved since the British left India some twenty-five years earlier: They said India was still someone else's *raj* (empire), not theirs. My colleagues and I were sure that television cameras used to expose violations of national laws and human rights would help villagers speak back to power sources, thus making it difficult for upper-caste people, large landlords, and men to continue to exploit lower-caste folk, landless day-wage laborers, and women. Most of us thought knowledge served as power under all conditions: All that was needed to dismantle caste, class, and gender abuse was the harsh glare of investigative documentaries and drama on local TV. We did not think about the lack of essential fair and honest legislative, judicial, and executive systems needed to support televised exposés.

The Kheda Communication Project, a federal government noncommercial unit of India's SITE project, pictured itself as an agency confronting an oppressive agricultural power structure. To illustrate this argument, I recall one of many episodes from twenty years ago. While the details may have blurred, the essence remains accurate. A producer and a writer for the local news show, called *Vaat Thumaaree* (Your News), drove to the experimental villages every morning to record incidents of injustice and exploitation as they happened, for immediate transmission that evening. The assumption was that exposing unfairness in this way would help resolve the situation promptly. Initially, the team focused on incidents of local government inefficiency, such as roads not being repaired and schools being run without teachers. The TV team interviewed victims and then responsible officials on camera to extract commitments and dates for resolving identified problems. After a reasonable amount of time, crews returned to these sites to report on whether problems had been resolved as promised. Several officials were thus shamed into efficiency.

The crew then moved on to more serious problems of exploitation, such as family agribusinesses not paying their labor the legal minimum wage. The plan was to feature daily interviews of this kind on the same topic in different villages so the heat would be too much to bear for the offending large farmers and local district government (equivalent of a county in the United States) officials who sheltered them. As the daily coverage continued, daily laborers could not believe the government agency was standing up for them against the local economic power structure, but neither could these economic powers. The federal government agency, full of physicists, TV producers, and social scientists, was dabbling in rural development. Large farmers began to protest by writing letters to the physicist–director, complaining that large farm owners were being incorrectly portrayed on their local TV station programmed by the space agency. They then marched to the TV station to protest this portrayal when nothing changed.

Televised interviews of abused labor continued as the harvest season began. Empowered by the coverage and the then Prime Minister's emergency program guaranteeing enforcement of minimum wage laws, laborers decided to strike against landlords for the legal minimum wage. The assumption was that landlords would have to negotiate at this time if they wanted their crops harvested. On the first day of the strike, the local news showed large farmers expressing shock. Disaster struck on the second day: Large farmers hired paramilitary gangs to burn down the huts of the strikers who had been interviewed on television. My TV production colleagues were safely in bed in their homes in the city two to three hours' drive away; the laborers they had interviewed saw their lives and livelihoods go up in flames. No police came, having been paid off by the large farmers. The laborers were not organized and had no political party to turn to. No villager would talk to Kheda Communication Project TV crew henceforth.

The power of TV had confronted the well-organized economic and political power structure of the village and had lost. The opposition of the formal federal political structure had no teeth in comparison to the well-orchestrated local political and economic forces. This anecdote is intended to show how the investigative journalism potential of the media can be constrained by the power structure in a society. It also indicates the need for social research at the interface of media and power structures to specify the conditions under which media power can be harnessed as a successful agent for change.

It was clear to the liberal, well-intentioned urban TV crew of the federally run Kheda Communication Project that they had been irresponsible and naive to think of taking on the village power structure alone, without a master plan or a supporting organization of landless laborers, lawyers, and state government officials. We learned firsthand that development and social change through communication technology alone was impossible. Public-service activists experience confrontations like this every day in every part of the world.

Rather than openly taking sides with the exploited as in Kheda, the Western commercial journalistic tradition has radio, TV, and the press playing a nonpartisan role, with the confidence that remedial action will occur through a relatively honest police and court system. This assumption is not justified, however, in that media systems in the industrialized North would not be able to sustain many investigative programs such as CBS's *60 Minutes*. Similarly, the assumption that honest government leaders will act to resolve problems in less developed societies is equally unjustified.

Privatization

In the latter half of the 1980s, as support for privatization of state activities grew in Washington, D.C., USAID grants to Johns Hopkins University's Population Communication programs focused developing country attention on private sector media formats, performers, and approaches to attract audiences for prosocial ends. Funding from the Rockefeller Foundation for entertainment–education projects followed. Early research has begun to investigate whether U.S. researchers of these current programs might be repeating possible conceptual and ethical errors made by Lerner and Schramm in promoting particular media and program formats (e.g., entertainment education) (Sherry, 1997).

Investors and telecommunication operators from saturated markets in Europe and North America have expanded into the less mined markets of Asia, Latin America, and the Caribbean since the mid-1980s. This is a time when state telecommunication entities have also been looking for investment capital and new technologies. With improved audio, video, and text transmission facilities, these agencies intend to meet the unmet demands of their business sectors and to compete in the increasingly global economy (Mody, Bauer, & Straubhaar, 1995).

THE CURRENT CONTEXTS OF POWER

To understand the possible role of media in support of human welfare in developing countries in the next century, it is necessary to update constantly our environmental analysis, as do private businesses and an increasing number of nonprofit businesses. Developing countries and communities must systematically identify the national development threats and opportunities that they face within their own power structures. Although there has been more progress reducing poverty in the past fifty years than in any comparable period in human history, still more than a billion people live in extreme poverty, lacking clean water, sanitation, electricity, and education (UNDP, 1998). Media specialists need to specify which media conditions and discourses (if any) and which power contexts might contribute to preferential development for the poor.

The external context of developing countries has become increasingly private and corporate in the last fifteen years: Over half of the largest economies are not represented by countries, but by private profit-making corporations. The discourse on development in the mainstream media and in the trade press focuses on removing restrictions on private capital rather than on public service applications, such as health, education, and welfare. The collapse of Communism and a weak Russia have been accompanied by Anglo-American unity and regional power blocs based on a variety of factors, including fundamentalist religious resurgence, primordial ties, personal authoritarianism, and military might. As the polarizing Cold War reasons for official development assistance disappeared, rich industrialized country members of the Organization for Economic Cooperation and Development (OECD) reduced their foreign aid. In 1997, OECD countries gave less than 1/4 of 1 percent of their gross national product in foreign aid, with the small Nordic countries continuing to give the most (1 percent of their GNP), in contrast to the United States donating only 0.08 percent (World Bank, 1998).

As states become increasingly financially strapped, they tend to follow IMF advice to provide opportunities for foreign capital investment and to allow competition. In the process, states are losing their control over agriculture, health, and industry. Along with the recent adoption of privatization and competition in the developing world, the United Nations Conference on Trade and Development (UNCTAD, 1997) has documented a widening of resource gaps between the industrialized North and the less-developed South, as well as within developing countries. The gap between industrialized countries and Latin America has grown most quickly, but other differences, such as the level of resources between industrialized nations and those in Africa, persist. Within developing countries, the income share of the richest 20 percent has risen consistently since the introduction of privatization, deregulation, and competition. Thus, most countries appear to be losing proportionately their middle classes, as discrepancies between skilled and unskilled labor grow in this age of capital-intensive, labor eliminating technology.

Limited media access

Although the processes and effects of mediated communication have changed in major ways since the 1960s, there is still limited access to media technologies in many areas. Current statistics show that for every 1,000 people in developing countries, there are only 185 radio receivers, 145 TV receivers, 39 main telephone lines, 3.6 cellular subscribers, 6.5 personal computers, and 0.5 Internet users (UNDP, 1998). Yet, the ownership of radio, TV, and telecommunications has become less state centered and more private. The availability of foreign capital has increased the number of main telephone lines. Even when they continue to be state operated, operations of media are financed by advertising and are focused on private profit maximization. Regional satellite systems, such as STAR in Asia, provide direct-to-home systems and national cable operators with current Hollywood shows. News channels that antagonize national political regimes are willingly withdrawn from programming, so commercial interests are not hurt, as in the case of STAR dropping the BBC from its satellite feed to China.

In addition, domestic productions imitate foreign formulas and genres. The format of domestic and foreign broadcasts becomes increasingly similar to action–adventure fantasies, for example, sometimes imported and cheaply dubbed, with plots having little resemblance to everyday problems in Los Angeles or Nairobi. Where necessary, media producers use minimum “localization” of foreign formats and stories to attract the right demographic audiences for advertisers. Moreover, only 3 percent of Internet host computers are in developing countries, which include more than three-quarters of the world’s population (Mody, 1999).

MASSIVE DEVELOPMENT CHALLENGE, LIMITED MEDIA

One out of six people in the world still lives in poverty, most being in developing countries. The current private sector approach to development seems to be benefiting the rich rather than the poor.

As we enter the next century, communication media continue to be sparsely available. They are increasingly financed through advertising and thus are programmed with entertainment that attracts the largest audience with purchasing power. A little more than forty years ago, development communication was proposed in the United States as the strategic application of communication technology in response to an international Cold War agenda, ending up as the transmission of particular messages by states in developing countries to achieve the objectives of their ruling regimes. The reach of the ruling regime was extended, through the power of the media, to large numbers of people (hence low per-unit cost) simultaneously (hence speedily), in attempts to effect compliance through manipulation of cognitions, values, and behavior. With current trends against state control, communication for public welfare and development for the poor seem to be left to nongovernmental organizations (NGOs), financed by foreign and domestic civil organizations.

Research on communication processes in developing countries must evolve beyond communication and development as a mechanistic strategy with associated tactics, to a full-blown disciplinary perspective on communication-in-society, sophisticated enough to be specific to particular developing country time-and-place conditions and universal enough to be comparable. There are lessons to be learned from communication research and praxis elsewhere; most importantly, the research agenda for communication in developing countries needs to avoid mistakes of context-free research and ungrounded theory.

A new research agenda for communication in developing countries is recommended, moving beyond state initiatives to nongovernmental civic movements. Like the formal school system, media represent another input into affecting social values. It is crucial, then, that we identify the domestic and external conditions in a society's power structures, as well as the political and economic conditions in their media systems, which may positively influence both opportunities for food, shelter, and education for the billion-plus poor and the awareness of human neighborly responsibility of the five billion not poor others.

REFERENCES

Boyd–Barrett, O. (1977). Media imperialism: Toward an international framework for the analysis of media systems. In J. Curran, Gurevitch, M. & J. Woollacott (Eds.) *Mass communication and society* (pp. 116–141). London, UK: Sage.

Cardoso, F. H. & Faletto, E. (1979). *Dependency and development in Latin America.* Berkeley, CA: University of California Press.

Dizard, W. P. (1966). *Television: A world view.* Syracuse, NY: Syracuse University Press.

Fahey, L. & Narayanan, V. K. (1986). *Macroenvironmental analysis for strategic management.* St. Paul, MN: West Publishing.

Guback, T. H. (1969). *The international film industry.* Bloomington, IN: Indiana University Press.

Hornik, R. C. (1989). The knowledge–behavior gap in public information campaigns: A development communication view. In C. T. Salmon (Ed.), *Information campaigns: Balancing social values and social change* (pp. 113–138). Newbury Park, CA: Sage.

Lerner, D. (1958). *The passing of traditional society.* Glencoe, IL: Free Press.
Lowery, S. & DeFleur, M. (1995). *Milestones in mass communication.* New York, NY: Longman.
McClelland, D. (1966). *The achieving society.* New York, NY: Free Press.
Mody, B. (1979). Programming in SITE. *Journal of Communication,* 29(4), 90–98.
Mody, B. (1983). First World technologies in Third World contexts. In E. M. Rogers (Ed.), *Communication technology in the U.S. and Western Europe* (pp. 134–149). New Jersey: Ablex.
Mody, B. (1987). Contextual analysis of the adoption of a communication technology: The case of satellites in India. *Telematics and Informatics,* 4 (2), 151–158.
Mody, B. (1988). From communication effects to communication contexts. *Media Development,* 3, 35–37.
Mody, B. (1997). Cold War to world business system. *Journal of International Communication,* 4(2), 1–2.
Mody, B. (1999). The Internet in the other three quarters of the world. *Aspen Institute of Information Studies Annal,* April.
Mody, B., Bauer, J. M., & Straubhaar, J. (1995). *Telecommunication politics: Ownership and control of the information highway in developing countries.* Mahwah, NJ: Lawrence Earlbaum.
Mody, B. & Borrego, J. (1991). Mexico's Morelos satellite: Reaching for autonomy? In G. Sussman & J. Lent, (Eds.), *Transnational communication: Wiring the Third World* (pp. 150–164). Newbury Park, CA: Sage.
Rogers, E. M. (1976). *Communication and development: Critical perspectives.* Thousand Hills, CA: Sage.
Rostow, W. (1960). *The stages of economic growth: A non–Communist manifesto.* London, UK: Cambridge University Press.
Samarajiwa, R. (1987). The murky beginnings of the communication and development field. In N. Jayaweera & S. Amunugama (Eds.), *Rethinking development communication* (pp. 3–19). Singapore: AMIC.
Schiller, H. I. (1969). *Mass communication and American empire.* New York, NY: August M. Kelly.
Schiller, H. I. (1973). *The mind managers.* Boston, MA: Beacon Press.
Schramm, W. (1964). *Mass media and national development.* Stanford, CA: Stanford University Press.
Schramm, W. & Lerner D. (1976). (Eds.) *Communication and change: The past ten years and the next.* Honolulu, HI: University of Hawaii Press.
Sherry, J. (1997). Prosocial soap operas for development: A review of research and theory. *Journal of International Communication,* 4(2), 75–101.
Simpson, C. (1994). *Science of coercion: Communication research and psychological warfare 1945–1960.* New York, NY: Oxford University Press.
Tunstall, J. (1977). *The media are American.* London, UK: Constable.
United Nations Conference for Trade and Development (UNCTAD) (1997). *Trade and development report 1996.* Geneva, Switzerland: UNCTAD.
United Nations Development Program (UNDP) (1998). *Human development report 1998.* New York, NY: Oxford University Press.
World Bank (1998). *Assessing aid: What works, what doesn't and why.* New York, NY: Oxford University Press.

15

Accounting for Power in Development Communication

Karin Gwinn Wilkins

Development communication refers to the strategic application of communication technologies and processes to promote social change. Although currently the theoretical approaches and research findings of development communication are seen as applying to any community actively engaged in strategic social change, historically development discourse has been concerned with project interventions in an international setting, funded through wealthy agencies and implemented in nation–states with comparatively fewer financial resources.

Future trends in development communication need to consider power more explicitly in theory and in practice. This approach builds on a reflexive stance of scholars and practitioners, who recognize the limitations of current discourse and intervention.

ACCOUNTING FOR POWER

Power should be a central consideration in reconceptualizing the theory and practice of development communication. There are many different ways to understand and define power. Lukes reminds us that no one definition of power will serve all cases (1986, p. 5). There are many debates concerning the conceptualization of power, such as whether we are concerned with the production of intended effects or the capacity to produce them (Aron, 1986), or the degree to which resistance might be relevant or feasible (Lukes, 1986).

These differences over definitions stem from perspectives of power. Olsen and Marger (1993) describe different approaches, beginning with a Marxist perspective, which emphasizes the economic and material foundation of society and describes social change as occurring inevitably through a dialectic process of class conflict. An élite perspective, in contrast, recognizes the ability of a small, cohesive group to control resources, but also considers social change to be more circumscribed by the very institutions, such as the government, military, and media, that support this élite group. Thus, gradual change may be possible, as conflicts occur not between classes but within élite groups (Prewitt & Stone, 1993).

Instead of insisting on one particular perspective, I suggest that we consider how frameworks of power help us understand processes of social change. For the purpose of this chapter, I consider power as an ability to shape social contexts, building on Lukes's third level of power. This third level subsumes both a first level, referring to decision-making power that affects others' actions, and a second level, concerning the power to prevent activities from occurring.

Within an interactive, dynamic system, agents of powerful institutions have the capacity to shape the contexts in which problems and solutions are determined. In this framework, power is unevenly held but established through interaction (Simmel, 1986) within existing networks (Foucault, 1986). Moreover, power is not conceived as the property of an individual (Arendt, 1986), but is manifest in the institutions that offer certain high-level agents authority (Simmel, 1986), functioning within political and economic systems (Habermas, 1986). This structure involves a network of people and institutions, through organizationally based power in economic, political, military, and ideological domains (Dumhoff, 1993).

Maintaining power requires securing legitimacy among those who are governed (Arendt, 1986; Skocpol, 1993). This legitimation may be promoted through the ideological production of discourse (Foucault, 1986). Gramsci (1971) articulates a process of hegemony, through which powerful groups attempt to maintain consent by controlling ideological institutions. Downing explains that this ideological domain represents "a terrain of struggle for organized political forces . . . in their attempt to claim control over the direction of society's development" (1996, p. 200).

These theoretical understandings of power offer a great deal to our reconceptualization of development communication. Seeing development as a discourse, we may examine the assumptions implicit in the frameworks justifying strategic intervention. Through discourse, institutions create knowledge about groups of people, through their representation in constructed categories. Seeing development as a practice within a global economic and political system, we may illuminate the conditions through which certain problems and groups attract visibility and become reconstituted for the purpose of intervention. Seeing development as organizational intervention, we may explore the organizational contexts and projects' characteristics that guide implementation. Although some of the concerns raised more generally about development are relevant to a discussion of power, development communication may be seen as a special case in which institutions engage in ideological production through strategic intervention using communication processes and technologies.

INSTITUTIONAL DISCOURSE

I begin by conceptualizing development as a discourse and then review how this discourse has shifted over time in offering visibility to different issues and groups. By discourse, I refer to an understanding of development as a set of interpretations that are structured through institutional statements about people, places, and problems. As Crush explains, development discourse becomes "constituted and reproduced within a set of material relationships, activities and powers—social, cultural and geo-political" (1995, p. 6). These relationships are manifest through the actions of development institutions, working in their global context. Discourse perpetuates the interests of the agency promoting these interpretations and therefore should be understood as political and not neutral (Escobar, 1995a). The categories constructed through development discourse not only shape problems and those perceived to suffer from those problems, but also legitimize appropriate solutions (Rakow, 1989; Schön, 1979). Within this process, some agents hold more power than others to structure frameworks of issues and interventions.

This power to shape reality about the very nature of social change is then held by institutions acting within historical and geographical contexts (Crush, 1995; Escobar, 1995b). Power of this nature is rooted in an ability to articulate knowledge, specifically about others. In reference to Orientalism, Said suggests that to "have such knowledge . . . is to dominate it, to have authority over it" (1978, p. 32). Said (1978, 1993) and Escobar (1995b) agree that development has worked historically as another form of colonizing discourse.

Early approaches to development privileged economic conditions within the nation–state. President Truman's 1949 speech, suggesting that global poverty might be resolved through strategic industrialization, urbanization, and technology, launched this U.S. perspective (Escobar, 1995b; Melkote, 1991). Schramm (1963), Lerner (1962), and others believed that communication would foster this path toward universal modernization by encouraging individuals to act and think in more empathic ways and establishing the infrastructure needed to facilitate commercial growth and democratic governance.

As the documented conditions of many in impoverished nations did not improve despite the introduction of many development programs, the development model was critiqued on several grounds from the 1970s on (Melkote, 1991; Rogers, 1976). The initial premise that all societies would evolve along similar paths was replaced with a more contextual understanding of development. In addition to moving away from a universal path or goal, equity and distribution grew in import relative to an earlier emphasis on economic growth. This was also the era of the "basic needs approach," emphasizing the fundamental resources people need for survival. Still, these new approaches did not question the very premise that development would alleviate problematic conditions.

In addition, others raised serious concerns regarding the receipt of development aid as perpetuating dependence of poorer countries on wealthier bilateral and multilateral agencies. This concern with development as a form of cultural imperialism, perpetuating dependency, moved the focus from modernization within a nation–state to concern with an international structure of nation–states with different degrees of power. Dependency scholars reminded us then of the power structure within which developing countries work, situating power in the hands of wealthier nations (Schiller, 1991).

Against the dominance of a global market system, some groups organize to promote the idea of a global civil society, recognizing the importance of postmaterialist values (Calabrese, 1997). While some insist on conceptualizing the development process within a global structure, others point to local, community-level efforts as appropriate domains for examining social change (Huesca, 1995; see also Escobar, this volume, for discussion of global–local distinction). Recent attention to social movements complements participatory approaches by emphasizing the ability of marginal communities to control their own social change, but also by situating these processes within contexts differentiating levels of power (Gamson & Wolfsfeld, 1993).

New approaches to development, referred to by some as "postdevelopment," establish social movements as radical alternatives, promoting marginal interests against dominant development structures and ideologies (Escobar, 1995b; Moore, 1995). In this regard, social movements are not seen as a way to transform or improve development, but as "symbols of resistance to the dominant positions of knowledge and organization of the world . . . for the reimagining of the 'Third World' and a post–development era" (Escobar, 1995b, p. 227). This understanding of social change corresponds with Freire's (1983) approach to using communication processes, through dialogue, as a way to recognize and then resist oppression.

Several scholars are now beginning to remark upon a "crisis" in development, questioning the entire project (Moore, 1995; Parpart, 1995). To do so, they examine development discourse (Crush, 1995), not only in terms of its historical claims, but also in terms of its current concerns, such as sustainable development, structural adjustment, and population. The latter issue, population, tends to be connected with environmental degradation (Williams, 1995) or limitations (Mitchell, 1991), proposing a balance between demography and geography. Several authors (such as Mackenzie, 1995; Moore, 1995; Williams, 1995) suggest that these frameworks objectify and subjugate the very people they intend to serve.

Similarly, sustainable development, as an approach that articulates the need to serve a current generation without compromising the interests of a future generation, is critiqued on several levels. First, this approach reclaims the importance of economic development, albeit with an added interest toward environmental preservation, and second, it assumes that the earth can and should be managed, by changing the irrational behavior of the poor (Escobar, 1995a). This discourse legitimizes and rationalizes economic growth and efficiency within a global capitalist system, ignoring "destructive social consequences and human costs" (Ferguson, 1995, p. 130).

Development discourse involves the institutional production of texts, justifying intervention. Through this discourse, people, as well as places and conditions, are categorized through a bureaucratization of knowledge. This process involves the creation of "techno-representations," in Escobar's words, "endowed with complex political and cultural histories" (1995a, p. 213) that create visual structures of groups without allowing them to be heard. Development institutions then have the ability to create knowledge about and represent others (Escobar, 1995a; Said, 1978, 1993).

Examining development discourse over time, one can see that groups and issues shift in their importance. The visibilities of rural poor and women, for example, grew during the 1970s (Escobar, 1995a). The issue of Women in Development (WID) became more prominent by 1975, when the United Nations launched the Year of Women. This discourse valued women's contributions as economic producers and as human reproducers (Staudt, 1985). Attention to WID gradually shifted toward a concern with "gender and development" (GAD), changing the frame toward an understanding of gender as a socially constructed category (Wilkins, 1997). Recent literature proposes a new shift toward "international feminisms" (Sreberny-Mohammadi, 1996), recognizing differences across class, race, and other social categories (Mackenzie, 1995).

Despite this shift in discourse, women still dominate the focus of attention in development communication in health, population, and nutrition projects, particularly in their role as reproducers (Wilkins, 1999). Thus, in practice gender appears to operate in a way that essentializes women according to their biological conditions rather than account for their social, political, and economic relationships. Moreover, women in these projects tend to be targeted as individual consumers, assuming that they will facilitate social change through their successful purchase of suggested services and products.

Another important trend in representation is the emergence of the "consumer" as an explicit category of beneficiary (Wilkins, 1999). This implies that communication interventions are targeting those with the capacity to purchase products or services, in the process of improving their conditions. This category implies a different metaphor of social change than working with the "poorest of the poor," whose circumstances may preclude active participation in the marketplace.

Development communication projects, like many Western communication campaigns, tend to represent their beneficiaries as individuals in need of information or persuasion (Salmon, 1989). This interpretation of a beneficiary is problematic, blaming individuals for the very problems the interventions claim to intend to resolve (Mody, 1991). In this regard, the cause of the social problem addressed is located within an individual decision to change, rather than a problematic structure that limits the distribution of resources or even a normative climate that constrains the possibilities for change.

Development institutions produce these categories in their production of knowledge about the people they intend to help and the problems they believe to be relevant. Formative research used in the design of these interventions, summative research used to evaluate, and managerial monitoring of planning and implementation are all used in the process of constructing communities, problems, and interventions.

INSTITUTIONAL PRACTICE

One may locate power within the development institutions engaged in its practice. Development communication, as a strategic intervention, is implemented by agencies working within organizational contexts, conditioning the norms of interpretation, and political–economic structures, constraining the possibilities for decision making. Situating development communication within structures of power implies that the interventions themselves need to be contextualized beyond a simplistic media effects model. Instead of focusing on the reception of communication campaigns, this framework would ask us to consider the organizational contexts within which social problems and their solutions are articulated. Organizational contexts encompass both structural (in terms of interorganizational relations) and normative (in terms of shared approaches to social problems and their solutions) conditions (Putnam & Pacanowsky, 1983).

A range of institutions may be involved in the process of using communication to promote strategic social change. Development projects tend to be supported through bilateral and multilateral institutions, along with national agencies and nongovernmental organizations (NGOs). Each organization may play multiple roles: as a donor distributing resources to another organization, as a recipient receiving resources, and even as a referent to other organizations engaged in similar activities. The funding relationship may be characterized in terms of the degree of concentration or control exhibited or the extent of autonomy restricted. A development agency rarely serves exclusively in either a donor or a recipient role but acts in different capacities in relation to different organizations. An NGO, for example, may receive bilateral funding, but then in turn supports other development agencies. These relationships compose a structure of institutional activity, which guides the process of implementation.

Governments, along with other agencies, create programs to promote social change within their own territorial domains. Within states, the politically powerful may be seen as holding the ability to control political, economic, and ideological institutions (Olsen & Marger, 1993). States must deal not only with the internal divisions of power, but also within a global system of nations with different levels of access to resources. States with adequate resources to do so have the capacity to act as bilateral agencies, sponsoring projects in other countries. The U.S. Agency for International Development (USAID) is one of many bilateral institutions, with comparatively more resources to invest in the development project than many other agencies. Because of its prominence as a donor and as a referent, it is critical to observe trends in USAID practice, such as its movement toward the private sector in its economic and social development programs (Mitchell, 1991; USAID, 1993; Wilkins, 1999). One might also study internal dimensions of development organizations, such as the distribution of resources and the establishment of offices devoted to particular concerns (Staudt, 1997).

Multilateral agencies combine resources from two or more government institutions to support development projects. Many United Nations (UN) organizations, such as the UN Development Programme (UNDP) and the UN Population Fund (UNFPA), fit this category. Similar to bilateral institutions, multilateral agencies have been accused of promoting projects that do not question existing power structures, thereby serving a global élite (Escobar, 1995a; Williams, 1993).

Although some point to NGOs as important actors in the development sphere (such as Mody, 1991), it is not easy to generalize the function of this category of agency. Some NGOs receive a high concentration of funding from government sources, while others limit or deny this source of revenue. Those that do rely on government funding may be co-opted within the process of creating and implementing strategic interventions (MacDonald, 1995). Some NGOs though are able to resist promoting the agendas of larger agencies, either through strongly establishing their own strategic interests or through limiting the nature or proportion of received resources. Some community groups, collectively promoting social movements, do not represent formal NGO status but merit attention due to their critical role in engaging alternative visions of social change.

Development communication interventions are implemented by agencies and communities working within a global system. Recent conceptualizations of development argue that social change processes may be more adequately conceived on different spatial or local levels, in terms of social movements, connected through global rather than national parameters (see Escobar, this volume). These trends toward globalization are explained through the growth of international agencies and global forms of communication and production (Schiller, 1991).

This global power system appears to be dominated by a few wealthy nation–states, particularly the United States, and transnational corporations (TNCs), sharing interests and practices toward markets and consumers (Schiller, 1991, p. 21). These powerful institutions may enforce co-optation as well as control of media technologies and industries, with little consideration of inequities in use or access (Steeves, 1993). While global capital may not be homogenizing communities around the world, these processes may be consolidating heterogeneous groups for the purposes of consumption and tourism (Escobar, 1995b, p. 99).

Development discourse itself may be seen as legitimizing global capitalism as a natural and universal system (Moore, 1995, p. 7). A trend toward privatizing development interventions (Wilkins, 1999) corresponds with broader policy shifts toward deregulation and privatization within and across political boundaries (Mohammadi, 1997; Moore, 1995). These trends serve the interests of those agencies that benefit from the growing dominance of a global capitalist system, limiting the efforts of poorer communities and nations in their quest for capital to direct their own social change.

STRATEGIC INTERVENTION

As a strategic intervention, development communication works with communication technologies and processes to promote social change, engaging many substantive fields, such as health, nutrition, education, population, agriculture, and microenterprise. Whether explicit or implicit, frameworks of development communication posit a source of power in their conceptualizations of the social change process. Both modernization and dependency frameworks share an assumption that media have a great deal of power to affect audiences, while participatory and social movement approaches highlight the ability of communication processes and technologies to facilitate the strategic interests of marginal communities.

Although communication interventions may be united by their assumption that information may be an appropriate means to resolve social concerns, they are divided in their approaches to intervention. Social problems, and consequently the interventions designed to resolve them, are constructed by practitioners working within organizational contexts, which are guided and constrained by normative climates and political–economic structures. Those groups and persons participating in the construction of communication campaigns have power with respect to their ability to define problems, appropriate solutions, and beneficiaries (Gergen & Gergen, 1983; Salmon, 1989). Some issues are then selected over others for intervention.

Communication interventions use communication technologies and processes in many ways, for a variety of purposes. Among other functions, communication technologies may be used as low-cost loudspeakers, as motivators of demand, or even as legitimators (Hornik, 1988); these technologies may also be directed toward individual, social, institutional, or policy change. Communication processes may be used to facilitate the planning, implementation, or dissemination of an intervention. Involving beneficiaries in these communication processes may help avoid the failure of development communication interventions to account for peoples' existing knowledge and concerns (Mody, 1991).

Communication interventions may fail for a variety of reasons. Hornik's (1988) review of development communication projects suggests that many fail due to inappropriate theoretical approaches, poor program implementation, inadequate resources, or lack of political support. Understanding the political and economic contexts in which these projects are introduced may also allow us to have a better sense of how these interventions are interpreted. For example, one might need to assess the commercial context in which social messages are introduced, in order to gauge the environment in which beneficiaries are being asked to respond. Evaluations of communication projects tend to focus on the social conditions of individuals within defined groups, ignoring other salient conditions, such as other messages supported through the media in accordance with dominant political and economic agents.

An underlying issue here is who might be engaging in the production of these interventions and for whose benefit. When strategic interventions for social change encourage individuals to consume, then the interests of the commercial and public systems do not diverge. The social marketing model (McGuire, 1989) follows this trend, suggesting that individuals may improve their problematic conditions through prudent choices in the marketplace. Social marketing coincides with a broader trend toward commercializing social issues, such as public health. For example, many development agencies have devoted substantial resources to education about and distribution of oral rehydration solutions (ORS), a critical resource in alleviating devastating dehydration that accompanies diarrhea in infants. Now multinational corporations are absorbing this function, creating cereal-based ORS to market to adults as well as infants (Basic Support for Institutionalizing Child Survival, 1998).

Through this approach, beneficiaries of public programs are constructed as consumers, media are deemed useful to the degree they change behavior, and social change is situated within individual responses to market conditions. Characterizing social change within a commercial structure resonates with globalization trends privileging the role of multinational corporations as dominant institutions. Social marketing is quite popular among USAID projects, working within existing power structures to promote gradual change in support of a global capital system.

Other models of intervention differ from social marketing in their approaches to social change. Some efforts, for example, attempt to influence decision makers who have the capacity to change policies of key institutions or to foster gradual normative change about particular issues. While a variety of institutions implement projects attempting structural change, multilateral agencies and NGOs tend to orchestrate projects intending to educate over the long term.

Another model suggests that information be offered for its own merit, as a human right, leaving aside the potential outcome of the intervention. A participatory model that conceptualizes participation as an end in itself would fit this mold (Melkote, 1991). This approach to communication intervention engages a social process by which groups with common interests jointly construct messages to improve their situation or change unjust social structures (Mody, 1991). Communication, then, enables people to recognize their oppressive circumstances, and then perhaps act collectively to transform their situation (Freire, 1983). NGOs and local community organizations tend to support these approaches in attempts to contest dominant frames and structures.

Although these interventions may seem valuable as a potential form of resistance, there are a number of concerns with their implementation. In their attempts to address local needs, some interventions may result in perpetuating inegalitarian power structures, particularly across gender, within communities. Moreover, participation, without concomitant changes in structural conditions, may not be sufficient to foster substantive social change (Escobar, 1995b; Mody, 1991).

Media provide critical sources of information and socialization in many of our communities. In development communication, interventions are designed to use these technologies or processes strategically to promote defined social change. As in media studies, key questions regarding strategic communication intervention include: Who controls the production of knowledge, and by extension, mediated messages? Who has access to this production process? And what are the constructions of people, problems, places, and solutions embedded in this discourse? An assumption here is that the production of strategic communication, as in any other media industry, conveys the interests of dominant agents within a global system, becoming a site for ideology to be produced and reproduced (Mody, 1991). Instead of focusing on media as isolated tools, we need to focus on the processes of power that contribute to the production of communication intervention.

The selection of channels within an intervention may rest on several concerns. At times projects may include implementation decisions based on political considerations, such as a need to legitimate or elevate a sponsoring political agency through an élite medium, like the Internet or television. When projects have more independence from these concerns, decisions may be grounded in a concern with the access of beneficiaries to the channel, or even in assumptions made about the various effects mediated and interpersonal channels might have. Some assume, for example, that people may be more persuasive than media in the process of social influence; Hornik (1989), however, recognizes the potential for mediated technologies, particularly when people both recognize intervention concerns as their own and have the capacity to act on them.

The potential for an intervention either to engage resistance or to support dominant institutions is not inherent within a channel but contingent upon the context in which it is introduced. Melkote (1991) demonstrates how folk media may be used in many ways, as participatory tools for community action or as government means for disseminating information. Some groups who wish to engage in more radical visions of social change may opt for using alternative instead of dominant media systems, particularly if they believe that certain media industries will not portray their interests favorably.

Some new trends appear to do more to support the existing global economic system than to question it, positioning social change as a gradual process to facilitate at an individual level. Enter–educate strategies, for example, expand upon social marketing ideas by using popular media to promote social messages. This has become an increasingly popular strategy in many countries around the world, including India and Brazil, since a Peruvian radio drama was broadcast in 1969, highlighting a young woman's advancement through her skillful use of a Singer sewing machine (Singhal & Rogers, 1989). While this type of intervention is intended to influence individuals toward socially beneficial goals by attracting their attention with enticing media formats, enter–education projects may be seen as promoting social change in a way that does not question existing economic or political systems.

Similarly, new communication technologies are being used in development projects in support of global, rather than national, economic domains. Some see new communication technologies as advancing "irreversible social and political change" (Bugliarello, 1995, p. 76). This framework assumes movement toward a global economic structure to be neutral and automatic, instead of recognizing political connections. Communication technologies then move from being constructed as tools for modernization toward being vehicles for privatization.

Current enthusiasm for new communication technologies replaces an earlier emphasis on public programs within the nation–state with a drive toward privatizing public interventions within a global context. Many emerging programs using new communication technologies for development attempt to integrate participants into a global information economy (Wilkins & Waters, forthcoming). Like many other projects, a central tenet of this approach is that private sector investment is necessary to build an information infrastructure. Consequently, for less wealthy nations to "participate" in this globalization, they are urged to privatize their cultural industries just as the industrialized nations have done. The potential risks from engaging in this global community include loss of control over cultural industries, loss of capital to multinational corporations, and loss of power over policy decisions.

This integration into a global economy raises again potential concerns with dependency. As Reeves (1993) argues, the ability to produce and use new technologies is concentrated in an élite group of multinational corporations and nations (such as the United States and Japan). For a less wealthy nation to use these technologies, it would need to acquire hardware, software, and maintenance from these wealthier groups, thus reinforcing structures of dependency (Schiller, 1991). Such an investment would not only increase foreign debt but also allocate resources away from needed health, education, and other social services. Thus, a push from large bilateral or multilateral organizations, or even large NGOs to invest in technological infrastructure may encourage local government officials to serve commercial interests rather than meet social needs.

Another approach to understanding the role of new technologies in social change focuses on the use of these as tools for participation and empowerment, particularly among marginal groups. Research in this area is just beginning, but some studies document the use of computers to promote dialogue among women's organizations (Moseley, 1995; Owen, 1998), labor unions (Drew, 1998), and other marginal groups (IDRC, 1992).

Although projects designed to promote commercial global modernity and alternative participatory processes command substantially different levels of resources and articulate vastly divergent goals, their discourse on the importance of new technologies is remarkably similar (Wilkins & Waters, forthcoming). These varied projects seem to concur on the benefits of this globalization through digitized information, whether as linking the global marketplace or activist communities. Neither framework appears to question the broader parameters of a system that invites poor communities to participate in a global commercial system.

RECONCEPTUALIZING DEVELOPMENT COMMUNICATION

Reconceptualizing the field in terms of power demands that we consider development communication as an intervention created and justified through institutional discourse operating within a global system. We need to reconsider what difference these structures and dynamics have made in attempts to promote social change through strategic intervention. An analysis such as this might begin with locating power sources, in order to ascribe responsibility to powerful agents and to identify potential avenues for resistance (for example, see Mody, this volume). Using communication technologies and processes to promote social change need not necessarily follow a patriarchal approach. To escape this cycle, we need to recognize problematic patterns and attempt to change them.

REFERENCES

Arendt, H. (1986). Communicative Power. In S. Lukes (Ed.), *Power* (pp. 59–74). Oxford, UK: Basil Blackwell.

Aron, R. (1986). Macht, Power, Puissance: Democratic Prose or Demoniacal Poetry? In S. Lukes (Ed.), *Power* (pp. 253–278). Oxford, UK: Basil Blackwell.

Basic Support for Institutionalizing Child Survival (BASICS) (1998). *Social Marketing Matters,* 6, April, The Partnership for Child Health Care, Inc.

Bugliarello, G. (1995). The Global Generation, Transmission, and the Diffusion of Knowledge: How Can the Developing Countries Benefit? In *Marshaling Technology for Development: Proceedings of a Symposium* (pp. 61–82). Washington, DC: National Academy Press.

Calabrese, A. (1997). *Global Trade, the Information Society and the Ambivalence of Social Movements.* International Association of Media and Communication Research Conference.

Crush, J. (1995). Introduction. In J. Crush (Ed.), *Power of Development* (pp. 1–26). New York, NY: Routledge.

Domhoff, G. W. (1995). The American Power Structure. In M. E. Olsen & M. N. Marger (Eds.), *Power in Modern Societies* (pp. 170–182). Boulder, CO: Westview Press.

Downing, J. (1996). *Internationalizing Media Theory: Transition, Power, Culture.* London, UK: Sage Publications.

Drew, J. (1998). *Global Communications in the Post–Industrial Age.* Ph.D. Dissertation. University of Texas at Austin.

Escobar, A. (1991). Anthropology and the Development Encounter: The Making and Marketing of Development Anthropology. *American Ethnologist,* 18(4), 658–682.

Escobar, A. (1995a). *Encountering Development: The Making and Unmaking of the Third World.* Princeton, NJ: Princeton University Press.

Escobar, A. (1995b). Imagining a Post-Development Era. In J. Crush (Ed.), *Power of Development* (pp. 211–227). New York, NY: Routledge.

Ferguson, J. (1995). From African Socialism to Scientific Capitalism: Reflections on the Legitimation Crisis in IMF–ruled Africa. In D. B. Moore & G. J. Schmitz (Eds.), *Debating Development Discourse: Institutional and Popular Perspectives* (pp. 129–148). New York, NY: St. Martin's Press, Inc.

Foucault, M. (1986). Disciplinary Power and Subjection. In S. Lukes (Ed.), *Power* (pp. 229–242). Oxford, UK: Basil Blackwell.

Freire, P. (1983). *Pedagogy of the Oppressed* (M. B. Ramos, Trans.). New York, NY: Continuum.

Gamson, W. & Wolfsfeld, G. (1993). Movements and Media as Interacting Systems. *The Annals of the American Academy,* 528: 114–125.

Gergen, M. M. & Gergen, K. J. (1983). Interpretive Dimensions of International Aid. *New Directions in Helping,* 3, 329–348.

Gramsci, A. (1971). Class Consciousness. In G. Lukacs (Ed.), *History and Class Consciousness: Studies in Marxist Dialectic* (pp. 46–82). Cambridge, MA: MIT Press.

Habermas, J. (1986). Hannah Arendt's Communications Concept of Power. In S. Lukes (Ed.), *Power* (pp. 5–93). Oxford, UK: Basil Blackwell.

Hornik, R. C. (1988). *Development Communication, Information, Agriculture and Nutrition in the Third World.* New York, NY: Longman.
Hornik, R. C. (1989). The Knowledge-Behavior Gap in Public Information Campaigns: A Development Communication View. In C. T. Salmon (Ed.), *Information Campaigns: Balancing Social Values and Social Change* (pp. 113–138). Newbury Park, CA: Sage.
Huesca, R. (1995). A Procedural View of Participatory Communication: Lessons from Bolivian Tin Miners' Radio. *Media, Culture and Society,* 17, 101–119.
International Development Research Centre (IDRC) (1992). *101 Technologies: From the South for the South.* Ottawa, Canada: IDRC.
Lerner, D. (1962). *The Passing of Traditional Society.* 2nd Printing. Glencoe, IL: Free Press.
Lukes, S. (1986). Introduction. In S. Lukes (Ed.), *Power* (pp. 1–18). Oxford, UK: Basil Blackwell.
MacDonald, L. (1995). NGOs and the Problematic Discourse of Participation: Cases from Costa Rica. In D. B. Moore and G. J. Schmitz (Eds.), *Debating Development Discourse: Institutional and Popular Perspectives* (pp. 201–229). New York, NY: St. Martin's Press, Inc.
Mackenzie, F. (1995). Selective Silence: A Feminist Encounter with Environmental Discourse in Colonial Africa. In J. Crush (Ed.), *Power of Development* (pp. 100–114). New York, NY: Routledge.
Marger, M. N. (1993). The Mass Media as a Power Institution. In M. E. Olsen & M. N. Marger (Eds.), *Power in Modern Societies* (pp. 238–250). Boulder, CO: Westview Press.
McGuire, W. (1989). Theoretical Foundations of Campaigns. In R. E. Rice & C. K. Atkin (Eds.), *Public Communication Campaigns,* 2nd Edition (pp. 43–66). Newbury Park, CA: Sage.
Melkote, S. R. (1991). *Communication for Development in the Third World.* New Delhi, India: Sage.
Mitchell, T. (1991). America's Egypt: Discourse of the Development Industry. *Middle East Report,* 21(2), 18–34.
Mody, B. (1991). *Designing Messages for Development Communication: An Audience Participation-based Approach.* New Delhi, India: Sage.
Mohammadi, A. (1997). Communication and the Globalization Process in the Third World. In A. Mohammadi (Ed.), *International Communication and Globalization: A Critical Introduction* (pp. 67–89). London, UK: Sage.
Moore, D. B. (1995). Development Discourse as Hegemony: Towards an Ideological History—1945–1995. In D. B. Moore & G. J. Schmitz (Eds.), *Debating Development Discourse: Institutional and Popular Perspectives* (pp. 1–53). New York, NY: St. Martin's Press, Inc.
Moseley, E. S. (1995). *Women, Information, and the Future: Collecting and Sharing Resources Worldwide.* Fort Atkinson, WI: Highsmith Press.
Olsen, M. E. & Marger, M. N. (1993). Theoretical Perspectives on Power. In M. E. Olsen & M. N. Marger (Eds.), *Power in Modern Societies* (pp. 75–87). Boulder, CO: Westview Press.
Owen, C. (1998). *New Technologies and Women's Movements in Mexico.* MA Thesis, University of Texas at Austin.
Parpart, J. (1995). Post–modernism, Gender and Development. In J. Crush (Ed.), *Power of Development* (pp. 253–265). New York, NY: Routledge.
Prewitt, K. & Stone, A. (1993). The Ruling Elites. In M. E. Olsen & M. N. Marger (Eds.), *Power in Modern Societies* (pp. 125–136). Boulder, CO: Westview Press.
Putnam, L. & Pacanowsky, M. E. (Eds.). (1983). *Communication and Organizations: An Interpretive Approach.* Beverly Hills, CA: Sage.

Rakow, L. (1989). Information and Power: Toward a Critical Theory of Information Campaigns. In C. Salmon (Ed.), *Information Campaigns: Balancing Social Values and Social Change* (pp. 164–184). Newbury Park, CA: Sage Publications.

Reeves, G. (1993). *Communications and the Third World.* London, UK: Routledge.

Rogers, E. (1976). Communication and Development: The Passing of the Dominant Paradigm. *Communication Research,* 3(2), 121–133.

Said, E. (1978). *Orientalism.* New York, NY: Pantheon Books.

Said, E. (1993). *Culture and Imperialism.* New York, NY: Alfred A. Knopf.

Salmon, C. (1989). Campaigns for Social "Improvement": An Overview of Values, Rationales, and Impacts. In C. T. Salmon (Ed.), *Information Campaigns: Balancing Social Values and Social Change* (pp. 19–53). Newbury Park, CA: Sage.

Schiller, H. I. (1991). Not Yet the Post-Imperialist Era. *Critical Studies in Mass Communication,* 8, 13–28.

Schmitz, G. J. (1995). Democratization and Demystification: Deconstructing 'Governance' as Development Paradigm. In D. B. Moore & G. J. Schmitz (Eds.), *Debating Development Discourse: Institutional and Popular Perspectives* (pp. 54–90). New York, NY: St. Martin's Press, Inc.

Schön, D. (1979). Generative Metaphor: A Perspective of Problem-Setting. In A. Orthony (Ed.), *Metaphor and Thought* (pp. 254–283). Cambridge, UK: Cambridge University Press.

Schramm, W. (1963). Communication Development and the Development Process. In L. Pye (Ed.), *Communications and Political Development.* Princeton, NJ: Princeton University Press.

Simmel, G. (1986). Domination and Freedom. In S. Lukes (Ed.), *Power* (pp. 203–210). Oxford, UK: Basil Blackwell.

Singhal, A. & Rogers, E. (1989). Prosocial Television for Development in India. In R. Rice & C. K. Atkin (Eds.), *Public Communication Campaigns.* 2nd Edition. Newbury Park, CA: Sage.

Skocpol, T. (1993). The Potential Autonomy of the State. In M. E. Olsen & M. N. Marger (Eds.), *Power in Modern Societies* (pp. 306–313). Boulder, CO: Westview Press.

Sreberny-Mohammadi, A. (1996). International Feminism(s): Engendering Debate in International Communications. *The Journal of International Communication,* 3(1), 1–3.

Staudt, K. (1985). *Women, Foreign Assistance and Advocacy Administration.* New York, NY: Praeger.

Staudt, K. (1997). Gender Politics in Bureaucracy: Theoretical Issues in Comparative Perspective. In K. Staudt (Ed.), *Women, International Development, and Politics: The Bureaucratic Mire* (pp. 3–34). Philadelphia, PA: Temple University Press.

Steeves, H. L. (1993). Creating Imagined Communities: Development Communication and the Challenge of Feminism. *Journal of Communication,* 43(3), 218–229.

U.S. Agency for International Development (USAID) (1993). *The Substance Behind the Images: USAID and Development Communication.* Washington, DC: USAID.

Wilkins, K. (1997). Gender, Power and Development. *The Journal of International Communication,* December, 102–120.

Wilkins, K. (1999). Development Discourse on Gender and Communication in Strategies for Social Change. *Journal of Communication,* 49(1), 44–64.

Wilkins, K. & Waters, J. (Forthcoming). Current Discourse on New Technologies in Development Communication. *Media Development.*

Williams, G. (1993). Modernizing Malthus: The World Bank, Population Control and the African Environment. In J. Crush (Ed.), *Power of Development* (pp. 150–175). New York, NY: Routledge.

Index

ABOUT THE CONTRIBUTORS

Edna Einsiedel (Ph.D., Indiana University) is Professor of Communication Studies at the University of Calgary. Her extensive research on development communication and other issues has resulted in more than thirty articles, book chapters, and monographs.

Arturo Escobar (Ph.D., University of California, Berkeley) is Associate Professor in the Department of Anthropology at the University of Massachusetts at Amherst. A recent recipient of a Guggenheim Fellowship (1997), Escobar has published extensively on the subjects of development and social change, including two critical volumes: *Encountering Development: The Making and Unmaking of the Third World* and *The Making of Social Movements in Latin America: Identity, Strategy and Democracy.*

Ronald Walter Greene (Ph.D., University of Illinois) is Assistant Professor in the Department of Speech Communication at the University of Texas at Austin. His research focuses on the relationship between citizenship and modernity. He is the author of *Malthusian Worlds: US Leadership and the Governing of the Population Crisis.*

Robert Huesca (Ph.D., Ohio State University) is Assistant Professor of Communication at Trinity University, San Antonio, Texas. His research interests include alternative media and participatory communication for social change. His publications have appeared in *Journal of Communication, Gazette, Media, Culture & Society,* and *Communication Studies.*

Thomas L. Jacobson (Ph.D., University of Washington) is Associate Professor and Chair at the Department of Communication, State University of New York at Buffalo. He is also section president for the Participatory Communication Section of the International Association for Media and Communication Research. With Jan Servaes, he has a co-edited book now in press on *Theoretical Approaches to Participatory Communication.*

Brij Kothari (Ph.D., Cornell University) is Assistant Professor at the Ravi J. Matthai Center for Educational Innovation, in the Indian Institute of Management, Ahmedabad. His varied research interests include literacy development, primary education, popular culture, mass media, and other information technologies.

Srinivas Melkote (Ph.D., University of Iowa) is Professor in the Department of Telecommunications at Bowling Green State University. His research interests include the role of communication in social change and empowerment, health communication, and international communication.

Bella Mody (Ph.D., Gujarat University) is Professor in the Department of Telecommunication in the College of Communication at Michigan State University. A native of India, she has published and worked widely in the areas of international political economy of media systems, audience interpretations of media programs, and the design of media campaigns for public service applications in developing countries.

Mark Pedelty (Ph.D., University of California, Berkeley) is Assistant Professor in the General College at the University of Minnesota. He is the author of *War Stories: The Culture of Foreign Correspondents,* an ethnographic study of journalists in El Salvador. After publishing this book and related articles in anthropology and mass communication journals, Pedelty turned to the study of musical subcultures in Mexico. He holds a faculty position in the General College of the University of Minnesota.

Clemencia Rodríguez (Ph.D., Ohio University) is Assistant Professor of Communication at the University of Texas at San Antonio. Since 1984 she has worked closely with grassroots media projects in Nicaragua, Catalonia (Spain), Texas, and in her native Colombia.

H. Leslie Steeves (Ph.D., University of Wisconsin–Madison) is Associate Professor in the School of Journalism and Communication, University of Oregon. Her research interests include gender and communication in developing countries, especially in sub-Saharan Africa.

Douglas Storey (Ph.D., Stanford University) is Senior Research Officer for Asia and the Former Soviet States at the Center for Communication Programs in Johns Hopkins University's School of Public Health. A former Peace Corps volunteer (Belize and Malaysia), he has been working in the field of development communication for more than twenty-five years. Since 1986 he has lived, worked, and travelled extensively in rural South and Southeast Asia.

Jody Waters (M.A., University of Calgary) is a doctoral candidate with the Department of Radio–Television–Film, University of Texas at Austin. She has worked extensively with projects supported by the Canadian International Development Agency.

Karin Gwinn Wilkins (Ph.D., Annenberg School for Communication, University of Pennsylvania) is Assistant Professor with the Department of Radio–Television–Film, University of Texas at Austin. Her publications on development and international communication issues have appeared in the *Journal of Communication, International Journal of Communication, Peace Review,* and *Media Asia,* among others.